OUTCASTE

LIBRARY OF ANTHROPOLOGY

Editor: Anthony L. LaRuffa

Editorial Assistants: Patricial Kaufman and Phyllis Rafti

Advisory Board: Edward Bendix, Robert DiBennardo,
May Ebihara, Paul Grebinger, Bert Salwen, Joel Savishinsky

SAN CIPRIANO   Life in a Puerto Rican Community
Anthony L. LaRuffa
THE TRAIL OF THE HARE   Life and Stress in an
Arctic Community
Joel S. Savishinsky
LANGUAGE IN AFRICA   An Introductory Survey
Edgar A. Gregersen
OUTCASTE   Jewish Life in Southern Iran
Laurence D. Loeb

Other volumes in preparation

OUTCASTE
Jewish Life in Southern Iran

Laurence D. Loeb
University of Utah

GORDON AND BREACH
NEW YORK   LONDON   PARIS

Copyright © 1977 by

Gordon and Breach Science Publishers Inc.
One Park Avenue
New York, NY 10016

Editorial office for the United Kingdom

Gordon and Breach Science Publishers Ltd.
42 William IV Street
London WC2N 4DH

Editorial office for France

Gordon & Breach
7–9 rue Emile Dubois
Paris 75014

Library of Congress Cataloging in Publication Data
Loeb, Laurence D   1942–
    Outcaste : Jewish life in Southern Iran.

    (Library of anthropology)
    Bibliography: p.
    Includes index.
    1.   Jews in Shiraz – Social life and customs.
2.   Shiraz – Social life and customs.   I.   Title
DS135.I65L6   301.45′19′240557   76–53663
ISBN 0–677–04530–1

For Roni, Gabi and Adina

Behold! The Guardian of Israel neither slumbers nor sleeps.
(Ps. 121:4)

Introduction to the Series

One of the notable objectives of the *Library of Anthropology* is to provide a vehicle for the expression in print of new, controversial, and seemingly "unorthodox" theoretical, methodological, and philosophical approaches to anthropological data. Another objective follows from the multidimensional or holistic approach in anthropology which is the discipline's unique contribution toward understanding human behavior. The books in the series will deal with such fields as archaeology, physical anthropology, linguistics, ethnology and social anthropology. Since no restrictions will be placed on the types of cultures included, a New York or New Delhi setting will be considered as relevant to anthropological theory and method as the highlands of New Guinea.

The *Library* is designed for a wide audience and, whenever possible, technical terminology will be kept to the minimum required. In some instances, however, a book may be unavoidably somewhat esoteric and consequently will appeal only to a small sector of the reading population – advanced undergraduate students and graduate students in addition to professional social scientists.

My hopes for the readers are twofold: first, that they will enjoy learning about people, second, and perhaps more important, that the readers will come to experience a feeling of oneness with humankind.

New York City   *Anthony L. LaRuffa*

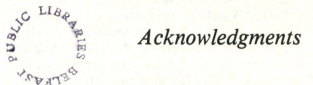

Acknowledgments

Field research in Iran and Israel, from August 1967 through December 1968, was sponsored by grants from the Memorial Foundation for Jewish Culture, the Cantors Assembly of America, and the Jewish Theological Seminary of America. A Herbert Lehman Fellowship (12-LF-66) from the State of New York, which generally supported my graduate studies, was used, in part, to finance some of the research.

In the initial phase of field study in Iran, the American Joint Distribution Committee was particularly understanding and helpful. Thanks go especially to Mr. Morris Rombro, the director of JDC operations in Iran at that time, to Miss Donna Garson and Messrs. Qanuni and Havari of the Shiraz office.

The aid and advice of Mr. Me'ir Ezri was most valuable. Mr. Menahem Eldar provided a number of useful introductions to Jews located in some of the more remote settlements. The warm interest and help of Mr. Alan Gilbert and other personnel of the USIS is greatly appreciated. Dr. Bruno Nettl's efforts in arranging my temporary affiliation with the Teheran Research Unit of the University of Illinois, as well as the assistance of its director, Dr. William Archer, are also acknowledged with thanks.

Historical research in Israel was facilitated by the Zionist Archives of the Jewish Agency and by Mr. Me'ir ben Eliyahu, who provided access to the files of the Ben Zvi Institute. In New York, the Yivo Institute was also of help in the preparation of historical materials. The Jewish Theological Seminary provided me with an opportunity to examine some of their Judaeo-Persian manuscripts.

My interest in the Jews of Iran stems from a suggestion made in 1964 by Professor Johanna Spector of the Jewish Theological Seminary, that an attempt be made to study this community *in situ* before it vanished. Dr. Spector readily allowed me to make use of many music recordings from her personal tape collection and encouraged me to explore various approaches to this study. I thank her for her guidance and personal interest in this project. To the faculty of the Department of Anthropology

ix

of Columbia University and especially to Robert Murphy, Morton Klass and Abraham Rosman, I owe a debt of gratitude for their encouragement of my studies as well as this research.

My thanks to Rabbi David Shofet, a good friend and excellent informant, who generously translated numerous documents and books from Persian. To Mr. Yussef Haridim-Yazd who provided many insights into the behavior and attitudes of Persian Jewry, I am much indebted. Thanks to Seymour Parker, Emmanuel Marx, Shlomo Deshen and Walter Zenner for their comments on some of the problems posed herein. I am grateful to Barbara Fry, David Vandevert, Lucia Ann McSpadden and William Royce who read earlier drafts of this book and contributed their ideas to the formulation of some of the issues raised.

To Dawn Bott, Karla Shobe and most especially Ursula Hanly my sincere appreciation for their diligence in typing the manuscript.

Without the help of the many Iranian Jews, both in Iran and in Israel, who patiently answered our many questions, offered my wife and myself their hospitality and shared their experiences with us, this study would have been impossible. I cannot cite them individually here, although some appear with pseudonyms in the text. Their friendship and cooperation will be forever valued and cherished.

Most of all, to my wife Nomi, whose tireless efforts in the field, helpful editing, proofreading and pertinent comments have nurtured this offspring:

> Her children rise and call her blessed,
> And thus her husband praises her:
> "Many daughters have done excellently
> But you excel them all."
> She opens her mouth with wisdom;
> And the teaching of kindness is on her tongue.
> And let her own works praise her in the gates
> Give her the fruit of her hands.

(Proverbs)

Table of Contents

List of Tables

List of Figures

List of Musical Examples

xiii

List of Plates

Author's Note

This book is an extensively revised version of a Ph.D. dissertation I wrote for Columbia University, 1970, entitled *The Jews of Southwest Iran: A Study of Cultural Persistence.* It is not intended as a theoretical *tour de force,* although it does break some new ground. It is rather a contribution to the ethnography of ethnic groups. More particularly, by means of description and analysis, I endeavor to penetrate and understand the world of the oriental Jew. The events and observations dealt with, extend through December of 1968, supplemented by sporadic reports received from informants through the summer of 1976.

Living informants are referred to throughout by pseudonyms. Only historical figures or those whose identities could not possibly be hidden anyway, are referred to by their real names.

At the time of fieldwork, the Iranian *rial* was being exchanged at 75 to the U.S. dollar.

Dates cited in this book use the designation B.C.E. (before the common era) and C.E. (of the common era). Biblical references are cited in the standard manner and Talmudic citations, unless otherwise indicated, refer only to the Babylonian Talmud with book abbreviation, folio and leaf indications, e.g. (Meg. 32a).

For the reader's convenience, a glossary of specialized Hebrew, Persian and Judaeo-Persian terms is appended. Holiday names and their significance are to be found in Table 11.

In the course of this ethnography the terms "Sfardim" or "Sfardic" and "Ashkenazim" or "Ashkenazic" are used. Sfardim are those Jews of Spanish and Portuguese descent, who settled in the Balkans and all of the lands bordering on the Mediterranean Sea after their expulsion from Spain and Portugal at the end of the fifteenth century. Their ritual traditions, to some extent, replaced the indigenous traditions, and a hybrid rite peculiar to the Oriental Sfardim evolved. Ashkenazim are Jews primarily from Central and Eastern Europe. Their ritual tradition has been widely adopted by Jews in North America and throughout the English speaking world.

The following organizations are frequently referred to in the course of this work:

The Jewish Agency (Sokhnut): A non-government agency "recognized by the State of Israel as the authorized agency to work in Israel for development and colonization, the absorption and settlement of immigrants and the coordination of activities of Jewish institutions and associations operating in these fields" (American Jewish Year Book, 1967:496).

ORT (Organization for Rehabilitation through Training): "Trains Jewish men and women in the technical trades and agriculture; organizes and maintains vocational training schools throughout the world" (American Jewish Year Book, 1967:478).

JDC (American Jewish Joint Distribution Committee): "Organizes and administers welfare, medical, and rehabilitation programs and services and distributes funds for relief and reconstruction on behalf of needy Jews overseas" (American Jewish Year Book, 1967:478).

Alliance Israélite Universelle: A French aid organization, whose main function today is the administration of a system of Jewish schools, primarily in Asia and North Africa.

Otsar Hatorah: An American orthodox Jewish organization operating numerous Jewish religious schools in the Middle East.

ABOUT IRANIAN JEWISH HISTORY

In the course of research, it was determined that there was a lack of comprehensive materials on the history of Iranian Jewry, making diachronic analysis of socio-cultural stability and change all but impossible. I deemed it necessary, therefore, to attempt a partial reconstruction of this history from a mixture of primary and secondary sources. Until some competent social historian can develop a more complete picture of the events and conditions of Iranian Jewry, any conclusions derived from this evidence must be regarded as tentative. Nevertheless, the historical data reveal a surprisingly extensive chronicle of apparent persecution of Jews at the hands of the dominant population. Despite having had a previous effort (Loeb, 1970) calling attention to these circumstances and their consequences labeled "traditional minority persecution" literature (Fischer, M., 1973:328), the reader is advised to read and evaluate the historical material carefully. I especially draw your attention to Appendix I, which provides a brief outline of Iranian Jewish history.

ABOUT TRANSLITERATION

In an attempt to simplify the transliteration problems arising from the use of Hebrew, Persian and Judaeo-Persian terminology, the following plan is being adhered to:

Hebrew Letters

$'$	–	'alef	l	–	lamed
v	–	vet	m	–	mem
b	–	bet	n	–	nun
g	–	gimmel	s	–	samekh
d	–	dalet	$'$	–	'ayin
h	–	he	f	–	fe
v	–	vov	p	–	pe
z	–	zayin	z	–	zade
h	–	het	q	–	quf
t	–	tet	r	–	resh
y	–	yod	sh	–	shin
kh	–	khaf	s	–	sin
k	–	kaf	t	–	tav

Vowels are transcribed approximately as pronounced. Some terms, occasionally occurring in English usage, are transliterated according to a standard spelling as found in Webster's New Collegiate Dictionary (1953), e.g. yeshiva.

The same system is used in transliterating the Persian and Judaeo-Persian, necessitating the addition of several symbols, as follows:

j is pronounced as in "*joke*".
ch is pronounced as in "*ch*urch".
gh is a glottal not occurring in English.
dh is pronounced as in "*th*is".
th is pronounced as in "*th*in".

Place names are often given a standard spelling. Not too much attention is paid to careful vocalization of place names, as this was found to be individually as well as regionally variable. Place names, proper names, and some special titles are capitalized, but, generally not italicized. The Hebrew word *Siddur* (prayer book) is capitalized and italicized. Otherwise, most Persian, Hebrew and Judaeo-Persian words are italicized.

Preface

In August, 1967, after a short stopover in Israel, my wife, Nomi, and I, newly wed, arrived in Iran to begin 16 months of field study among the Jewish minority of that country. I had chosen to come to Iran because I felt at the time, that there was an urgent need to better understand the realities of everyday life of Jews living in a Muslim country. With few exceptions, previous anthropological studies of oriental Jews were done by reconstruction rather than *in situ,* thus lacking the all-important elements of observation and participation on the part of the researcher.

With the cooperation of the Iranian authorities, we settled in Shiraz, a provincial city in Southern Iran, whose mild climate made it a most attractive residence. The Jewish community there dates back well over 1000 years and despite the inroads made by emigration, it remains substantial and fairly well organized. We rented an appartment in a house owned by a young Jewish goldsmith, located in one of the new Jewish–Muslim mixed neighborhoods, about ten minutes from the old Jewish quarter. It was our very good fortune to have lived with this most hospitable and cooperative family for most of our stay and we were delighted to have shared that residence with one of the community's most respected men: Bash-e Khan Mulla Aqa Yaqobi, chief *gabay* of Shiraz, informant and friend. In the spring of 1968, we lived with a young spinner and his gracious wife and family in the heart of the old Jewish quarter. We also traveled throughout the country, meeting Jewish families in nearly every community, large and small.

Nomi and I divided the research labor along task and sex lines. A psychiatric social worker by profession, Nomi took advantage of her access to women to gather data on their problems and attitudes, focussing on interaction within the family and the enculturation process. Excluded from that feminine sphere for many reasons, I devoted much time to the analysis of economic conditions, formal education, religious life and political structure – more acceptedly the male domain. While we divided our efforts among the rich and poor, pious and secular, our primary interest lay in the *Mahalleh,* the old Jewish quarter, most of whose in-

xxiii

PLATE 1　Author's rented room in the old Jewish quarter.

habitants were lower ranked economically and prestige-wise. Often our motives were questioned by the elite Jews, who having no interest themselves in their poorer brethren nor their problems, could not understand why we spent so much time among them and, more particularly, why we had to live among them in such relatively primitive conditions.

Our choice of work area and the need to reside in the Mahalleh for six weeks was largely influenced by the problems I wished to explore: how does an isolated, intimidated pre-industrial urban minority community survive? What effects do environmental and social conditions have on community organization, attitudes and religious practice? Much of the material, it was felt, could be found amidst the traditional segment of the population still residing in the Mahalleh. We had ample opportunity to also interact with middle and high ranked members of the community whose life-style and comments provided a useful and necessary counterpoint to that of the Mahalleh people.

Coming to Shiraz as observant Jews permitted us immediate entrée to many community activities while providing us with prestige amongst the traditional segment of the community not always accorded foreigners. As a coreligionist with extensive familiarity with a variety of Jewish traditions, I saved much time not having to learn what otherwise might be called "basic" Judaism. However, while this proved to be highly advantageous, such an approach is not without its hazards and I am certain that some behavior I took for granted and did not subject to closer scrutiny could have provided grist for an anthropologist with a somewhat different perspective. Despite my biases and probable preconceptions, I have tried to fairly present the Shirazi Jewish world view while consciously attempting to evaluate impartially their statements, behavior and implicit assumptions.

We spent relatively little time with Muslims, Bahais, Zoroastrians and Christians, because it was felt that too much contact of that kind would be both diverting and a source of concern to our Jewish informants. Instead, when the need arose, as it did every few months, to break off contact with the Shirazi Jews in order to renew our energies and perspectives, we would leave Shiraz and visit communities to the north and east where we could collect similar data for purposes of comparison.

We were often approached by informants and friends for advice concerning education, career, health care and emigration. We tried to be helpful whenever possible. In retrospect, it would be hard to evaluate our personal impact on Shirazi Jewry, but we hope it has been and will continue to be positive.

Laurence D. Loeb

CHAPTER I

Introduction

In the Autumn of 1910, immediately following the High Holyday penitential period, the last major pogrom was initiated against the Jews of Shiraz. Murder, pillage, rape and extensive vandalism were reported to have left the entire community of 6000 virtually homeless and terrorized.

Shortly after arriving in Shiraz I had occasion to talk with several elderly informants about the events surrounding this incident. There was surprising agreement about why it happened:

A wedding was held in the house of Mayur Kohanim, already a wealthy man and progenitor of one of the wealthiest families in modern day Shiraz. Among the invited guests to this affair was the wife of the Qavam, then provincial governor of Fars.[1] She noted that the groom gave his bride a very valuable jeweled ring. The Qavam's wife was most envious and when she reported her observations to the governor, he replied: "these people are getting rich and that is dangerous for me". He attempted to extort a large sum of money from the community. When the Jews sent word that they would be unable to pay, he had a young boy killed and accusing the Jews of ritual murder, stirred the populace to riot in the Mahalleh. He then ordered his own soldiers to rob the Mahalleh and kill anyone who opposed their activity.

The explanation given provided no profound insights into the political importance of this incident. Nor did it contain any significant comment on the kind of interaction which daily transpired between Jew and Muslim, or the nature of the deep seated hostility that could give rise to so emotional an outbreak.

I was struck rather by the mundane humanizing of an almost surrealistic happening into concrete personal terms – in this case, the jealousy over ostensible Jewish wealth, by the Qavam. It was even then readily apparent that this Shirazi model was beautifully simple, avoiding the philosophic complications and contradictions a more insightful construct might evoke.

---

[1] He was actually *Kalantar* (magistrate) at that time. The family allegedly descended from an apostate Jew (see Chapter III).

1

This book is a study of a society's adaptation, not to a harsh physical environment, but to a hostile social clime. It is hoped that the descriptions and interpretations offered here will allow a greater understanding of some aspects of the relationship between a dominant population and an isolated, intimidated pre-industrial urban minority. The viewpoint adopted here is sympathetic to that minority through whose eyes we try to understand their world.

Those familiar with studies made of the urban poor in the industrialized city, will find many of the attitudes and behavioral patterns displayed by Shirazi Jews reminiscent of those exhibited by many contemporary urban poor.[1] Elsewhere (Loeb, 1970) it has been shown that there is an unmistakable close correspondence between Shirazi Jewish culture and the model constructed by Oscar Lewis (1966) to typologize the "culture of poverty". As Oscar Lewis puts it:

When we look at the culture of poverty on the local community level, we find poor housing conditions, crowding, gregariousness but above all a minimum of organization beyond the level of the nuclear and extended family. (Lewis, 1966: xlvi)

Populations living in a "culture of poverty" not only share in the "lack of economic resources, segregation and discrimination, fear, suspicion or apathy and the development of local solutions for problems", but there is a corollary "lack of effective participation and integration . . . in the major institutions of the larger society" (Lewis, 1966: xlv).

The Shirazi Jew not only displays the aforementioned traits, but likewise exhibits strong feelings of marginality, helplessness, and dependence, a

present-time orientation with relatively little ability to defer gratification and to plan for the future, a sense of resignation and fatalism, a widespread belief in male superiority,

provinciality, concern primarily with personal problems, lack of class consciousness but high sensitivity to status distinctions (Lewis, 1966: xlvii–xlviii).

Despite these numerous similarities, Shirazi Jews cannot be properly categorized as living in a "culture of poverty". Their condition is not primarily the result of economic circumstances, nor is it associated chiefly with differences of "class" as is true of the "culture of poverty". Their situation cannot be said to have arisen from the breakdown of a

---

[1] Many of the patterns of behavior and some of the attitudes professed by Shirazi Jews are shared in some measure by their urban-poor neighbors. It must be argued however that Jews were less well off than their Muslim neighbors who in their frustration would, at times, turn against the Jews, making their life even more miserable.

stratified social and economic system, from imperial conquest in which natives are maintained in servile colonial status or from the process of detribalization (Lewis, 1966: xlv). While the "culture of poverty" seems unstable and transitional, the culture of Shirazi Jewry is of a type that is long-lived and durable.

The Jews of Shiraz are what Sjoberg calls an "outcaste group" (1960: 133–137). By no means a rare phenomenon in the pre-industrial city, this kind of grouping, frequently defined by ethnicity, was relegated to the lowliest of professions and the lowest social ranking. Sjoberg feels that the Jews usually belong to the higher strata of social outcastes "because of their domination of strategic aspects of urban economic life" (1960:134). However, this was not true for Shirazi Jews, who were truly the lowest of the low. The outcaste group is viewed as being needed to provide certain essential services such as commerce and entertainment, but as a "potential disseminator of new and heretical ideas" (Sjoberg, 1960:136), it is a danger to the power structure. Sjoberg's perceptive insights will be supported in the course of this work.

While studies of overseas Indian and Chinese communities abound in the literature, their culture has not been viewed in terms of Weber's (1952: 336–55) "pariah people" or Sjoberg's "outcaste group" nor has their adaptive strategy been evaluated or contrasted with that of the industrial poor living in a "culture of poverty". But if pre-industrial urban pariah societies do have aspects of their cultures in common, then Shirazi Jewish culture may possibly be archetypical.

In such a culture, it may be expected that while employment may be high, it will be limited to marginal professions. A stable nuclear family, probably living in an extended household, is one important adaptive alternative necessitated by marginal low-income employment and high population density, providing some stability at this fundamental level of community organization. Some kind of political structure, however informal and ephemeral, would make decisions affecting the internal dynamics of the semi-autonomous community and vis-à-vis the dominant population.

Religion could provide an ideology for ethnic survival, a means of expression, an area for intellectual achievement, a source of permanence and stability in an otherwise insecure environment and a means of uniting and integrating the entire community. Religious differences between the dominant and subject populations may lead to mutual revulsion and a notion of "pollution", thereby reinforcing the outcaste status of the minority through segregation, but simultaneously strengthening its ethnic identity. There are undoubtedly other traits, such as food hoarding, and the hiding of cash for emergencies, passivity with respect to the dominant population and various mechanisms of defense, which would have special adaptive value for a pariah population.

One of the basic distinctions between the pre-industrial-urban pariah culture and the industrial-urban "culture of poverty" lies in a fundamental dissimilarity in the respective relationships of the dominant and subject populations. In the "culture of poverty" situation, the dominant population exhibits a passive lack of interest in the subordinate population, whose survival may be considered irrelevant, while actively enforcing discrimination and segregation. In the pre-industrial city the dominant population is actively hostile towards the subject population while enforcing segregation.

Populations existing in a "culture of poverty" survive as loose family units with a generally weak sense of community identity and ideology. In the "pariah culture", community and ethnic identity are well developed, as is ideology, and the subject population is aware of, and identifies with, communities of the same ethnicity struggling to survive elsewhere.

Yet "pariah culture" as well as the "culture of poverty" societies share the unwelcome circumstance of being trapped within a negative-feedback homeostatic loop, in which their own *survival* provides the necessary negative reinforcement to maintain the systemic equilibrium. The uncoordinated and generally passive response to the pressures of the dominant population ensure stable relations and continued exploitation of the subordinate community.

SETTING

Iran is a country of 628,000 square miles, approximately three times the size of France (Fischer, 1968: 3). The country is rimmed by mountain ranges, within which are located interior desert basins. Most of the 32 million inhabitants of the country are rural, settled in some 50,000 villages along the mountain chains. But the urban population is rapidly increasing.

The Jews of Iran reside in almost every large city in the country.[1] Their number is currently estimated at about 85,000,[2] most of whom

---

[1] The author visited the Jewish communities of Teheran, Kerman, Yazd, Isfahan, Hamadan, Burujerd, Nahawand, Kermanshah, Sanandaj, Rezayeh, Mashhad, Firuzabad, Meymand and Bushehr.

[2] The 1966 census count was 67,800 (Iran Almanac, 1968:529), but this figure is assumed to be conservative.

FIGURE 1   Map of Iran

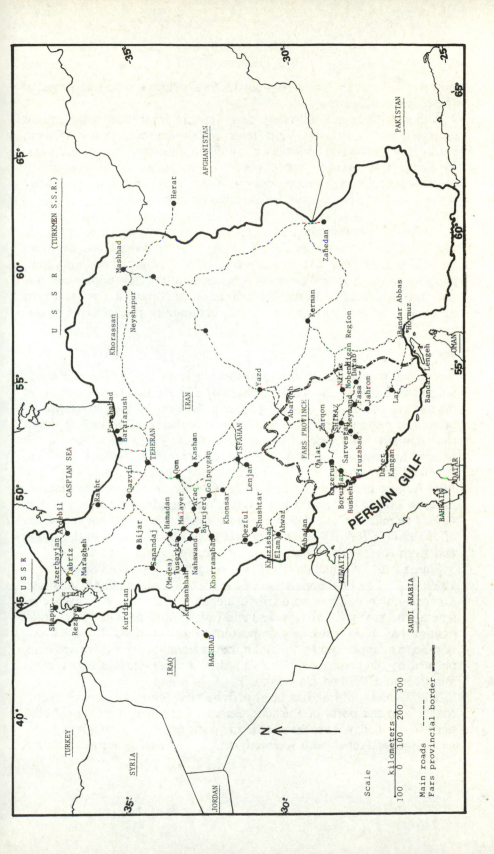

now live in Teheran. Not more than 1–2% are rural dwellers and most of these live in Kurdistan.

Although there are still many poor Jews in Iran, most belong to an emerging middle "class". Most Jews are shopkeepers, many of them working in the bazaar as sellers of cloth, carpets, trinkets and antiques. In Teheran, a Jewish upper "class" is emerging, consisting of importer–exporters, automobile dealers, spare parts distributors, factory owners and others engaged in lucrative enterprises.

Although Jews all over the country identify with one another there is no nation-wide community. The Teheran community tends to speak for all, being the largest and closest to the seat of power; but decision-making in that large and fragmented community is tedious and complicated. In order to avoid the complications of the new population mix and large dispersed population groupings of the capital, it was decided to make a traditional, provincial, Jewish community the focus of study.

SHIRAZ

Shiraz, the capital city of the southwestern Iranian province of Fars, is located at Latitude 29° 42' N, Longitude 52° 30' E. This location is at the western end of a 125-km-long basin in the heart of the Zagros Mountains. The basin is well watered and the city receives 240 to 700 mm of rain annually – an average of about 350 mm – 90% of which falls in autumn and winter. The daily average temperature extremes of 39 °C in summer and minus 7 °C in winter are rarely experienced. The July–August mean temperature is 25 °C while the December–January mean is 3.6 °C. During the hot months the humidity averages less than 40%. The mild climate, due in part to the city's relatively high elevation of 1539 m (5078.7 ft), attracts tourists from northern Iran in the spring and from the Persian Gulf region in summer.

Shiraz's urban population in the 1966 census was 318,086 (Bemont, 1969: 287). The total population of Fars was about 1,500,000, of which a considerable number were tribal, including Qashqai, Khamseh confederation, Arabs, Kowli (gypsies) and Lurs. Tribal influence on regional politics has been extremely important. Fars is ruled by a Governor-General appointed by the Shah, but regional politics there are complicated by the presence of Iran's southern armies, various tribes, court ministers and Pahlavi University.

Traditionally, Shiraz has been a trade city, located on the principal roads from the ports of Bushehr, Bandar Lengeh and Bandar Abbas northward. Today Bushehr is a minor port, and a major highway connects Bandar Abbas with Kerman, thereby bypassing Shiraz. Shiraz is just beginning to industrialize and the government intends to make it the center for Iran's electronics industry. Silver and goldsmithing, mosaic inlaying, carpet weaving and leather tanning are some of Shiraz's major crafts. Modern Shiraz was one of the first Iranian cities to have piped water, and was to be the first to have piped gas.

The Jewish population of Shiraz in the 1956 census was 8304 (Clarke, 1963:48) and due to emigration has remained about the same to the present day.[1] Before 1949, Jews comprised more than 15% of the city's population, but since then, the city's population has increased five-fold and Jews today comprise less than 2% of the total. Nevertheless, the Jewish population of Shiraz is exceeded in magnitude only by Teheran's approximately 50,000 Jews. The size of Shiraz's Jewish population has varied with time and the perspective of the reporters (see Appendix V). Factors affecting the size of the Shirazi Jewish community include:

1) *Forced conversions and pogroms* were, until recent years, important in inhibiting growth of the Jewish population.

2) *Earthquakes* have struck Shiraz frequently. In about 1853 a major quake killed some 330 Jews (Petermann, 1861, II:171). An informant claims that the last major quake, in about 1915, killed 333 Jews.

3) *Famine and disease* resulting from the filth and squalor of the Jewish ghetto, has caused population losses. In 1821 there was a major cholera epidemic (Fraser, 1825:84–85). In 1902, 400 Shirazi Jewish children died from smallpox, diptheria and typhoid (Alliance, 1903:105). In 1918, 10,000 of Shiraz's total population of 50,000 died of influenza (Sykes, 1930, II:515). According to informants, typhus struck the Shiraz region during World War II. Malaria, typhoid and hepatitis are endemic to Fars. Such non-fatal diseases as cataract, trachoma and leishmaniasis are also endemic.[2] Because of drought and perennial locust swarms, Fars has been very susceptible to famine.

4) *Floods and war* have affected the population adversely.

5) *Emigration to Israel* in this century has radically reduced the Jewish population.

---

[1] Shirazi Muslim informants insist that there are still at least 16,000 Jews in the city.
[2] During the period of research, an epidemic of leishmaniasis (a fly-borne protozoan disease) affected about 50% of the Jewish children ten years old or less. Medical informants reported, however, that the incidence of tuberculosis is quite low among Shirazi Jews as is generally true for urban-dwelling Jews the world over (Rakower, 1973).

PLATE 2   A Jewish home in the village of Meymand.

PLATE 3   The only Jewish head of household residing in Meymand with his wife and two unmarried adult daughters.

The Jewish population of Fars province, excluding Shiraz, numbering over 4500 (Ben Zvi, 1937:82) as late as 1930, has declined drastically in recent years as a result of emigration. The 1968 Jewish population centers of Fars outside of Shiraz included: Firuzabad 40 to 50, Niriz 4, Meymand 4, Bushehr 12, and Boruzjan 12 to 15 – totaling about 72 to 85.

THE PEOPLE[1]

Those first meeting Shirazi Jews would not notice any marked phenotypic differences from the Shirazi population at large. The observer soon becomes aware, however, that due to a high incidence of inbreeding some six or seven facial types tend to predominate and that certain types prevalent among Muslims are not found at all among Jews. Likewise, while most Jews tend to be a light olive complexion as is common among Mediterranean peoples, they are generally fairer skinned than local Muslims and very few are "black", as the darker skinned Muslims are referred to as being. Shirazis tend to be short to medium in stature, with most men averaging between 157 and 172 cm and women ranging from about 152 to 160 cm. Rarely did individuals exceed these heights. Most women maintain a weight proportional for their size, though frequent childbearing, hard physical labor, poor nutrition, and general disregard for their figures may be responsible for many mothers with sagging breasts and rounded pot bellies. Many women, teenaged and up, walk with the gait of one in the latter stages of pregnancy, even when not actually carrying a child. Hair color for both sexes is usually dark brown or black, though the use of *henna* often gives the hair a reddish tinge. There are proportionally more redheads than in the population at large. Wavey and straight head hair predominate over curly hair. Eye color tends to be dark brown or black, but some light colored eyes were observed. Teeth are yellowish-white and straight with little or no protrusion. Lips vary from moderately thin to full. There seem to be a great variety of noses, but no fleshy pug noses, sometimes seen among the Muslim population, were observed among Jews. The environment too leaves its effects on phenotype: extensive facial scarring from leishmaniasis is commonly noticed among all age groups and smallpox scarring is seen in those born before 1940. In middle age, toothlessness, glaucoma and cataract are not unusual.

---

[1] This material is based on the impressions of the author and his wife, and no claim is made for its "scientific" validity.

PLATE 4 A Jewish porter in Shiraz.

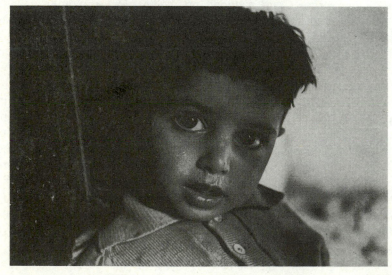

PLATE 5 A pensive three-year-old girl.

To the best of my knowledge, there was generally only limited evidence of maladaptive gene-linked aberrations. No attempt has yet been made to examine Shirazi Jews genotypically, so there would be no point in speculating on gene frequencies.

INTERCOMMUNAL MOBILITY AND COMMUNICATION WITHIN IRAN AND VIS-A-VIS THE OUTSIDE WORLD

Through the early Islamic period, Shiraz lay on a major trade route of Radanite Jewish traders and its Jews were under the indirect leadership of the Exilarch in Baghdad. As of the middle of the twelfth century, formal links bound the Babylonian and Persian Jewish communities. Religious pilgrimage brought many Persian Jews to holy sites within Babylonia (Adler, 1907:44). Nevertheless, as the *lingua franca* of the two countries began to change (Fischel, 1960:1156), a language barrier between the Jews of Persia and Babylonia materialized. The massive communication disruptions initiated by the thirteenth century Mongol invasions did not completely sever the ties between these communities. But by the early fourteenth century, for reasons unknown, Persian Jewry seems to have been largely cut off from the rest of the world, and each settlement survived in relative isolation from the others until the late nineteenth century.

Only during the Safavid period (1502–1722), especially during the seventeenth century were internal and external communications relatively good. In the early sixteenth century it was reported that the Jews residing in Tabriz were not permanent inhabitants but merchants on business from Baghdad, Kashan and Yazd (Grey, n.d., 171–2). The Jewish poet Babay ibn Lutf (Bacher, 1904; 1906–7) indicates that there was much traffic by Jews between the main cities of Persia and cooperation among them during the persecutions of Abbas I and II. Jews migrated to Baghdad and westward (Bacher, 1906:52:247), to Afghanistan (Fischel, 1960a:77) and even to India (Fischel, 1960a:81). Occasionally foreign Jews settled in Persia proper[1] (Bacher, 1906:51:91). Even the messianic movement of Shabbtay Zvi of Izmir embraced the Jews of Mazanderan, in 1666.

After the Afghan invasion of 1722, communications until the twentieth century were sporadic at best. Mail was exchanged between com-

---

[1] One informant claimed that his family came to Shiraz from Algeria in the seventeenth century, but he offered no evidence to support this assertion.

munities at irregular intervals. Except for the Zand period (1750–1794) when Baghdadi Jews were reported to be present in Shiraz (Sassoon, 1949:129),[1] most movement by Jews during the eighteenth and early nineteenth centuries was to the north and within the northern part of the country. Mashhadi Jews set up trade settlements all over the north (Wolff, 1832:67). Jewish merchants from Hamadan worked in Ardebil (Descos, 1908:109). The Jewish traveler, Neumark (Yaari, 1947:73), says that religious leadership in Kermanshah came from Mashhad and Yazd. On the other hand, Shirazis report that occasionally merchants would come there from the north but never stayed very long.

From time to time, Jews were given permission to emigrate, usually with the restriction that they remain in Persia. In the eighteenth century, Jews from Dalman (Salmas) who had moved to Qazvin were settled in Mashhad (Ben Zvi, 1961:98). Under the Qajars (1792–1925), Jews attempting to escape difficult conditions, fled from Yazd to Mashhad (Wolff, 1832:32). Yazdis also settled in Kerman. Some Shirazis settled in Kashan (Alliance, 1907:85), as did Yazdis and Araqis. Emigrants from villages and towns settled in provincial capitals, e.g., Fars' Jews from Lar, Jahrom, the Nobendigan region, Fasa, Zarqon, Firuzbad, Kazerun, Borazjan and Bushehr came to Shiraz. However, until Pahlavi times, surprisingly few Jews came to Shiraz from distant cities.

A few Jews sought to leave Persia altogether. Some fled to Baghdad and others emigrated to Palestine. A trickle made their way to India, where they contributed to the revitalization of Indian Judaism (Fischel, 1960a:80–88). Some of the emigrants to Calcutta maintained commercial and spiritual ties with their native communities: reportedly wine and *maẓẓa shmura* (specially prepared unleavened bread for Pesaḥ) were shipped from Shiraz to Calcutta in the mid-nineteenth century and the latter community sought religious legal opinions from Shirazi scholars with respect to Shirazis then living in India (Musleah, 1975:66, 70).

Beginning in the early eighteenth century, a trickle of emissaries came from Jerusalem, mainly to the cities of the north. They collected money and sometimes acted as teachers. The unique Persian prayer liturgy (Adler, E., 1898:601), began to change to the Sfardic rite, perhaps due to their influence.

By the mid-nineteenth century, letters were exchanged between Persian and European Jews which eventually led to active intervention by the latter on behalf of their Persian co-religionists.

During periods of poor communication the Jews of Shiraz felt particularly isolated. In Qajar times it was said:

---

[1] At least one Persian Jew found his way to Vienna in the 1750s (Ben Zvi, 1958).

The traveler who passes safely through the realm of the Governor of Shiraz is universally held to be fit subject for congratulation. (Arnold, 1877, II:155)

On a twenty-two day journey from Shiraz to Isfahan, Joseph Benjamin (1859:235–7) reports that his caravan of 2000 was attacked three times; this was not considered abnormal.[1]

While travel was hazardous for anyone, the Jew was in especially great personal danger, and Shirazi Jews are still reluctant to travel alone. Benjamin reported while traveling through Fars,

One day, when I was on the point of putting on my Tephilim in preparation for prayer, I heard with terror the words: "A Jew is among us!" – I turned round; a Persian pointed his gun at me and fired, but the bullet whistled by me. The caravan-Baschi, who with many others had run to the spot, snatched the weapon from the hands of the perpetrator, who cried out in a rage: "A Jew is daring to pollute our company!" (1859:227)

Jews usually sought traveling companions who would agree to protect them, but such protection, bought at a high price, was not very secure.

Several horsemen who were conveying the annual taxes from Shiraz to Teheran had come up with a couple of Jewish shopkeepers, whom they first insulted, and afterwards, passing from insult to injury were about to lay violent hands upon. One of our company, a Persian, happening to be present, had pity on the poor Jews, stood up in their defense and took the impudent fellows from Shiraz rather roughly to task for their unbecoming conduct. One of the horsemen, a hotheaded young fellow, became so enraged at this interference, that he lifted his rifle and shot at the Jews. He afterwards pretended that the whole thing had been a joke, that he intended only to frighten one of the Jews by sending a bullet through his tall fur cap, but unluckily he missed his aim and hit, instead, the Persian's arm. (Vambery 1865:99)

Jews were heavily taxed at every inn *en route* (Benjamin, 1859:260). Jewish entertainers were forced to perform for the guests as part of their tax (Browne, 1950:243). The murder of Jewish travelers, especially merchants was a common occurrence (Alliance, 1892, *et seq.*).

Aside from the problem of safety, any trip in the years before bus service, was a major undertaking. Although Shiraz was a trade center, its main port, Bushehr was eleven days away by mule. Isfahan was at least a fifteen day trip and Teheran – more than a month. One informant, who made a pilgrimage to the tomb of Ezra in the vicinity of Baghdad in 1920, was *en route* four months and six days.

After the British restored communications in 1918, emissaries from Baghdad and Jerusalem began to arrive in Shiraz more regularly. Since

---

[1] Until the mid-1960s, Fars roads were still considered dangerous and subject to banditry.

about 1935 Shirazi Jews have been able to travel freely around the country. Many have been to Isfahan and Teheran.

THE LINGUISTIC HIATUS

While the relative isolation of Shiraz and other Persian–Jewish settlements from the outside necessarily contributed to the development of a uniquely Persian–Jewish culture, over time the communities began to diverge culturally. What is more, a linguistic drift occurred, giving rise to a large number of mutually unintelligible dialects of Judaeo-Persian.

Jews in each locality speak a distinctive variation of Judaeo-Persian. While these dialects have certain features in common, such as usage of Hebrew loan words, similar vocabulary and common phonetic characteristics, informants report difficulty in understanding Jews from other cities. One school teacher from Shiraz, who spent two years in Isfahan, reported that it took him several weeks to understand the dialect there and a number of months before he was adept at speaking it.

Some dialects are more closely related than others. For example, Kerman was first settled by Yazdis during the middle of the nineteenth century and later immigrants were also from Yazd, thus the dialects of these two cities are mutually intelligible. It is claimed that the dialects of Isfahan, Hamadan and Kashan are closely related (Abrahamian, 1936:3). The dialect of the main city of a region, is largely understood by the population of the smaller settlements of the area.

An inspection of the Comparative Kinship Terminology of Jews in Iran (Appendix IV) reveals numerous differences between the Shirazi dialect and other Judaeo-Persian dialects, even within the limited corpus of terms presented here.

Preliminary analysis of the Shiraz dialect indicates a grammar, distinctive from modern Persian. While syntax and morphemic structure are similar to Persian, phonetic differences are substantial; loan words and metathesis contribute to its unintelligibility to non-Jewish Persians. Jews claim that the dialect is a defense against the Muslims and its importance for identification and secrecy cannot be overestimated. Many people in Shiraz initially tried to prevent the author from learning to understand "*judi*".

The Shirazi dialect is considered substandard by educated Iranians and is highly disapproved of in the schools; Jewish children are discouraged from speaking it by their teachers. Most children understand the dialect, but many can no longer speak it. I am told, nevertheless, that Jewish children can quickly be identified as such by that speech pattern.

A popular record, " *'Eshq Yahud-e-Shiraz*" ("Teheran", No. 1713) rather good-naturedly mocks the Shirazi Jew's dialect.

Besides these dialects, Jews all over Iran speak mutually intelligible variations of "*letra'i*" ("not Tora-like"). This jargon consists of special terminology primarily related to business. It does not seem to have ever been a full-fledged language. The vocabulary is mostly Hebrew, but the grammar is Persian. Few Muslims understand the regular Jewish dialects, but none at all understand "*letra'i*".[1]

"*Zargari*", the "goldsmith" language, is utilized by Jews in that profession and follows the general trend of goldsmith jargons in that part of the world. Its "secret" is the interpolation of nonsense syllables into the flow of speech.

The relative isolation of Shiraz and other major urban centers limited the extent of their mutual interdependence. Iranian Jewish communities were for the most part socially, spiritually, economically and politically independent of each other. Yet subject to common conditions, Jews remained vitally concerned about the wellbeing of co-religionists everywhere and, whenever feasible, came to their aid.

---

[1] See Mizrahi (1959) for a short description of this jargon.

CHAPTER II

"Outcaste": Shi'a Intolerance

"PROTECTED" MINORITY

Proclaiming a spiritual debt to Judaism, the seventh century Arab conquerors of Persia bestowed upon Jewry the title: "People of the Book". Together with Christians and Zoroastrians, Jews were henceforth to be considered *dhimmi,* a "protected minority". The concept of "protection" was an ideological rationale for permitting unbelievers to continue to live among the "faithful". In return for this privilege, *dhimmis* were obliged to pay a special poll tax, the *jaziyeh,* and were denied some of the rights (and obligations) of full citizens. Provided the *dhimmis* lived up to their obligations, Islam offered to protect them from foes within the greater society and from without. The penalty paid for this guardianship was second class citizenship, economic exploitation and social discrimination.

INTIMIDATION

The incidence of Jewish persecution in the distant past is difficult to evaluate, due to the dearth of relevant accounts. But from the beginning of the seventeenth century, through 1925, Jewish survival was in constant danger, as Iranian hostility towards them increased. The harassment, intimidation and restrictions directed toward the Jews seems sufficient cause for the development of certain Jewish behavior patterns and attitudes discussed later.

The proclamation of Shi'a Islam as the state religion has greatly contributed to the suffering of Iranian Jewry.[1] The Shi'a clergy has frequently led hostile action against the Jews. Today, the Shah's friendly policy towards Israel has engendered bitter opposition to his rule from the clergy (Iran Almanac, 1968:532). During the June 1967 Six Day

---

[1] See Appendix III for an explanation of the unique circumstances of the *dhimmi* condition under Shi'a Islam.

16

War, the clergy was instrumental in effecting a boycott of Jewish business in Shiraz, Teheran and elsewhere. In some cities the clergy prevented the sale of bread and other food to Jews for as long as three days, until the government intervened.

The restrictive code, *Jam Abbasi,* (see Appendices I and II), decreed in the seventeenth century and based on the so-called Code of Omar, was the work of the clergy, as were later restrictive codes. These codes and the pogroms directed at the Jews were for the expressed purpose of converting them. Murder, expulsion and robbery were only secondary considerations.

The type of restrictions placed on Jews and the methods of harassment have been numerous and varied (see Appendix II). They affected so many aspects of communal and personal living, that they must be considered in some detail.

1 FORCED CONVERSION

Forced conversion of Jews in Iran is known as early as the fifth century (see Appendix I). Since the period of Abbas I at the beginning of the seventeenth century, these have occurred regularly. In the reign of Abbas II, (1642–1667), all the Jews of Iran were converted to Islam and, many communities remained Muslim. All the Jews of Mashhad became *jadid al-islam* (new converts to Islam) in 1839 (Wolff, 1846:395). Attempts were made to convert some of the smaller communities in Fars at the beginning of the twentieth century.

More often, individuals were singled out and forcibly converted. Usually it was a life or death choice given to those caught in a compromising situation (doctors were especially susceptible to such extortion), but sometimes victims were selectively kidnapped and tortured.

2 LAW OF APOSTASY

In order to encourage Jews "voluntarily" to accept Islam, the Law of Apostasy was promulgated in the seventeenth century. It remained in effect officially until 1881, though it continued to be enforced unofficially until Reza Shah was induced to end the practice (Yishay, 1950:70). This law stated that should a Jew convert to Islam he becomes the sole heir of all members of his family (lineage). This economic incentive was likely responsible for most of the "voluntary" conversion to Islam, which may have been considerable. A 1903 emissary to Shiraz indicates that when he visited there was not a single Jewish family without a *jadid al-islam* waiting for a relative to die so that he might inherit from him (Alliance, 1903:107).

3 MURDER

Murders were commonly associated with riots and pogroms, but travelers and itinerant merchants were also frequent victims. Even when witnesses could be found, the murderer of a Jew was subject, in most cases, only to a *fine* (Benjamin, J., 1859:259), or, at worst, a beating. The murder of Jews by unknown assailants, often without apparent motive, occasionally occurs in the present day. Due to improved communications, rumor of such murders now spreads quickly and widely throughout the country.

4 BEATINGS

Beatings and torture of Jews are often reported. Whereas prominent members of the community were often singled out for government administered beatings, any Jew who ventured into the streets could be beaten and stoned by a mob. It is said that when a Jew was beaten he would immediately begin to scream and feign excruciating pain, claiming he had been wounded to death. Persians call this *jud baazi,* "Jew game".[1] The slowest, most painful torturous death a Persian can conceive of is known as *jud kosht,* "Jew murder".

5 KIDNAPPING AND MOLESTATION OF JEWISH WOMEN

The kidnapping of Jewish women, especially young virgins (married women were fair game too!), was frightening to Jews. Lotfali Khan-e Zand took girls from Isfahan and Shiraz for his harem (Levi, 1960, III:489), but lesser men too seized Jewish women for themselves. An informant told me that several years ago, a Muslim army officer was living in a Jewish home. A teenaged girl in the house was attractive and outgoing. One evening, he arranged for a jeep to come by and invited the girl for a drive. He made off with her, taking her from Shiraz to Ahwaz from where her parents received a letter that stating she had married him. The police did not interfere because she was sixteen and therefore of legal age.

Formerly, in contrast to the veiled Muslim woman, the Jewess was not permitted to cover her face in public. She was thus immediately identified as a Jew by Muslim men, who would then annoy her. An informant reported:

---

[1] See Chapter IX for another interpretation of *jud baazi.*

Jewish women used to spin wool for carpets. When their spools were finished they would take them to the bazaar where they were told to put their heads against the wall while their work was inspected. Upon obeying this order, they would be hit over the head and stunned, while their wool was stolen. When such incidents reccurred, Jewish women stopped going to the bazaar.

Today, when even Muslim women are pinched and handled by Muslim men, Jewish women are singled out for special treatment because they are not protected by their kinsmen. The latter do not intervene for fear they would be beaten or even killed.

6 BLOOD LIBEL

Blood libel accusations, an idea probably imported from Europe, became common in Iran during the nineteenth century. The usual form was to accuse the Jews of ritually murdering a Muslim child. Sometimes a dead child would be placed in front of a Jewish home to support the accusation (Stuart, 1854:325–6). The last major pogrom in Shiraz, in 1910, began as a blood libel (Alliance, 1910). As recently as 1945, Jews in Shiraz were accused of ritual murder (Yishay, 1950: 305).

A second sort of libel involves the profanation of Shi'a saints and Imams. Informants confirm that during the nineteenth century Shirazi Jews were accused of representing Husseyn by a dog's head in the synagogue during Ashura, a day of Shi'a mourning. (See Chapter X.)

7 EXPULSION, LIVING RESTRICTIONS AND RESTRICTED TRAVEL

Expulsion was an occasional alternative to conversion, but was dangerous because of hazardous travel. Fars at the beginning of the twentieth century was an area which saw a number of communities expelled, including Lar, Jahrom, Nobendigan and Darab. Periodically, Jews were forbidden to live in certain places or were permitted only with special restrictions. Thus fourteenth century Abarquh (northern Fars) could not be settled by Jews (Mustawfi, 1919:120) and in the 20th century, only temporary residence was permitted. Jews were also prohibited from residing in Semnan (Curzon, 1892, I:291). In late nineteenth century Qom, Jews could not sell wine or keep a shop (Bishop, 1891, I:170). Today there are no residence restrictions, but the twelve Jewish families in Mashhad and the seven in Tabriz are made to feel very unwelcome. Most interesting is the fact that in the nearly 450 km between Zarqon (25 km north of Shiraz) and Isfahan, there is not now, nor apparently was there previously a town or village with permanent Jewish settlement. Jews were forced to get permission to move from one area to another, and this was only infrequently granted. This effectively prevented Jews from escaping especially difficult circumstances.

8   RITUAL POLLUTION

The Jew is considered *najas* "unclean". He is both ritually polluted and polluting and the Shi'a Muslims in Iran take numerous steps to avoid contact with him. Many of the traditional restrictions on the Jews were in support of this avoidance behavior.

a) The Mahalleh, a separate ghetto area to which Jews were restricted, was instituted in Iran long ago. In Shiraz, its size was very carefully regulated and a Jew's attempts to purchase property from Muslims, thereby extending the size of the Mahalleh, was firmly opposed by the Muslim clergy.

b) Physical contact with *dhimmis* generally was abhorred by the Muslim, but the Jew could understand this attitude as he had similar fear of pollution by the "*arelim*" or "uncircumcised", i.e. Christians and Zoroastrians. Nevertheless;

It is more easy to get the Mussulmans to eat food with the Parsis than with the Jews, whose religion ranks higher than Zoroastrianism in the popular regard. (Malcolm, 1905:108)

A Jew who would enter the house of a Muslim would be expected to sit on a special rug. The water pipe, tea or food would not be offered to him. Any object, especially food, touched by a Jew could not be used by a Muslim; thus animals slaughtered by Jews, if judged not ritually fit, could not then be sold to Muslims.[1]

A Jew, planning on purchasing something, could not handle or sort the merchandise, on penalty of being forced to purchase the entire lot at a price to be fixed by the Muslim merchant. This practice, now largely eliminated in Shiraz, is still observed in Burujerd, Hamadan and elsewhere in the north of Iran.

Water was considered the most common agent of pollution, therefore Jews were not permitted to use the public baths. In recent years, they have been permitted to do so in Shiraz, but in Yazd for example, they are restricted to their own bath or that of the Bahais. The possibility that

---

[1] By contrast, in modern-day Shiraz, the hotels buy their beef from the Jewish butchers because it is fresher and cleaner and because Muslim butchers specialize in selling lamb.

rain-water might splash off a Jew onto a Muslim led to the *prohibition of Jews walking in public during the rain*! One informant from Shiraz, told the following anecdote:

When I was a boy, I went with my father to the house of a non-Jew on business. When we were on our way home it started to rain. We stopped near a man who had apparently fallen and was bleeding. As we started to help him up, a Muslim *akhond* (theologian) stopped and asked me who I was and what I was doing. Upon discovering that I was a Jew, he reached for a stick to hit me for defiling him by being near him in the rain. My father ran to him and begged the *akhond* to hit him instead. The surprised *akhond* did not hit anyone and we were permitted to continue homeward.

Fear of pollution by Jews led to great excesses and peculiar behavior by Muslims. In nineteenth century Qom:

the few (Jews) who are allowed to reside here come from Koshan and Ispahan, and the ostentatious vocation which they pursue is peddling; but as the pious living in the religious atmosphere of so many descendants of the Prophet would be shocked at the idea of touching anything that has passed the hands of a defiled and impure Jew, they have had recourse to a more profitable traffic, the sale of spirituous liquors. (Stern, 1854:184–5)

It was also reported that

Christians and Jews according to Persian law are not subject to decapitation as they are considered unclean by the Mohammedans and not sufficiently worthy of this privilege. (Adams, 1900:120)

In Barafarush on the Caspian Sea it was believed that disinterment and dispersion of the Jew's remains to the wind would be efficacious in obtaining rain. Jewish dead were burned and their ashes scattered by Muslims for this purpose (Mounsey 1872:274; Stern 1854:264).

c) The badge of shame was an identifying symbol which marked someone as a *najas* Jew and thus to be avoided. From the reign of Abbas I until the 1920s,[1] all Jews were required to display a badge. The badge has been described as

a little square piece of stuff; two or three fingers broad, sewed to their *Caba* or Gown in the middle of their Breasts, about two fingers above the Girdle, and it matters not what stuff the piece be of, provide the colour be different from that of the Cloaths to which it is sewed. (Thevenot, 1687, II:110)

---

[1] The patch had to be worn in Shiraz until about 1920 according to informants and was required until the beginning of the twentieth century in Teheran (Alliance, 1898:137), Yazd (Malcom, 1905:51–2) and other places.

Jews were sometimes required to wear a special hat such as the one prescribed by Abul Hassan Lari. In Teheran it was the practice for Jews to wear the traditional nightcap, *shubkolah,* all the time (Wills, 1887:135). The Jews of Isfahan were "not permitted to wear the *kolah* or Persian head-dress", (Curzon, 1892, I:510). In about 1800, Jews in Bushehr were forced for a short time to wear the red Turkish Fez (Wills, 1887:314). To this day, the head covering remains the Persian ethnic identification mark *par excellence,* although the Jew no longer wears a distinctive one.

Jewish women were required to wear a black *chador,* (an all enveloping cloak), while exposing their faces (Benjamin, 1859:230). This may explain the present-day Shirazi women's preference for a white *chador.*

9   POLL TAX

The *jaziyeh* (poll tax) was universally applied to Jews in Muslim countries in return for their status as a *dhimmi* or "protected minority". The entire community shared the burden of its collection.

10   NAME CALLING

One of the great insults in Iran is to call someone a Jew or "Jud" (Fraser, 1825:511). So low is the Jew thought, that the Turks once cursed Abbas I saying:

I hope also from the divine Majesty, that in the Day of Judgement he will make you serve instead of Asses to the Jews, that that miserable Nation which is the Contempt of the World, may mount and trot with you to Hell. (Sykes, 1930, 1:178–8)

11   JUSTICE

It was mentioned previously that Jewish life was considered almost worthless by the courts. A Jew could never win a case in court against a Muslim, and, even today, a Jew will go to any length to avoid court action. Muslim–Jewish disputes used to be settled by an *akhond,* (muslim theologian) with a fine or beating as the Jew's normal due. Children too, were dragged before the *akhond* and beaten for alleged wrong doing. The Shirazi Jewish mother still threatens her misbehaving child with the words: "the *khond* will get you!"

Since Reza Shah, the courts have become more equitable. But only Muslims are permitted to practice law – perhaps because so much national law is based on Islamic law.

12   PUBLIC DEGRADATION

The public greeting of the king or governor by the assembled population was described by Chardin in the seventeenth century (1923:208). In Qajar times,

... at the arrival of a new provincial governor, the Jews are compelled to sacrifice an ox in his honour upon the high road at some distance from the town. The headman of the Hebrew community has to run with the bleeding head of the animal, imploring the governor's countenance and protection, until he is beaten off by the farrashes. (Wills, 1887:231)

Morier witnessed the procession of the Shah in early 19th century Teheran, in which the minorities participated as follows:

They, (Armenians) all began to chant Psalms as His Majesty drew near and their zeal was only surpassed by that of the Jews, who also had collected themselves into a body, conducted by their Rabbis who raised on a carved representation of the wood of the tabernacles, and made the most extravagant gestures of humiliation, determined that they at least should not pass unnoticed by the Monarch. (1818:388) [1]

Wills describes the Jews' greatest public humiliation in bitter terms:

At every public festival – even at the royal salaam, before the King's face – the Jews are collected, and a number of them are flung into the *hauz* or tank, that King and mob may be amused by seeing them crawl out half-drowned and covered with mud. The same kindly ceremony is witnessed whenever a provincial governor holds high festival: there are fireworks and Jews. (1887:231)

During the Qajar period, a very difficult time for all Iranian Jews, Shiraz was reputed to be the place where the Jews were most ill treated (Binning, 1857, II:120; Curzon, 1892, I:510–11). Harassment was a concomitant of living.

It was said that one religious fanatic, Sayid Sharif, upon catching a Jew, would cut off his side whiskers, shave part of his chin, make his hat into an ass's bonnet, tear his clothes into shreads and send him away after having given him several blows on the head (Alliance, 1903:110).

Muslims used to intrude into the houses of Jews, drink their wine and liquor, seize any household object to their liking and remove it to their homes without any overt objection of the Jewish owner. If a Muslim decided to sell a house to a Jew, he would demand a price five times its

---

[1] In 1975, upon the Shah's proclamation of single "Resurrection" Party Rule, the Teherani Jewish establishment demonstrated its unquestioned support for the Shah and his policies at a public ceremony, which by most accounts was both embarrassing and humiliating to Persian Jewry.

worth, and even after the transaction was completed the Muslim could find a way to reclaim his property (Alliance, 1903:111).

When a Jew marries, a rabble of the Mahommedan ruffians of the town invite themselves to the ceremony, and, after a scene of riot and intoxication, not infrequently beat their host and his relations and insult the women of the community; only leaving the Jewish quarter when they have slept off the drink they have swallowed at their unwilling host's expense. (Wills, 1887:231)

Nearly as frightening as the actual physical harassment were the threats made daily against the Jew. Verbal abuse continues even to the present day. During World War II, Muslims used to tell Jews, "Hitler is in the cameo around my neck." They went around Shiraz selecting which houses they would take when Hitler took over Iran.

Although more subdued than in the past, verbal and physical abuse of the Jew still occurs in Shiraz during the month of Muharram and especially on Ashura, the day of mourning for Husseyn. Jews are very circumspect to avoid offending Muslims at this time. On Ashura itself, Jews pretended not to know the author in order that on this day, especially, he would not be identified with them. Nevertheless, rumor (untrue) spread through the city that the author had been jailed for three days for taking pictures of the Muslims' ritual pageant.

In the Spring of 1968, Jews, who normally close their stores on Yom Ha'azma'ut (Israel Independence Day) in order to picnic in the gardens, remained open because the Muslim masses were upset about the military parade scheduled for that day in Jerusalem. Yom Ha'azma'ut eve, over 500 men and women assembled in a Mahalleh synagogue to read psalms and penitential prayers — hoping for a peaceful parade.

Threats by the Muslim clergy kept the Jews at home during the 1967 Six Day War. The synagogues were closed for nearly ten weeks until Tish'a B'av. Informants claimed that during the war the *goyim* tried to break into the Mahalleh, but were stopped by the police. Others said that some Jews were beaten up. One informant claimed that after several days, one member of the *Anjoman* (Central Committee) asked everyone to open his store and to keep it open on the Sabbath and on Shavu'ot to demonstrate that Shirazi Jews were *not* in sympathy with Israel. The same informant said that many Jews did as he asked.

The presence of SAVAK, the secret police, adds to the Jews' anxiety. There was an unconfirmed story that a Yeshiva student was arrested by them for publicly praising Israel after the Six Day War. One student activist claimed that whenever Zionist programs take place, the secret police carefully question him about them.

It is readily apparent that Shi'a intolerance must have necessitated many adaptive responses on the part of Shirazi Jews. Choice of occupation, the nature of kin networks and political structures, self-perception and world-view will be seen to have been pervasively affected by the passive strictures and active hostility of the dominant population and the authorities.

While *dhimmis* have been set apart in Iran as pariahs, generally without recourse to political power or influence, this is not to say that the *dhimmi* ethnicities were viewed by the populace as equivalent (*cf.* Fischer, 1973; Schwartz, 1973), although they were all "untouchable" outcastes, distinctive in their relative lack of esteem. Jews nevertheless believe themselves to have been singled out for special mistreatment by the Muslims. The Jew presumes that "the hand of God" has fated the Jew to be thus punished for his "sins": "This has truly been *galut* (exile)," say the Shirazis. "The *goyim* have severely oppressed the Jews and we have had no place to flee."

CHAPTER III

Shiraz in Jewish History

It is not reliably known when Jews first came to Fars province or more particularly, to Shiraz.[1] However, it would seem reasonable to assume that since Jews were living in the Persian capital of Susa (Khuzistan) in the sixth century B.C.E., they would have settled soon after in the other large cities of Persia, including those of nearby Fars. One scholarly traveler claimed to have found Hebrew inscriptions at Persepolis, dating, allegedly, to the period in question (Vambery, 1884:120). The Jews themselves have a tradition that they came in the days of the First Exile (586 B.C.E.) and refused the call of Ezra to return to Judea.[2]

An informant recounted the following tradition:

We were settled as captives in a village known as Holelar (Khullar?) near to Shiraz, where there were good vineyards for wine. We were also settled in other villages in the area. Under pressure from the *goyim* (Muslims), we slowly drifted into Shiraz, then a small city criss-crossed by water channels extending into the city from the river.[3] At first we camped along the channels, but the *goyim* gave us no peace there, so we eventually bought land and built houses on it. We have occupied the same area (the Mahalleh) ever since, and God has prospered us, and the land we own is the best in the entire city.

The city of Shiraz may be very ancient and is perhaps identical with Shira-its-tsi-ish mentioned in the sixth century B.C.E. Elamite tablets from Persepolis (Arberry, 1960:31). At first overshadowed by Achaemenian Persepolis and later by Sassanian Istakhr, Shiraz was made the preeminent city of Islamic Fars by Muhammad, brother of the viceroy Hajjaj ibn Yussuf, in 693 C.E. (Arberry, 1960:31).

Reportedly, during the Arab period, the Jews of Fars were more numerous than any other minority excepting the Zoroastrians (Fischel, 1953:115). Eldad the Danite (*c.* 880) reported the presence of a

---

[1] See Appendix I for a brief history of Iranian Jewry.
[2] Similar traditions are reported among Yemenite (Brauer, 1934:21) and Jerban Jews (Slousch, 1927:258)
[3] The river, Rud-e Khoshk, has been dry for many years.

26

sovereign Jewish kingdom living in the mountains near the Persian Gulf, whose chief means of subsistence was sheep herding. These Jews from the tribe of Yissakhar,[1] allegedly spoke Hebrew and Persian and were well organized, with "leaders of hosts" and a judge (Adler, E., 1966:7). Two other "lost" tribes, Zvulun and R'uven, were living in the Paron (probably Zagros) mountains. They, too, appear to have been nomads and may have been bandits as well. These Jewish tribes wandered and settled in "a country ten days journey by ten days" (Adler, 1966:7). Eldad's reports, which most historians tend to regard as fabricated, may not be so fanciful as they believe.

An early 19th century visitor to Fars reported finding "Calaa-i-Jahudan" (Jews' Castle) supposedly dating to the tenth century, not far from Kazerun (Ouseley, 1819:302).

More importantly, the tenth century Muslim geographer Istakhri claimed:

All of the land from Isfahan to Tustar (Shushtar) was settled by Jews in such large numbers that the whole area was called Yahudistan. (Fischel, 1935:526)[2]

It is thus quite possible that there were Jewish pastoral nomads in ninth century rural Fars. One might even speculate that these nomads were transhumants utilizing many of the same migratory routes later adopted by the Kurds and more recently, the Qashqais.

The Jews of tenth century Fars were dispersed and settled in several communities. They considered themselves independent, and when the Exilarch, David ben Zakkay, officially recognized head of the Jewish community of all the lands of the Eastern Caliphate, sent his son there to collect the revenue due him, the latter was rebuffed. He was forced to ask the Persian emir for help and threatened the local Jews with excommunication when they refused to pay. These pressures had their desired effect (Dubnov, 1968:357). Such conflict suggests the feebleness of the bonds then linking Fars and Babylonian Jewry. Although indirect ties continued for several centuries through the office of Sar Shalom in Isfahan,[3] and thereafter by means of sporadic pilgrimages by Fars' Jews to shrines in Babylonia as well as infrequent commercial and religious emissaries in both directions, by the onset of the fourteenth century,

---

[1] The name Yissakhar is perhaps more than coincidentally similar to the name of the Sassanian religious capitol of Fars: Istakhr.
[2] It is noteworthy that the Bakhtiari tribes who currently migrate as pastoral nomads in the northern portion of this area wear a white garment with black stripes remarkably reminiscent of the traditional Jewish *tallit* (prayer shawl) — minus the ritual fringes.
[3] See Appendix I.

there is no further evidence of contact between the Jews of Southern Iran and the religious centers of Babylonia.

During the Arab period, Shiraz was the hub of several important trade routes. One linked Hormuz on the Persian Gulf with Isfahan, Kashan, Sultaniyya and Kerman (Arberry, 1960:36). It also served as a link in the probable Jewish Radanite trade route to India. In 867, Shiraz was made a provincial capital by Ya'qub ibn Laith of the Saffari dynasty. The Buwayids made it their capital and built there a large hospital. From 932 to 1055, Shiraz was a center for the arts. Under the Seljuqs (1055), colleges were established there. In 1148, Fars became independent under the Salghurids. Later in that century, Fars was racked by civil war, famine and disease, but Shiraz at least was spared the ravages of war suffered during the Mongol invasions. At first, tribute was paid to the Il-Khans, but in 1265, Fars came under their direct control.

Meanwhile, Jewish nomads seem to have disappeared from Fars, since Benjamin of Tudela (*c.* 1169) makes no mention of them. On the other hand, the urbanization of Fars' Jewry was already an established fact, as Shiraz's Jewish population approached 10,000 (Adler, M., 1907:58). No satisfactory explanation has, as yet, been offered for this demographic shift.

Under the fourth Mongol Il-Khan, Arghun, the Jewish vizier Sa'ad ad-Daula appointed a Jewish governor, Shams ad-Daula, over Fars (Fischel, 1937:104). Shirazi Jews were the beneficiaries of the Jewish vizier's large charitable contributions. Among the libels spread about Sa'ad ad-Daula was that he had prepared a list of seventeen Shirazi notables for execution, including "divines and theologians" (Browne, 1920:34). It is not known whether Shirazi Jews, like their brethren in Tabriz and elsewhere, were forced to pay a price in blood and wealth at the demise of Sa'ad ad-Daula.

The Mongol era, the thirteenth and fourteenth centuries, saw in Shiraz the development of some of Persia's finest poetry, that of Sa'adi and Hafez. Both poets enjoyed immense popularity among Iranian Jews who transliterated their works into Judaeo-Persian (Fischel, 1960:1162) accompanied by beautiful painted illuminations in the characteristic miniature style of the times.

Fars was the center of Persian–Jewish culture from the fourteenth through the sixteenth centuries. Persian Jewry's greatest poet, Maulana Shahin, lived and worked in mid-fourteenth century Shiraz (see: Bacher, 1908). His lifework was a poetical commentary on the Bible entitled *Sefer Sharh Shahin al Hatora*. Written in Judaeo-Persian in the epic style of Ferdosi, this composition synthesizes Biblical and Rabbinic literature together with material from the Islamic tradition and Persian classical poetry (Fischel, 1960:1166). Shahin manuscripts are to be found throughout the Judaeo-Persian speaking world. Until recently. Shahin's works were read each Sabbath afternoon in Shiraz and elsewhere.

In sixteenth century Safavid-era Shiraz lived another poet, Amrani, who imitated the style of Shahin. He too showed a familiarity with Jewish and non-Jewish sources in his *Fath-Nameh* (1523) "Book of Conquest" and *Ganj Nameh* (1536) "Book of Treasures". The latter is a poetical paraphrase of the Mishnaic tractate *Avot* (Fathers). Amrani continued Shahin's commentary on the Bible, by writing poems on the Early Prophets. Other important poets in Fars during this period were: Yehuda Lari (*Makhzan al-Pand*, "The Treasure House of Exhortation") and Yosef Zarqani (*Shabbat Nameh*, "Book of the Sabbath").

This kind of scholarship and art set the standard for Persian Jewry. Its emphasis on exegesis and legend and its lack of emphasis on Jewish law and Hebrew grammar have strongly influenced Iranian Jewish scholarship to the present day. Never again did Fars Jewry attain such heights of scholarship, nor did its religious leadership reattain such influence in Iran.[1]

Fourteenth century Shiraz was "a pleasant city", but filthy (Mustawfi, 1919:120) and densely populated (Ibn Battuta, 1962:299). Mustawfi adds that people

are much addicted to holy poverty, and they are of strict orthodoxy, so they are content to do but little trade! Hence there are many poor folk ... (1919:113)

Shirazis, Jews as well as Muslims, still enjoy the twin reputations of laziness and orthodoxy. But despite its piety and reputation for charity (Ibn Battuta, 1962:300), Shiraz was noted for its lack of justice (Mustawfi, 1919:114).

In all probability, the Jewish population of Shiraz during this time was substantial. But while urban Jews seem to have enjoyed some measure of security, settlement in the rest of Fars seems to have been restricted. Thus, in Abarquh, on the northern fringe of Fars, it was said:

If any Jew remains but forty days, he dies; hence there are no Jews here; and should any come hither on some important business, in less than forty days he must go hence. (Mustawfi, 1919:120)

The ensuing absence of Jews in northern Fars continuing to the present day may well date to this period. With the exception of the Safavid

---

[1] Shirazi immigrants in Jerusalem in the early twentieth century, dominated the religious life of the Persian community there (see: H. A. Cohen, 1970).

period (1502–1722), when Jewish settlement in Fars was comparatively unrestricted for commercial reasons, there have been no Jews settled in the 450 km between Zarqon (25 km north of Shiraz) and Isfahan. No matter its reasons, such restricted residence led Fars' Jewry to a consequent feeling of isolation from Jews elsewhere in Persia.

Southern Fars was visited by a number of European travelers during the seventeenth century. Port cities to the southeast of Fars, such as Hormuz and Bandar Abbas were inhabited by Jews, according to the reports. Sir Thomas Herbert (1677) reports that Jews were said to have founded the town of Jahrom, naming it for Kiryat Y'arim in Israel. In Lar, most of the inhabitants were Jewish silk farmers (Thevenot, 1687:131). Lar also seems to have been a center for scribes, who translated the Bible into Judaeo-Persian; Giambattista Vechietti brought back Judaeo-Persian manuscripts from Lar, in 1601 (Fischel, 1960:1169).

During the Safavid period (1502–1722), the Jews of Shiraz suffered the consequences of Persia's shift of state religion from orthodox Sunni to sectarian Shi'a Islam. They were among the first to face the vengeance of the renegade Jew, Abul Hassan Lari (1622), who attempted to humiliate his former coreligionists by forcing them to dress outlandishly so to be mocked by their Muslim neighbors (see Appendix I). Extensive restrictive codes, such as the Jam Abassi[1] were instituted. Between 1653 and 1666, the communities of Shiraz, Lar and Bandar Abbas were ordered to convert to Islam. The following account of the events which subsequently transpired in Shiraz is based on the chronicle of Babay ibn Lutf (Levi, 1960:330–343; Bacher, 1906;90–91, 96–97).

When news (of the Shah's decree) reached Shiraz, the people mourned, prayed, asked forgiveness, gave charity, blew the *shofar* (ram's horn), said penitential prayers and recited confession. The Jews were assembled by the leaders of the city, and read the royal decree. They were then given a choice of forfeiting all their possessions and going into exile outside the city, or converting to Islam. They chose exile, but tried to stall its implementation. The city's leaders insisted that the decree be enacted immediately. Through appropriate bribes, the Jews were able to live temporarily just outside the city. They camped in tents near a swamp. One night, the camp was raided and women and children kidnapped. The Jews returned to the city to protest to its leaders of the iniquity which had been visited upon them. They cursed the perpetrators of the crime and threatened divine retribution on Judgement Day. The mayor of the city was angered by the Jews' harsh words and ordered them to be whipped unless they converted. Many Jews, especially Priests and Levites accepted martyrdom, rather than conversion to Islam. Numerous others committed suicide. Finally, Jewish women from Lar and Shiraz were delegated to ask the intercession of the Shah's mother on their behalf.

---

[1] See Appendix II.

These entreaties apparently had the desired effect, as the Shah finally abrogated his decree.[1]

The effects of these persecutions persisted and numerous new converts to Islam remained Muslims.[2] The Jam Abbasi was reinstated in Fars and Fryer observed in 1676, that the Jews of Lar were again wearing the "badge of shame", although the Isfahani Jews were not so compelled (1912:247–8).

Despite the persecutions of the Safavid period, there is little evidence that Shirazi Jews were especially poor. It was noted in fact, that Persian Jews tried to give the appearance of being poor, whether they were or not (Tavernier, 1684:160). It may well have been the Afghan wars that left the Jews of Shiraz in the state of abject poverty so often described in the nineteenth and twentieth centuries. The chronicle of Babay ibn Farhad indicates that when Shah Ashraf abandoned Shiraz in 1730, the Jews were required to give up their gold and were left completely penniless (Bacher, 1907:94). Neither the Afghans nor Nadir Shah bothered Shirazi Jews beyond that.

From 1750 to 1794, under the Zands, Shiraz was the capital of Persia. Karim Khan-e Zand ruled from 1750 to 1779, and, while harsh to the Jewish leaders he captured in the siege of Basra, he was fair to the Jews of Fars (Levi, 1960:488).

In 1786, one traveler noted:

The Jews at Shiraz have a quarter of the city allotted to themselves, for which they pay a considerable tax to the government, and are obliged to make frequent presents; these people are more odious to the Persians than those of any other faith; and every opportunity is taken to oppress and extort money from them; the very boys in the street being accustomed to beat and insult them, of which treatment they dare not complain. (Francklin, 1790:60)

The Jewish quarter stood near to the new citadel of the Zands. The advantage of such a location lay in the immediacy of government protection, when needed. In reality, despite the harassment described by Francklin, Jews suffered more from the propaganda of the Muslim clergy and their inability to cope with increased economic competition than from actual violence (Levi, 1960:487). The temporary preeminence of Shiraz led to a restoration of direct contact with Baghdadi Jewish

---

[1] See Chapter X for the traditional mythic explanation.
[2] Until recently, Muslim villagers in Fars used to give Jewish itinerant peddlers old Hebrew prayer books and phylacteries which they claim had been in their families for many generations. They had no idea what these objects were or why they had kept them.

merchants and bankers, who, for a brief period, visited Shiraz on business (Sassoon, 1949:129).

"I shall not forget that it was a Jew,[1] Hajji Ibrahim, who had helped raise the Kajars to the throne." In these words Nasser ad-Din Shah addressed Adolphe Cremieux in Paris, July 12, 1873 (Fischel, 1950:123). Sykes called Hajji Ibrahim a "king maker" (1930:285). Under the Zands he had been *Kalantar* (chief civil magistrate) and throughout the Qajar period, 1796–1925, his family maintained this position in Shiraz. He had, at first, won the throne for Lotfali Khan (Zand), but after a dispute with him, seized Shiraz and held it for Aqa Mohammad Khan, the first Qajar. Under the latter he was made grand vizier and he held the throne for Mohammad Khan's successor, Fath-Ali Shah. As had been the fate of court Jews before him, Hajji Ibrahim was assassinated at the order of the Shah, but the power of his family, which by then had converted to Islam, was not diminished. His daughter married the new Prime Minister, while his son succeeded to the position of *Kalantar* and took the title *Qavam ul-Mulk* (Support of the Kingdom). The family was known by the title *Qavam* to the end of the Qajar period, and is still eminent in Shiraz.

Despite such an auspicious beginning, the Jews of Fars suffered continual persecution and indignities at the hands of the Qajars (see Appendix II). The Austrian Jewish court physician, Polak (1865:28), claimed that the Qavam family had, in 1859, taken the Jews under their protection, but no one else confirms this. Indeed, some fifty years later they themselves engineered a pogrom against the Jews.

Rabbi David d'bet Hillel reported that a forced conversion of Shirazi Jews took place shortly before his trip to Persia in about 1827 (Fischel, 1944:225). Israel Benjamin (1859:229) may have been referring to the same event in his account, in which he declares that 2500 of 3000 Shirazi Jews converted to Islam. Stern, a Jewish-Christian missionary, confirms that "all of the silk merchants in the bazaar Vekeel, the most extensive market, are proselytes." Jews, "in order to save themselves from a violent death, constantly renounce the religion of their fathers" (1854:128). The situation became so desperate, that a number of families fled from Shiraz to Kashan, despite the dangers of such a trip (Alliance, 1907:85). Yet neither the Babis (whose movement began in Shiraz) nor church missionaries had any great success in obtaining

---

[1] Hajji Ibrahim's alleged Jewish origin is disputed by some scholars (William Royce, personal communication). But see *Khanevadeh Qavam Mulk* by A. Qasimi (Teheran, 1950:5) cited in Fischer, M., 1973:330.

proselytes from amongst the Jewish remnant in Shiraz. Those who survived clung tenaciously to Judaism.

The condition of the Jews of Fars continued to deteriorate towards the close of the nineteenth century. Two political factors were of significance in this decline. The first was the Qajars' increasing loss of control over Fars. The second was the emerging importance of the Jew as tool of international politics; in this case, he was a hostage to be used as leverage in dealing with the European powers.

In 1892, several Jews were murdered in Shiraz (Alliance, 1892:52). Twenty Jews were murdered and three synagogues were burned down in 1897 (Alliance, 1897:87). Pogroms, forced conversion and expulsion swept Zarqon, Lar, Jahrom, Darab, Nobendigan, Sarvestan and Kazerun (Alliance, 1900–1910). Jews abandoned Lar and Jahrom, which were never resettled, and emigrated to Shiraz and thence to Palestine, where they joined the numerous Shirazis who had previously escaped. Just after the holiday of Sukkot in 1910, a pogrom organized by the apostate Qavam family resulted in thirteen deaths, injury, theft, vandalism and near starvation for the 6000 Jews of Shiraz (Alliance, 1910:229–245). The Qavam brothers, who led the Khamseh confederacy against the Qashqais, were attempting to discredit the latter in the eyes of the British by blaming the pogrom on them. [1]

In the midst of this turmoil, in 1903, the first foreign Jewish agency to help Shirazi Jewry, the Alliance Israélite Universelle, founded a school in Shiraz. Its operations were terminated in the 1920s, but while active, it provided an education for some 300 boys and 70 girls, annually.

With Europe's attention diverted from Persia by World War I, the Jews of Fars too, slipped back into a more routine existence. Under the Pahlavis (1925–present), the various indignities previously imposed upon Fars' Jewry, were removed. Hostile behavior by Muslims has since been limited to occasional blood libels, religious harangues from the clergy, and boycotting of Jewish businesses. Violence is seldom reported. For the first time in hundreds of years Jews have been permitted to purchase large tracts of land; gardens and whole villages were bought and Jews now own large holdings along Shiraz's main streets.

Since the modern period is discussed in detail throughout this book, only a few highlights will be mentioned here. In 1947, Otsar Hatorah opened the first of several schools in Shiraz. In 1950, the American Joint Distribution Committee (JDC) began operations, which included a feeding program for school children, medical services and a sanitation

---

[1] Sykes tries to place the blame on Sawlat ad-Daula, chief of the Qashqais (1930:469), but informants who lived through those events confirmed personally the Qavam's guilt.

program; in June 1964, a medical clinic was opened in the Jewish quarter.

The 1950s witnessed a large emigration, especially of the poor, from Shiraz and the villages of Fars to Israel. In the 1960s, numbers of Shirazis went abroad to college and for professional training, others entered Pahlavi University in Shiraz. New freedom of movement, modernization, and increased opportunity have led to changes in the settlement pattern, vocation and social life of the Shirazi Jew, while Fars' rural Jewry has all but vanished. Despite all of this change and a declining incidence of violence in recent years, Shirazi Jews are constantly alerted to the ever-present threat to their continued survival posed by the latent hostility of their neighbors.

CHAPTER IV

The Jewish Community in Shiraz

THE MAHALLEH

For as long as Shirazi Jews can remember, they have been living in the Mahalleh, a "quarter" set apart from the other inhabitants of Shiraz. The overcrowding and filth of this area horrified nineteenth century observers, leading one to remark that "the houses resemble the dens of animals rather than the habitations of men" (Wills, 1887:271).

Until the 1930s, the Mahalleh was a contiguous area of Jewish settlement located in the northwestern part of the old city. At that time a new street, Lotfali Khan-e Zand, was cut through the Mahalleh (see Fig. 2), with a consequent destruction of housing, synagogues and shops. Some Jews seized this opportunity to move out of the old city altogether, though most remained in the untouched areas of the Mahalleh, where housing the dispossessed placed an added burden on the population.

Prior to World War II, some thirty refugee families from Mashhad settled in the new city. For a number of years they continued posing as *jadid al-islam* (new Muslims), but eventually this guise was discarded and they assumed full Jewish status. By 1945 about fifty families, less than 4% of the total Jewish population, lived outside of the Mahalleh (Yishay, 1950:308). In 1962 it was estimated that about 25% of the Jewish population lived outside of the Mahalleh (Clarke, 1963:50).

Settlement outside of the Mahalleh occurred over a period of years and, gradually, predominantly Jewish neighborhoods were formed. Jews settled mainly to the north and west of the Mahalleh. Wealthier Jews settled along Karim Khan-e Zand Street (called "Zand"), on which they owned much of the property. Even Jews whose residence remained in the Mahalleh moved their shops out of the city bazaar and relocated them along Khiaban-e Daryush and Khiaban-e Lotfali Khan-e Zand.

In the late 1950s the northern section of the Mahalleh was partially divided by a new street, Nemazi, which was completed by joining it with Lotfali Khan-e Zand in about 1966. Thus the original pre-1930 Mahalleh was divided into three parts. The section to the south of Lotfali

35

Khan-e Zand is known as *Zire Takh* after its main *kuche* (alley) of the same name. The segment to the northwest of the intersection of Nemazi and Lotfali Khan-e Zand is referred to as *Ose Qarchi*. The northeastern section, closest to the bazaar, is the Mahalleh proper.

Until 1949, *Zire Takh*[1] was the largest area of the ghetto, having the highest density of population. Many of the well-to-do lived here in large houses; several of them owning small gardens nearby. In the past twenty years, the Jewish population of *Zire Takh* was diminished considerably, while Muslims have been gradually moving in. It is the dirtiest of the three sections and was believed to be the site of origin of a leishmaniasis epidemic which raged during the period of research. It was the only section whose main alleys remained unpaved. There are five synagogues in *Zire Takh* containing thirteen prayer sanctuaries, and four kosher butchers. There used to be a public bath there, which no longer exists. Some 355 families, totaling about 2100 people live in 187 houses. The population density is just over eleven per house, but the houses are generally spacious.

Ose Qarchi (Domain of the Mushroom) contains many recently constructed houses, and only one synagogue. The Jews here are outnumbered by Muslims and the standard of living is the highest in the ghetto. About 165 Jewish families, or nearly 1000 people live in 85 houses. The population density of nearly twelve per house is somewhat misleading, as the houses are generally larger than in other areas.

The Mahalleh proper consists of some 180 families or about 1100 Jews, living in 112 houses. The population density is about ten persons per house. Here, however, the houses are older and smaller than in the other areas. The Mahalleh is the smallest of the three areas, but in 1968 it remained 80% Jewish. Within it are four kosher butchers, and five synagogues housing eleven sanctuaries. The poorest Jews live there and much of the JDC's sanitation and relief efforts are directed toward improving conditions in this area. JDC's medical clinic is also located here. The Jewish community's only *hamum* (bath), privately owned but featuring a JDC installed *maqve* (ritual bath), is located near the clinic. Although the community's central Committee, the *Anjoman,* purchased land at the northern edge of the Mahalleh many years ago, the new

---

[1] The name *Zire Takh* was not defined by Shirazis but may be derived from *zir-e takht* (beneath the throne), as the area is not far from the palace of the Zands. William Royce (personal communication) offers the alternative "*zir-e taq*" or "under the arch" which may have once led into the area.

FIGURE 2   Map of Shiraz

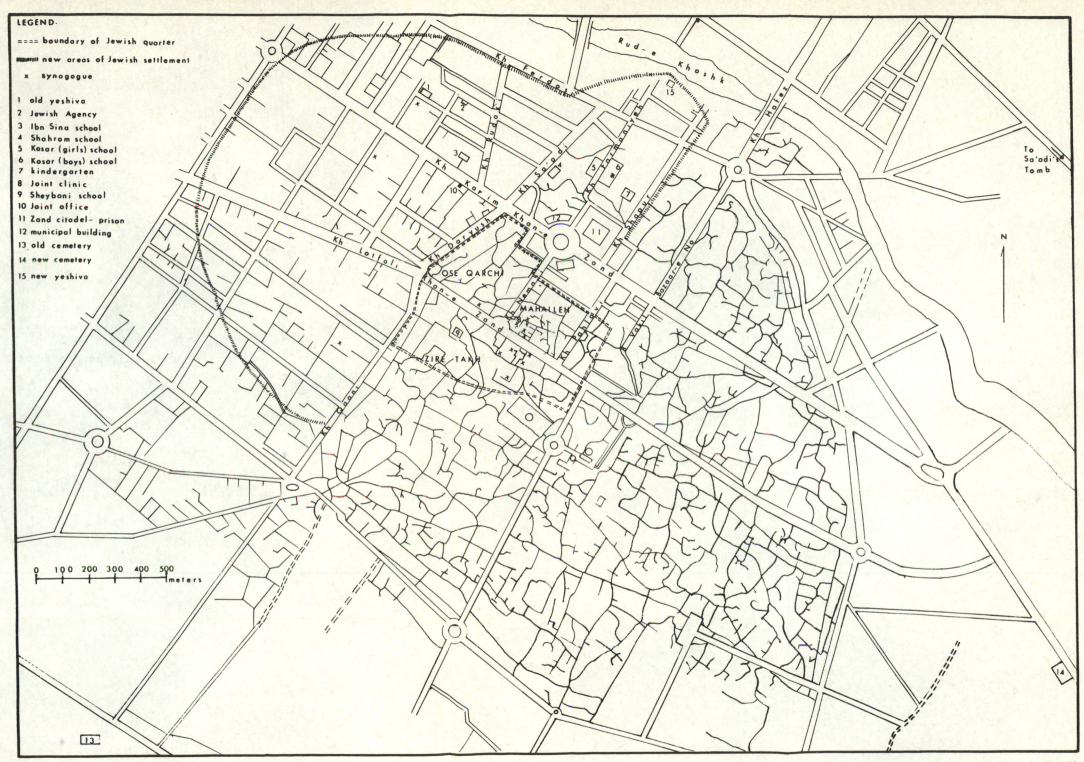

LEGEND:
==== boundary of Jewish quarter
〰〰 new areas of Jewish settlement
x synagogue

1 old yeshiva
2 Jewish Agency
3 Ibn Sina school
4 Shahram school
5 Kosar (girls) school
6 Kosar (boys) school
7 kindergarten
8 Joint clinic
9 Sheybani school
10 Joint office
11 Zand citadel- prison
12 municipal building
13 old cemetery
14 new cemetery
15 new yeshiva

0 100 200 300 400 500 meters

Facing p. 36 (Loeb)

PLATE 6   A large home in Zire Takh. The pool with its water tap is edged by fruit trees. The platform beds in the courtyard are provided for summer outdoor sleeping.

PLATE 7   The view from the main Mahalleh *kuche* across Kh. Nemazi which recently divided the Mahalleh from Ose Qarchi. The sheared off buildings attest to the proximity of this event to the author's sojourn. Nemazi serves as a pushcart market center for produce and second-hand merchandise.

hamum proposed for that site has never been built. The Friday fruit and vegetable market, and the used-clothing bazaar, are located in the center of this section; here men sit around resting from work and chatting.

Shirazi Jews use the term "Mahalleh" to designate the whole ghetto area and we shall adopt the same usage. Some 4200 Jews inhabit the Mahalleh, nearly 50% of the Shirazi community.

The Mahalleh is transversed by numerous alleys, both open and blind. Buildings used to extend (some still do) over the alleys at a height of about 170 cm. Doors facing on the *kuche* as well as the tunnel-like house entrances are still lower, averaging about 155 cm. Jews explain that the narrow, twisting alleys and high windowless walls, surrounding each house, along with the previously mentioned low entrances, protected the Jews from mobs and from mounted men.[1] Mahalleh dwellers frequently avoid walking the maze of alleys, by going over the flat connecting roofs of the houses.

HOUSING

Traditionally, Mahalleh housing has been constructed of sun-dried bricks; mud is used for mortar and plaster. Rooms are whitewashed inside. The house is built around a courtyard ranging in size from 3×2 m to 50×25 m. Many courtyards have a pool in the center surrounded by several fruit trees. Today, most houses have a water tap, electricity, an outhouse and a place for garbage disposal. Water for those without a tap may be obtained from neighbors, from the nearest synagogue or public tap. In the past, water was supplied by wells or from an open ditch called a *jub*. Outhouses are disinfected with carbolic acid at the urging of JDC. Garbage used to be thrown into the alleys and into a central dump, but now there are regular refuse collections and the alleys are swept twice per week by JDC or government employed sweepers.

Each house has a basement, which was formerly occupied, but is now used only for storage. Houses are either one or two stories high. All of the rooms have a wall facing the courtyard. That wall is lined with wooden shutters, which in the poorer homes are patched with cardboard, but in some homes have been replaced by glass. The inside room walls are lined with built-in storage niches.

The roofs, made from a mud and straw mixture laid over logs and matting, are at least 0.5 m thick. Each roof has several gentle depressions, canted towards the courtyard, to facilitate rain drainage.

---

[1] Habib Levi (1960, III:682) claims that the houses at the end of a narrow dark alley were more valuable since they were better protected against attack or intrusion.

PLATE 8   Porter stops to pose on main Mahalleh *kuche* with laden donkey and neighbor boy. JDC clinic is located in the modern building at the left.

Rain does not cause roof leakage, but heavy snow accumulations on the roofs often cause them to cave-in. Summer nights are spent on the roof, which provides a cool and comfortable sleeping area and is conducive to inter-family socializing. Roofs are unrailed and therefore dangerous. Falling from the roof presently constitutes the largest single cause of infant mortality and serious injury.

During the summer, Mahalleh inhabitants are bothered not only by heat, but by scorpions, mosquitoes, sand flies and roaches. In winter the houses are cold – the Aladdin wick-lamps and traditional *korsi* heater not being sufficient to relieve the discomfort. People go to sleep early and arise late in the winter months; everyone seems to be generally in low spirits during the cold and wet period from November through February.

The dried-mud floors of the Mahalleh house are covered by straw matting and inexpensive locally made carpets. Household utensils in-

PLATE 9   Main Mahalleh crossroads at dusk — a Jewish grocery.

PLATE 10   Neighborhood children traipse through one of the myriad of narrow Mahalleh alleyways.

PLATE 11   Wide alleys are favorite play spots. Here some boys play *gerdu baazi,* the nut game, similar to American marbles.

PLATE 12   Like most Iranian urban children, Jewish boys love to spin wheels.

PLATE 13   Typical wattle and daub Mahalleh roof.

PLATE 14   "Refrigerator" basket suspended from the roof at night safeguards family meat from prowling cats.

PLATE 15   Houses lacking water taps store water in huge pottery jugs — Muslim woman fills tea kettle at Jewish neighbor's yard.

PLATE 16   Storage niches in the wall are often decorated with pictures and amulets — two framed pictures of Moses holding the ten commandments adorn center niche.

PLATE 17 Separate room with charcoal stoves designated for Sabbath food warming.

PLATE 18 The entire family sleeps in one room – the infant's cradle is suspended above the other children.

clude numerous pots, pans, basins and trays, small glasses for tea, bottles for *sharbat* (fruit juice concentrate), some plastic or china dishes, spoons and knives. Cooking is done on an Aladdin stove or over a wood or charcoal fire. There is also a special Sabbath kitchen and stove. The "refrigerator" is a wood-framed screened cabinet, or a platform or basket suspended high above the yard out of the reach of cats, which abound in the Mahalleh. Most families own large thermos bottles which are filled with ice during the warm months and a handful of families have electric refrigerators. Most households have a radio and many have electric fans.

Formerly, overcrowding was a serious problem in the Mahalleh.[1] In 1883, the average density of the Jewish Mahalleh population was said to be about nine persons per house (Wilson, 1916:16). By 1903 it had reached 23 per house (Alliance, 1903:104). In 1905, it was more than 23 per house (Wilson, 1916:16). Prior to 1949, the population density peaked at between 27 and 30 per house, according to informants. Today the average density is about 11 per house. In 1904 it was reported that *20 families* might inhabit a three or four room house and 12 to 15 persons per room was not uncommon (Alliance, 1904:30). Today there are several large houses which are inhabited by five or six families. Rarely is there more than one nuclear family per room and usually there are several empty rooms per house. The average room occupancy is down to three to four per room.[2]

For heuristic purposes, the Mahalleh may be thought of in terms of neighborhoods. Each blind-alley, along which live several families, forms a unit. The women and children within this unit socialize continually, though patterns of friendship and enmity vary with time; socialization is by no means limited to this unit. Men socialize primarily in the synagogues and along the main *kuche*. Mahalleh women extend their range of acquaintances in the synagogue, at the *hamum* and at the market. There appears to be a tendency for kin to live in proximity to one another. In one blind alley, the families of two brothers, mother and unmarried sister occupied three of ten houses. In the Mahalleh, no one lives more than a three to five minute walk from a friend or relative. One reason families prefer to live in the Mahalleh, although they could afford to move out, is the ease of socializing with friends and neighbors; women particularly cherish these opportunities for social interaction.

---

[1] Clarke (1963:21) indicates that population density in the old city of Shiraz (including the Mahalleh) in 1956 was about 121.4 persons per acre, while in the new city it was only 20.2 per acre. The median number per dwelling was 4.3.
[2] The entire nuclear family sleeps together in the same room, even if other rooms remain empty.

PLATE 19   Mahalleh *hamum*.

All Mahalleh dwellers speak *judi*,[1] the Judaeo-Persian dialect of Shiraz. Many of the younger people make an effort to avoid its use, as it is considered substandard by the Ministry of Education. While older Mahalleh children speak it fluently, younger ones hardly speak it at all.

PUBLIC INSTITUTIONS

The Mahalleh adult has access to two central public institutions. The most important is the *knisa* (synagogue). The synagogue is central to the community's social and religious life as it is regularly attended by men and women; it will be examined at length in Chapter X.

The other is the *hamum* or "bath". Presently there is only one public Jewish bath in Shiraz, although once there were three. Mahalleh Jews have no baths in their houses and are dependent on the public one. Until

---

[1] Many of the terms used in this dissertation are *judi;* they are so identified in the glossary.

PLATE 20   In warm weather, young children are bathed in a basin at home.

recently, Jews were forbidden to enter a public bath utilized by Muslims for fear that the *najas* Jew might pollute them. Today Jews are no longer restricted to their own baths, and some living outside the Mahalleh regularly use non-Jewish public baths.

The Jewish bath contains a *maqve* (ritual bath), a large bath and a small bath. The old rooms are warm and moist and the bare walls are full of roaches. The rusted water taps are only about one meter above the stone floor, necessitating one's sitting or lying under them or rinsing with a pitcher or bucket. Washing is done with a coarse woolen cloth which rubs off a considerable amount of skin together with the grime. During the week, the large bath is utilized by the women and their children, while men make use of the small bath. On Fridays the procedure is reversed. Everyone makes an effort to visit the *hamum* once per week.

The bath house is heated; everyone sits on the floor. Women wash the young children at home in a copper basin during the warm months;

PLATE 21   Combing a cleansing clay through the hair in lieu of shampoo.

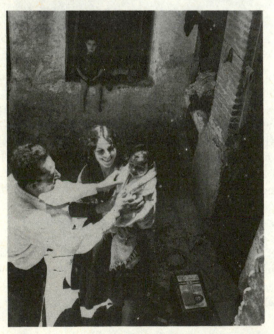

PLATE 22   Returning home for lunch, father affectionately reaches for his toddler daughter.

otherwise the children are bathed in the *hamum*. Women wash each other's hair with henna and gossip all the while. They often spend three or four hours in the bath.

Most men bathe on Friday, after work. They sit around swapping stories and jokes. It is said that some of them smoke the water pipe at the *hamum*, but this was not observed by the author. Several carters spend their Fridays assisting in the *hamum* by giving massages. Everyone enjoys the warmth and socializing, rumor-mongering and good-fellowship that the *hamum* offers.

The *maqve* is used by women for their monthly ritual immersion. Men formerly used the *maqve* for ritual immersion after becoming ritually polluted, but nowadays they go only on the day preceding Yom Kippur and on their wedding day.

MODESTY AND PRIVACY

The Jewish woman was not restricted to the *anderun* (harem) as was the Muslim. The Mahalleh woman is, nevertheless, circumspect regarding her behavior. She wars a *chador* (all-enveloping cloak) on the street and in the presence of strange men. Unlike Muslim women however, she never covers her whole face and rarely even covers her mouth. Jewish women prefer light, bright colors for the *chador,* whereas Muslims tend to wear black. Traditionally, the Mahalleh woman wore pants under her dress, but today this is not common in Shiraz. Nevertheless, she sits carefully on her haunches avoiding display of her feet, or, if she sits cross-legged, she covers her legs with a *chador*. Flesh in general, and legs in particular, are not to be revealed by her clothing – it is "ugly".[1] Exposure of flesh would be interpreted by Muslim men as an enticement, thus inviting an advance. Jewish men are said to eschew any immoral behavior with a married woman, and would be offended by any untoward behavior. Some scholars see the surveillance of women as the sole means of preventing their sexual abuse by Iranian men; since surveillance of Jewish women is relatively lenient, other sexual controls, mainly religious ones, are surmised to be operant.

Formerly it was possible to distinguish Jew from Muslim by dress, but this is no longer so. Modern Muslim women no longer cover their faces and some have dispensed with the *chador*. Men too are not distinguishable by dress; most wear Western style brimmed hats or no hat

---

[1] On the other hand, exposure of the breast for nursing, even in public, is perfectly proper.

PLATE 23   Escaping the early afternoon sun, women surrounded by neighborhood children gossip and spin under *kuche* overhang.

PLATE 24   Exposing the breast for nursing is not considered immodest; children are usually suckled on demand.

at all. Some wear the *tallit* (small prayer shawl), but this is concealed under the clothing.

Jewish men are less modest than women, but usually more modest than Muslim men. Mahalleh men rarely urinate in the street, whereas lower class Muslim men frequently do so. Jewish men only expose their bodies in the *hamum* and do not participate in body building by gymnastics and wrestling as do the Muslims.

Privacy is assured in the Mahalleh by having no windows facing the street, and a wall at least three meters high surrounding the house. Privacy is highly valued since it ensures non-visibility, an important defense against the Muslims.

TU KHIYABUN

The majority of Jews, now living *tu khiyabun* (outside of the Mahalleh; literally, "in the streets") live under somewhat different circumstances from those described above. Housing is far superior; roofs are of metal and are slanted, floors are tiled, and windows are large and glass-paned.[1] The courtyards are large, and the pool may be surrounded by a veritable orchard. Those living *tu khiyabun* often have electric refrigerators, gas stoves, fans and private baths. A growing number have Western furniture, and a few own automobiles.

Tu khiyabun, elite women and nearly all of the younger generation of females have discarded the *chador*. But women's social life is decidedly less rich than in the Mahalleh. Men do all the shopping, because in the course of the relatively long walk to the market their wives would be annoyed by Muslim men. Despite the fact that the neighborhood is Jewish, the blind-alley neighborhood unit is completely absent here. Socializing is largely limited to the family and visiting with them is less frequent than in the Mahalleh. *Knisa* becomes even more important to women living *tu khiyabun* since there, at least, they have an opportunity to gossip with old friends. Since most women have a private bath, they no longer visit the Jewish *hamum*. Jewish women *tu khiyabun* are also somewhat less careful concerning their ritual immersions; the *maqve* is but infrequently used, most women preferring to dip in the bathtub at home. One of the few links these women maintain with the Mahalleh is through the JDC medical clinic, whose services they still patronize. In sum, women living *tu khiyabun,* especially those who left the Mahalleh as adults, feel somewhat lonely and isolated, and miss the warm communal socializing

---

[1] Many houses have windows facing directly on the street.

PLATE 25　*Tu khiyabun,* housing and streets are more modern – many Jews live on this *kuche,* less than ten minutes walk from the Mahallen.

PLATE 26　Kh. Karim Khan-e Zand, Shiraz' main street.

PLATE 27   Municipal prison located in the former Zand citadel close to the old Jewish quarter.

PLATE 28   Washing clothes in the *jub* near the municipal building; these drainage channels were once widely utilized for many purposes, but now piped water has obviated their use by most Shirazi women.

PLATE 29   A professional letter writer pens a note at the behest of an illiterate woman – a thriving service in modern Shiraz.

PLATE 30   A mendicant *darvish*, a Sufi teller of tales, entertains young and old, a few steps from the Mahalleh.

PLATE 31 Author's wife chooses pomegranates at a fruit market near the Mahalleh.

PLATE 32 Copper-smiths' bazaar in Bazaar-e Vakil.

they enjoyed in the Mahalleh. Their new interests, fashionable clothes, movies and modern conveniences, are little compensation for greater seclusion and solitude.

Men's social life is little changed by moving out of the Mahalleh. Most of the day is spent at work and socializing is most commonly continued in *knisa*. Some men affiliate with the more modern and more prestigious synagogues *tu khiyabun,* but most continue to attend *knisa* in the Mahalleh. Men tend to be more conservative about changing their life styles *tu khiyabun.* They are as frugal with money as in the Mahalleh and this is a source of great conflict between husbands and their wives, who want more modern conveniences.

Tu khiyabun, Jewish children tend to play more with Muslim children than in the Mahalleh, and whereas most Mahalleh children go to American sponsored Otsar Hatorah parochial schools, children living *tu khiyabun* usually attend public schools. Most of the children living outside the Mahalleh continue their formal education through high school and some even go to college.

Acculturation to Persian and Western culture is greatly accelerated *tu khiyabun.* Reforming and liberalizing trends in community and religious life are largely instigated *tu khiyabun.* The movement of Jewish population out of the Mahalleh has been accompanied by the relocation of important community institutions such as the schools, the JDC office, the Jewish Agency office and others.

TRADITIONAL COMMUNITY ORGANIZATION

We have no information about Jewish community organization prior to the seventeenth century Safavid period, but there is little evidence that political organization differed significantly before that time. In an earlier era, other community structures must have existed. Nomadic Jewish populations living in Khorassan and throughout the Zagros mountains were completely self-ruled and independent in the pre-Mongol period. It is also likely that some sort of central rule over urban Jewish communities in Persia was administered by the Sar Shalom in 12th century Isfahan (see Appendix I). But all this appears to have ended with the thirteenth century Mongol invasions.

One of the most important functions of the Jewish political apparatus was to provide the government with the *jaziyeh* (poll tax) incumbent upon Jews as a "protected minority". The Jew responsible for the prompt payment of taxes was the *nasi* (prince). He was a highly respected Jew, probably the wealthiest, who by consensus was acknowledged the secular leader of the community. He may have been known also by the Persian term *kadkhoda*. He was normally chosen by the elders of the community to represent the community in secular affairs and in dealing with the authorities.

If the taxes were not paid in due time, or did not reach the amount requested, the Nasi could be dismissed by the authorities. On the other hand, if the authorities were satisfied, the Nasi might receive a sign of distinction and honor. (Fischel, 1953:119–120)

The poll tax on Jews was often farmed out to a high official who first promised a sum to the treasury and then proceeded to extort it from the Jews. During the reign of Abbas I, a renegade Jew functioned in just that way, squeezing the Isfahani community for 50% more taxes than in previous years (Fischel, 1953:119). Tax farming during the nineteenth century reduced the Jews to virtual serfdom.

The principle is very simple. The Jews of a province are assessed at a tax of a certain amount. Someone pays this amount to the local governor together with a bribe; and the wretched Jews are immediately placed under his authority for the financial year. It is a simple speculation. If times are good, the farmer of the Jews makes a good profit; if they are bad, he gains nothing, or may fail to extract from them as much as he has paid out of pocket – in that case, woe betide them. During the Persian famine the Jews suffered great straits before the receipt of subsidies sent from Europe by their co-religionists. The farmer of the Jewish colony in a great Persian city (of course a Persian Mohammedan) having seized their goods and clothes, proceeded, in the cold of a Persian winter to remove the doors and windows of their hovels and to wantonly burn them. The farmer was losing money, and sought thus to enforce what he considered his rights. No Persian pitied the unfortunates; they were Jews and so beyond the pale of pity. Every street-boy raises his hand against the wretched Hebrew; he is beaten and buffeted in the streets, spat upon in the bazaar. The only person he can appeal to is the farmer of the Jews. From him, he will obtain a certain amount of protection if he be actually robbed of money or goods; not from the farmer's sense of justice, but because the complainant, were his wrongs unredressed, might be unable to pay his share of the tax. (Wills, 1887:229–230)

Although the *nasi* was the most important secular leader of the community, decision-making was shared with the *'ene ha'eda* (eyes of the community), a council of elders. At times they opposed the *nasi* and, in at least one case, they appealed directly to the Shah to countermand the *nasi*'s wrongful behavior (see Appendix I). The *'ene ha'eda* were responsible for the schools, bath, cemetery and ritual slaughter.

Most of them are wealthy and distinguished, and, sometimes also loudmouths whom no one chose but nevertheless consider themselves the community representatives and leaders, both inter- and intracommunal. Sometimes one public-spirited member would organize the others and they would swear on their *z̦iz̦it* (prayer shawls) and on the Tora, to work together for the good of the community and to defend the interests of the community and its unity. The volunteer workers, especially the non-wealthy among them, labored for the sake of heaven and with surprising devotion. (Melamed, 1951:366, author's translation)

Often such volunteers were imprisoned for petitioning the Shah, or wounded or killed trying to quiet mobs of Muslims invading the Mahalleh.

The importance of the *nasi* and the *'ene ha'eda* in the secular affairs of the community, especially those externally directed, is rather apparent. But to a large extent, the community itself could function very well without them. This was due to a second political structure, largely invisible to the outside world, whose concern was the day to day problems of the community and whose membership sometimes overlapped with that of the *'ene ha'eda*. More will be said about this later in the chapter.

The government always tried to keep close watch on the Jewish community. In Safavid times there was a government office called the *diwan*, which regulated the external affairs of the Jewish community. This office handled all petitions, requests and complaints to the government as well as the registration of forcibly converted Jews. The *diwan* frequently employed Jewish renegades as "advisors" for spying on the Jews (Fischel, 1953:119). In Qajar times, the local government official in charge of Jewish affairs, known as the *karguzar* (agent) was attached to the Foreign Ministry (Wills, 1883:146–147). In Pahlavi times this office was eliminated.

RELIGIOUS LEADERSHIP

The religious leader of the community was called *dayan* (judge), *mulla* (master), *rabi* (Rabbi) or *ḥakham* (sage). Whereas the position *nasi* was bestowed, by consensus, on a most worthy member of the elite, the post of religious leader was usually inherited. For this reason, the religious elite and particularly the *dayan,* have carefully preserved their lineages, while other Jews have not.

The religious leader was the most influential individual in community internal affairs. The *dayan* could convene a court or *bet din* of three judges to decide all legal questions, secular as well as religious. The *dayan* was not empowered to sentence a person to death, but he could enact fines, grant divorces, publicly ridicule the guilty and have them ostracized. In addition the *dayan* usually doubled as *mohel* (circumcisor), *shoḥet* (ritual slaughterer), *sofer* (scribe), *darshan* (preacher), and *shaliaḥ ẓibbur* (precentor).

The office of *dayan* is passed from father to son, son-in-law or pupil. Succession has not always been smoothly accomplished. Informants report[1]

Years ago, a *dayan* died in Shiraz, leaving a very young son. A pupil was called upon to fill the position. When the son grew up, the student did not want to relinquish the position. The community, too, split over the question. People living in *Zire Takh* would not buy meat slaughtered by the *dayan* of the Mahalleh and vice versa. The dispute continued for several years and almost led to actual fighting. Finally it was reconciled, because the rift cut across too many kinship ties. The jealousy between the two families continues. Although the settlement favored *rabi* Y. over *mulla* S., it is the descendant of the latter who is today accepted as *dayan,* while the descendant of the former struggles for recognition.

The *shoḥet* too, was important in the community hierarchy, since taxes on ritually slaughtered meat were an important source of community revenue.

The post of *Shoḥet,* therefore, offered many possibilities of profit and personal enrichment which were only too often utilized, thus leading to conflict with the community and denunciation before the authorities. (Fischel, 1953:119)

The persecution of Isfahani Jews in the reign of Abbas I and the decrees of Abul Hassan Lari, are examples of mischief caused by this influential religious functionary (see Appendix I).

The *gabay* (treasurer, collector of money) was the third ranking community-wide religious position. The office is inherited, only so long as the son is trusted and acknowledged to be honest. A *gabay* is not chosen; he merely assumes the duties of collecting and distributing money for the poor – people either entrust their money to him or not, as they personally desire.

The chief *gabay* of the community co-ordinates the collection of money for various purposes. Money is distributed to the needy at Pesaḥ and at other holidays. The *gabay* used to provide burial funds for poor families, since no burial society, as such, existed in Shiraz. He was responsible for the community poor-house and is still the person to be relied upon to find quarters for impoverished families. Provision of dowries for orphaned females was also within his province.

---

[1] Melamed (1951:365) offers a similar anecdote.

COUNCIL OF THE PIOUS

The various religious functionaries of each *knisa* as well as from the community at large, constituted a "council of the pious". This council seems to have been the invisible political apparatus of the community. Called together in the privacy of a *knisa* by the *dayan* and *gabay,* the council would meet to solve the everyday problems of Shirazi Jewry. Since community funds including the ritual slaughter tax, charitable contributions and sale of ritual honors, passed through the hands of those present, the "council of the pious" had the full power to make important decisions. It is unclear whether the *nasi* or other secular elite took an interest in this council.

The invisibility of the organization is attested to by the dearth of reference to it by otherwise competent observers. Alliance directors in Shiraz omit any reference to community organization. During an emergency, one director reported:

Ten notables of the community, the rabbis at their head, risked leaving their homes in order to come inform me of the danger they were exposed to. (Alliance, 1905:97)

In 1910, reference is made to two chief rabbis (Alliance, 1910:231). Another observer speaks of two affines who vehemently disputed secular leadership of the community (Brawer, 1936:83); he claims too, that there was no proper community council in Shiraz (1946:333). Informants confirm that a "council of the pious" did indeed exist during this entire period. Even today this unofficial council meets, its power now reduced to decision-making within the religious sphere.

The dual, and apparently overlapping, political apparatuses were clearly advantageous to community defense strategy. Seizure of the secular leadership of the community, would leave the "council of the pious" unaffected and the community's vital functions unimpaired. The pious, except for the *dayan,* need never have been exposed to the authorities. On the other hand, the *'ene ha'eda* may not have been party to the decisions of the "council of the pious". As it was, the elite suffered for their apparent prestige and were happy to avoid any decision-making. Abnegation of power and authority remains a fundamental pattern of elite behaviour among Shirazi Jews. This refusal to exercise rightful authority may be a selfless act, necessitated by the harassment of visible leadership by the authorities and by a desire to maintain normal community functions in the face of these circumstances. But it most probably represents the belief that passivity is the best defense for exposed personages. Aloofness and selfish unconcern for the community may also contribute to this attitude.

THE KNISA

The necessity for a hidden body politic, fostered the increasing importance of the *knisa* in community life. There was no other community-wide institution which afforded invisibility from prying outsiders. Within its domain, political processes and aspects of social behavior generally inhibited in the Jewish community, were permitted to flourish, and, as we shall see in Chapter X, the synagogue developed an elaborate code of behavior and a proliferation of positions and roles.

THE INFLUENCE OF FOREIGN JEWISH ORGANIZATIONS

Since the beginning of the twentieth century, Shirazi Jews have been strongly influenced by foreign Jewish institutions and organizations.

ALLIANCE

From 1903 until sometime after World War I, a Jewish school system, set up and funded by the Alliance Israélite Universelle functioned in Shiraz. Its director, who by his own admission was looked upon as the Messiah (Alliance, 1904:31), directly intervened on behalf of the Shirazi Jewish community. During persecutions he requested direct intervention of foreign consuls. He was himself something of a consul, giving shelter to harassed Jews, while having command of several troops. The Alliance director arranged for famine relief and compensation for losses suffered by Jews in pogroms. The pattern of paternalism first fostered by Alliance, survives and is continued to this day by other foreign Jewish organizations operating in Shiraz.

Reliance on the director as an intermediary meant that for the first time, Shirazi Jews enjoyed the luxury of outside help. But the resulting exposure of the community to world Jewry was certainly a mixed blessing, as it soon became a pawn in regional, national and even international politics. Alliance left Shiraz in the 1920s, ostensibly because the community refused to provide a budget for the school. The Shirazis were happy to see them go, due as much to their interference in community affairs as for religious reasons.

For about twenty-five years after the departure of Alliance, foreign Jewish organizations had little to do with Shiraz. Emissaries from the Jewish Agency made occasional forays to encourage emigration to

Palestine, but they made little effort to interfere in community affairs.[1] In the late 1940s, Otsar Hatorah, an American sponsored orthodox Jewish school system moved into Shiraz with important consequences for the Jewish community (see Chapter VII).

JOINT DISTRIBUTION COMMITTEE (JDC)

The American Jewish Joint Distribution Committee, commenced its Shiraz operations in 1950. JDC, or "Joint" as the Shirazis refer to it, began by supplementing the Otsar Hatorah educational budget; later a school feeding program was instituted. A communal sanitation program was set up in the Mahalleh: outhouses were sanitized and made available to each household, piped water was provided free of charge at the synagogues while use of *jub* water was discouraged, and the collection of garbage and sweeping of the alleys was organized. A free vaccination and general health program was instituted in the Mahalleh, directed primarily at halting communicable disease. A health clinic, first proposed by the Youth Committee in the 1940s (Yishay, 1950:307), was finally opened in June 1964. The clinic provided free health facilities for the poor, stressing prenatal and pediatric care. A kindergarten and summer day camp were established for the children of poor families.

In 1968, JDC was Shiraz's largest single employer of Jews. At least 80 of its 93 workers were Jewish. JDC has actively participated in the community by making funds available to the chief *gabay* for relief efforts, founding a Ladies' Committee and promoting a strong official *Anjoman* (Central Committee).

JDC at first provided its services gratis to the community, but later it attempted to coerce the community into contributing to the operating budget by charging token fees for certain services. As these token payments have increased without corresponding improvement in service, the poor have expressed their resentment of "Joint". They claim that they are being cheated. One of their chief complaints is that the health clinic provides them with placebos and lectures instead of proper physical examinations. The doctors are said to be unconcerned about their patients – moneymaking alone interests them. When discontented Jews turn to government health clinics they are turned away with the explanation that the Jewish community provides its own health services. Shirazis are united in their opposition to paying for services rendered by foreign organizations. They boycotted the school feeding program when

---

[1] In 1932, an emissary attempted to reconcile a squabble among community leaders which was preventing establishment of a girls' school (Brawer, 1936:83–4).

the fee was raised and refused to enroll their children in kindergarten until tuition increases were rolled back.

Vastly improved living standards among Shiraz's Jewish population,
due, in part, to the efforts of Joint, have been a factor in the outright opposition to some JDC projects. In 1968, Joint attempted to persuade the
Central Committee to contribute to the school feeding program. Two
members of the committee objected that they were raising a generation
of beggars and that it was time to halt this business. The other members
abstained from voting and the matter was dropped. The JDC director,
confident that the poor would respond by pestering the Central Committee until they yielded, threatened to close the program. No such
response was forthcoming, so in 1968–1969, the school feeding program
was closed. By 1972, Joint operations in Shiraz were being drastically
reduced – to the delight of the Central Committee. Most Shirazis
accepted this development apathetically.

No doubt part of the resentment towards Joint derives from the many
years of foreign administration of the Shiraz operation. The director during the period of research, a female social worker, was persevering in her
efforts to effect positive social change, but her methods were ethnocen-
tric and thus often inappropriate to the particular circumstances. She
also chose *not* to speak Persian, necessitating the use of interpreters at
every formal and informal encounter. This tactic not only handicapped
the flow of communication, but engendered considerable hostility from
all segments of the community who considered her aloof and unsym-
pathetic. Furthermore, the elite especially resented any female, even a
westerner, trying to impose her will on the leadership. In sum, Shirazi
Jewish hostility to Joint expresses the common resentment of the socially
distant, lofty, paternalistic foreigner, a xenophobia not unusual to
Iranians in general.

THE ANJOMAN

Under the prodding of JDC, the traditional secular power structure has
been replaced by the *Anjoman*. The *Anjoman-e Kheyriy-e Kalimiyan-e
Shiraz* (Jewish Welfare Council of Shiraz), Shirazi Jewry's "Central
Committee", was granted official government recognition in 1967,
although it had been functioning unofficially for several years.

The present *Anjoman* membership consists of eleven self-appointed,
government approved, highly respected Jewish men. Within three years,
this *Anjoman* is to be replaced by an elected one, consisting of twelve
members. Future *Anjoman* members are to be elected by secret ballot,

after a widely publicized nomination meeting open to the entire community. Potential candidates must be Iranian, literate, aged thirty and over, having a reputation for being ethical and willing to abide by the *Anjoman* constitution. It is unclear as to how democratic this procedure will be. It is not clear whether the poor will be permitted to serve on the *Anjoman* and whether women can serve as members or even vote for the *Anjoman*. Until such time as elections are actually held, the *Anjoman* in effect, is very much like the traditional elite-dominated secular political structure discussed earlier.[1]

After elections, the *Anjoman* chooses its own officers, by a simple majority. These positions can be redistributed at the call of two-thirds of the membership. In routine matters, a majority of one effects a decision, but in case of a tie the side on which the *re'is* (chief/president) votes is declared the winner. Various checks and balances are built into the constitution to prevent misuse of community funds. Three-quarters of the *Anjoman* must approve the acquisition or sale of property. Bank drafts must be signed by the *re'is*, one vice-president and the treasurer. The officers of the *Anjoman* are assigned the task of checking up on each other. Meetings are held weekly and no one is permitted to miss more than a few. Decisions are announced in the synagogues.

The *Anjoman* has two active committees. The School Committee, whose chairman visits the Otsar Hatorah schools regularly to observe their operation, actually has very little effect on the administration of school programs. The Mahalleh Committee under the direction of chief *gabay,* distributes money to needy families. The chief *gabay,* the person most respected by Shirazis for his integrity, has held the position for thirty-six years. Having moved out of the Mahalleh some years ago, he remains the sole representative of the Mahalleh poor to the *Anjoman*.

The *Anjoman* has taken over the responsibility for administrating community funds by including among its membership the chief *gabay* (collector of money), the *dayan* (judge), and the *ḥazzan* (overseer) of the city's wealthiest synagogue. Through these people the *Anjoman* controls the community's local budget. All large appropriations, whether charitable or other, must receive the approval of the *Anjoman*. The shift in administration of community funds has weakened the still functioning "council of the pious" who previously exercised control over such funds. The *Anjoman*, however, does not consciously work in opposition to the "council of the pious" and both the *dayan* and chief *gabay* serve as

---

[1] Informants report that because these elections had not, as of 1974, been held, some of the younger elite, in protest, have considered reviving a long-defunct Youth Committee to develop alternative programs and policies.

liaison between the two committees. Unfortunately, the community's indigenous budget is miniscule as compared with the vast sums provided by Joint and Otsar Hatorah, so despite the control of local funds by the *Anjoman,* its real power over community affairs is decidedly limited.

The *Anjoman* is attempting to encourage more community participation in its affairs. Subcommittees have been organized, and each *knisa* has selected three young men to serve on them.

YOUTH COMMITTEE

Several years before the establishment of the state of Israel, young adults in Shiraz formed their own committee. Under the leadership of the son of one of the community's richest men, the *Kanun Javanan-e Yisra'el-e Shiraz* was founded to take "upon itself, not only the nourishment of the poor, but (to provide for) all of the needs of the Jews of the locality" (Yishay, 1950:307). They were said to have collected funds for building a wall around the cemetery, for synagogue repair, for founding a community Hebrew school and for setting up a free health clinic for the Mahalleh inhabitants. It was their intention to change the social order. How this organization of young people was diverted from its efforts to aid the Mahalleh people, is not known.

Eventually, a new organization, *Anjoman-e Daneshjuwan-e Yahud-e Shiraz* (Shiraz Jewish College Students Committee), replaced the other youth organization. The orientation of the new organization is towards Zionism and Jewish culture, with advice and materials provided by the Jewish Agency. Much of this Youth Committee's leadership is provided by Teherani students, who are largely unconcerned about the Mahalleh poor of Shiraz. Mahalleh youth are effectively excluded from membership, although it is supposedly open to all young adults.

One service provided by this committee was an activity program for young teenagers, the *Anjoman-e Javanan*. A club building with game-rooms and class-rooms was initially provided by JDC; now they use the Jewish Agency building. Youngsters' activities once included a summer club, games, hikes, an orchestra, a newspaper and speech therapy sessions to correct the "substandard" Jewish speech pattern. These activities came to an abrupt halt during the Six Day War and have been gradually resumed on a greatly reduced scale.

The Students' Committee's coed activities include: picnics, dances, lectures, films, Hebrew and English classes. They occasionally help to raise money for Israel, encourage synagogue attendance on Sabbaths and arrange for holiday meals for out-of-town students. Conservative elements in the community are concerned about the students' coed activities and generally impious behavior. Most Shirazi Jews are suspicious of the untraditional attitudes these youth display.

THE LADIES COMMITTEE

The first Ladies Committee, modeled after the Teheran Ladies Committee, was founded in 1957. The present Ladies Committee was begun in 1961. The Ladies Committee consists of about twelve members, all of whom are from elite families. They supervise the JDC kindergarten, provide part of its budget, and help distribute clothing to the poor. The Ladies Committee was closely regulated by the director of Joint operations in Shiraz, who provided leadership and direction to their activities. As yet, no effort has been made by them on behalf of women's rights and responsibilities.

SOCIAL RANK

Shirazi Jewish society can by no means be considered a stratified or classed society. Our designation and use of the term "class" is purely for the convenience of description. "Class" is understood to refer to an unbounded group of people of approximately the same financial means and similar overall rank.

Of Shiraz's 1968 population of approximately 1500 Jewish families, some 170, or 11.3% were on relief provided by JDC and the *Anjoman*. Some 25 to 30% more of the Jewish population while not on relief, were considered impoverished. Nearly all of the poor lived in the Mahalleh. As a group, they have the highest incidence of illiteracy, remain the most pious and are generally unaffected by Western values. Many of them have never been outside of Shiraz except on picnics.

About 120 families, or 8% of the Jewish population, are considered elite. The elite live outside of the Mahalleh, belong to traditionally prestigious families and are relatively wealthy. Associated with the traditional elite are college educated professionals and some *nouveau riche* businessmen. As a group, they have assimilated many Western values, traveled considerably throughout Iran and even abroad, and made extensive use of modern technology. Religion and community affairs are of little importance to most of them.

More than 50% of the Jewish population of Shiraz fit somewhere in between the two extremes. Most are skewed toward the lower end of the scale, and, while many live *tu khiyabun,* their style of living is similar to that of the ghetto dwellers. This group is by no means a "middle class" in the Western sense, but merely an in-between group, whose members tend to identify with either of the two polar groups. The membership of this "middle class" is pious, mostly literate, and, to some extent, acceptant of modern technology but not of Western ideas. Not so provincial as the poor, many have traveled to Teheran and some have been to Israel.

Shirazi Jews *do not* perceive "classes" within their society, although they vaguely acknowledge the presence of "elite" and "poor" polarizations and validate these polarities by differential behavior towards their respective members. In reality, a ranking system is operative.[1] Overall rank is a composite measure of relative prestige or influence, derived as a weighted product of several prestige scales. Prestige is gauged by kinship, affluence, occupation, religious knowledge, piety and education. The author was unable to assign a precise rank to all Shirazis because: (a) it is difficult to evaluate the relative weight given the various indices in each particular case (see Stirling, 1965:233) and (b) prestige is continually fluctuating due to gain and loss of honor during daily exchanges.

Generally, kinship, affluence and occupation are the most important indices of prestige and these tend to be closely interrelated. Social mobility in the past was limited, because kinship is not subject to major alteration, affluence is necessarily limited and a better occupation does not in itself guarantee acceptance by the elite. The traditional means of effecting upward social mobility is a long, tedious process which includes public examples of conspicuous consumption, demonstration of piety and religious knowledge, and participation in public face-to-face exchanges with the elite (see Chapter IX). Today, a few can circumvent this complicated procedure by shortcuts, such as becoming college--trained professionals or high-level government employees. Such position immediately propels one towards the upper pole of society.

In the past, the normal political prerogatives which accrued to those of high rank were usually denied to Jews. We have seen that achievement of high rank was a two-edged sword; on the one hand it entitled a Jew to a measure of respect and influence within the Jewish community, while, on the other, it exposed him and his entire household to hostile

---

[1] This ranking applies only within the confines of the Shirazi Jewish community. Until the present day it has little bearing on a Jew's position in the overall Shiraz social structure, although one's acceptance into prominent circles within Persian society may well influence one's prestige among Shirazi Jews.

government pressure. Despite the ambivalent position of the elite, high rank was apparently sought after. We surmise that this was due to a belief that prestige within the community and consequent deference, outweighed the dangers of external exposure. It is possible too, that striving to be at the top of society, no matter what the consequences, is a psychological universal. Today, the high-ranked wield greater political power than in the past, both within the community and *vis-à-vis* the authorities.

SOCIAL CONTROL

SETTLING DISPUTES

Shirazi Jews refrain from overt expression of derogatory opinions about other Jews. They do not believe there are Jews in the world who are irreligious. They do not accept the possibility that Jews do physical harm to one another and fighting among Jewish children was, indeed, rarely observed. Most subscribe to the myth, that in Shiraz, a Jew will not take a fellow Jew to court to settle a dispute — any such move is sternly repudiated by all.

In truth, disputes frequently do occur over the most trivial things, especially in *knisa* and in the guild. The major difficulty in settling disputes is that the party who gives in, suffers a serious loss of honor. Neither side can afford to do this, so a mediator or arbitrator must ultimately decide on the settlement. In *knisa,* the *ḥazzan* usually arbitrates; in business, it may be the guild elder. Otherwise, any respected member of the community can mediate in a dispute.

When the mediator comes to what he considers a fair decision, he pronounces it to the disputants and the angry words die away. He holds the head of each disputant with both hands and kisses him on the forehead. The parties then kiss each other on both cheeks and the dispute is over.

More serious disputes may require several mediators. Previously, Jews could turn to a *bet din,* a court of three judges, but this important institution disappeared many years ago. The present *dayan* is not considered qualified to act as a judge except in cases pertaining to marriage and divorce.

ACCESS TO POWER

While there are no rigid limitations on access to power within the Shirazi community, power remains largely in the hands of the elite. Among the elite themselves, there is differential access to political power derived from relative wealth, family position, occupation and "priesthood".

In Chapters VI and X we discuss the importance of the *kohanim* (priests) in Shirazi Jewish life. Although the *kohanim* do not function as a unit in secular affairs, they are heavily represented among the elite and powerful. The two richest extended families are priestly. The head of the community for the past twenty-five years and present president (*re'is*) of the *Anjoman* is a *kohen*. The previous community head (*nasi*) and then richest man in the city, was also a *kohen*. Five of eleven members of the *Anjoman* are *kohanim*; in addition to the *re'is,* they include: the vice-president (*nayab re'is*) and treasurer (*khazanadar*). The most powerful Mahalleh family is also priestly.

The relatively great influence of the *kohanim* in Shiraz is due to their larger numbers, their rightful claim to religious honor and the special power of blessing and curse attributed to them. But there is no evidence whatsoever that *kohanim* operate as a corporate group or even as a class-identity unit.

DECISION-MAKING

The decision-making process in Shiraz, in almost all circumstances, is by consensus. Actual voting on questions is rare and if a large vocal minority opposes some decision, be it in the *Anjoman,* the "council of the pious", *knisa,* or guild, a compromise is sought or the entire matter is dropped. On questions not thoroughly understood by the body considering it, factions form around influential protagonists in deference to their prestige rather than the merits of their reasoning. Decision-making then becomes tangled with personal honor and requires mediation as in disputes.

SOCIAL DEVIANCE

Certain conduct may be tolerated by Shirazi Jews while not actually condoned. In extreme cases, social deviance is publicly condemned and the individuals involved ostracized.

ALCOHOLISM

Heavy drinking was at one time, less a form of social deviance than a widespread and acceptable pattern of behavior. All informants point out that, in the past, sweet wine was joyfully imbibed daily; there was no easier way of blotting out the steady stream of indignities. Wine and *araq* cost very little then and everyone made his own.

At weddings and circumcisions each guest would be provided with 1½ litres of *araq*. On Sabbaths and holidays, groups of twenty or more young men would go to the gardens with ½ litre of *araq*, ½ litre of wine and half of a chicken per person. It is said that as late as 1949, the adult Shirazi Jewish male consumed about 6 litres of *araq* per month (Levi, 1960, III:1010). Informants claim, however, that they never got inebriated the way Muslims did, probably out of fear that the *goyim* would exploit the opportunity to victimize them.

Today, heavy drinking is less common. Musicians drink because it "improves their music". Butchers, too, are reputed to be heavy drinkers; they are said to maintain the custom of going to the gardens on Shabbat to indulge in heavy drinking and in licentious activity with the Muslim prostitutes that accompany them. Members of these two professions are among the lowest ranked in Shiraz and their heavy drinking may be a contributing factor to this evaluation.

Drunkenness is uncommon in Shiraz, although there are occasional reports of wife beating by men under the influence of alcohol. Two Jewish drunkards, known personally to the author, were the subject of constant ridicule by everyone.

DRUG ADDICTION

Drug addiction was also once fairly common, but only three active drug users remained in Shiraz during our research, the rest having emigrated. Opium and hashish are easily obtainable at a reasonable price. Two users are family men, whose wives and sons support the habit. Both have been partially cured, but neither can work. The third addict is a deformed beggar who eats hashish. His begging in the synagogues and on the street easily supports the habit. The community provides him with a small store-room to sleep in and a wheel chair for mobility. While they ridicule the drunkard, Shirazi Jews pity the dope addict.

BEGGING

The first Alliance emissary claimed that in Shiraz begging was strictly prohibited by Jews; he never saw a hand stretched in need (Alliance, 1903:107). The poor were supposed to turn to the *gabay* or *ḥazzan* of each *knisa* for help. But a traveler to Shiraz in 1851 reports that there were then many Jewish beggars and that they had to rely mainly on Jewish charity for support. An acquaintance told him that

PLATE 33   Muslim mother and son beg along a main street, as most passersby ignore them.

he had once been severely reproved by a moolah for giving alms to a poor Jewish beggar; and when he reminded the pious elder that the beggar was one of God's creatures, he was informed, by way of answer, that the Jew and all his nation were creatures only to be damned, and that it was unworthy in any Moslem, made to be saved, to entertain the least pity or sympathy for such wretches. (Binning, 1857, I:394)

Today, there are a number of full-time Jewish beggars. These men begin the day early by making the rounds of the synagogues and later they sit in the street, panhandling. The author knew four male Jewish beggars, two were alcoholics, one — a blind man and one a deformed drug addict;[1] only one female Jewish beggar was known to the author.

Many men, ostensibly not beggars, do not hesitate to supplement their income by collecting *ẓdaqa* (charity) in *knisa*. They are expected to turn in such money to the *gabay* or *ḥazzan,* but some keep their collections for personal use. Jews do not like beggars, but they pay off the more persistent ones to induce them to stop bothering them (*cf.* Heilman, 1975).

---

[1] Beggars in Iran make a special effort to display their infirmities and teach a child to cry, or pinch it to force from him real tears, in an effort to attract compassion from passers-by.

HOMOSEXUALITY

Masturbation is strongly opposed on religious grounds, but is said to be common. Informants claim that when a boy is old enough to ejaculate, he is taken to a Muslim prostitute; in the past he would be married-off to avoid the problem. Although Jews maintain that homosexuality is common among Muslim males, there is no agreement about its frequency among Jews, but it is generally assumed to be low.

It is also claimed that there is no homosexuality among females. However, a great deal of fondling and other physical contact among teenage girls was observed, perhaps to compensate for the lack of premarital heterosexual interaction.

PROSTITUTION

Muslim prostitutes living in the Mahalleh service only Muslim men; they are paid 50 to 100 *rial* for their compliance. Thursday afternoons and Fridays are the days of greatest activity, and the men wait on line for their turn. Jewish opposition to the Mahalleh Muslim prostitute is vigorous. Prostitutes are completely ostracized by their Jewish neighbors, and the police are occasionally summoned to halt their activities. The prostitutes themselves are not considered dangerous, but the men they attract were observed to harass the neighbors and to make a nuisance at nearby synagogues.

Jewish prostitution is not readily discussed by the people. It is claimed that there were some in the past, but that they had emigrated. Informants say that Jewish prostitutes used to be dealt with severely.

About fifty years ago, Mulla Dayanim exposed a Jewish prostitute after having hid in her house, where she was observed to have been alone with an unrelated Jewish man. The *bet din* ordered her to be punished. She was brought into the Great Synagogue and beaten on the hands and wrists. Her head was shaven, she was placed backwards on a brown ox and led about the city while people threw stones at her.[1] Not long after, she became a Muslim and told Muslims secrets which eventually led to the blood libel and pogrom of 1910. Since then, the community has been reluctant to punish Jewish prostitutes.

There seem to be several Jewish prostitutes still active in Shiraz. It is said that some of the wine sellers' wives, provide such service for Muslims who come to the *sharab khane* (wine-house) to drink.

---

[1] Muslims are reported to punish adulterers in a like manner (Wills, 1883:377). Similar practices are reported among Kurdish Jews (Brauer, 1947:155) and elsewhere in the Islamic world (*cf.* the movie "I Love You Rosa").

One Jewish woman, the married mother of five children, comes from a city known for the licentious behavior of its women. She leaves the Mahalleh for varying periods during the day and it is alleged that she goes to the homes of Muslim men and provides her services there. It is further alleged that her husband, a poor porter, knows of his wife's activities, but says nothing since he can by no means afford the five to ten rial daily allowance he gives his children, nor the jewelry his wife occasionally buys. His fourteen year old daughter was rumored to be engaging in similar activities and was quickly married-off to an out-of-towner.

Some husbands are said to pander for their wives; others merely look upon these activities as a needed additional source of income. Most husbands, however, would immediately divorce their wives if they would so much as speak to a Muslim man. Extra-marital relations between Jewish partners is thought to be very rare, but some informants expressed concern that the "enlightened" elite have fewer scruples about such behavior.

Most Jewish girls at matrimony are said to be unaware of the nature of sexual intercourse, but it is said that many Muslim girls studying at the Jewish girl's school are prostitutes who happily describe their adventures in minute detail. Marriage comes considerably later than in the past, and, with no heterosexual activity or even mixed socializing condoned for single females, it is surmised that there may be considerable sexual curiosity as well as frustration among Jewish girls. Jewish girls caught having Muslim boy friends suffer a tarnished reputation. Such "bad" girls are married off quickly or sent to Israel. Nevertheless, girls do risk these consequences, and the Jewish school authorities carefully censor the girls' mail in an effort to prevent such liaisons.

SOCIAL CONFLICT AND FRAGMENTATION

Jewish community organization characterised by a ranking system allowing for a moderate degree of mobility, communal identity, and the Mahalleh as the hub of social activity, displays a certain amount of cohesiveness. Yet over the past 300 years, there is evidence that dissent is common to Iranian Jewish communities. To some extent this can be blamed on community structure itself, wherein the roles and positions of protagonists are not clearly defined. Decision-making by consensus may serve as a defense against external pressure, but it leaves room for discord. Such dissent had ominous consequences for a community which has suffered from pogrom, forced conversion and the defection of its members.

No matter what the circumstances, factions and dissent have been a part of Shirazi life. In the early twentieth century there was a dispute between *Zire Takh* and the Mahalleh, as described earlier in the chapter. In 1932 there was a leadership dispute between two affines which hampered efforts to provide schooling for Jewish children and paralysed the visible political apparatus of the community (Brawer, 1936:83–85; 1946:333, 340–343). In 1967, during the Six Day War, there was a dispute over whether to stay home and pray in support of Israel, or go to work.

Today there are tendencies towards a community schism into two strata and two locations, namely the wealthy-elite-non-Mahalleh-dwellers versus the poor-Mahalleh-dwellers. The Mahalleh is slowly beginning to take on the appearance of a separate community. It has to some extent developed its own social structures and its own leaders. The "council of the pious" remains effective in the Mahalleh, whereas it has less influence outside; decisions of the *Anjoman* have more weight outside than inside the Mahalleh. Communications within the Mahalleh are much quicker and more effective than outside. Some Mahalleh leaders, known for their brutishness, are not above physically attacking *goyim* who are offensive to Jews, a pattern of behavior unheard of outside the Mahalleh. Joint and Otsar Hatorah have become powerful and influential inside the Mahalleh, while outside they have considerably diminished impact.

The elite, by choice or accident, have little to do with the Mahalleh. Their women never come to the Mahalleh, even for shopping, claiming it is dirty. Acculturation is rampant among those living outside the Mahalleh, while inside it remains dormant.

Yet there are factors operating to inhibit such a potential community schism. Social mobility is less restricted than in the past and there are no restrictions at all on physical mobility. Many of those living outside the Mahalleh, still live as do their co-religionists inside, and for most, the Mahalleh, its synagogues, shops and people remain the focus of Jewish life.

SOCIAL RELATIONS WITH OTHER MINORITIES

The other minorities are no longer of importance in Shiraz. There are several Armenian and Zoroastrian families as well as a number of Bahais. The Armenians and Zoroastrians are called *'arelim* (uncircumcised) by the Jews, a stigma which makes them ritually more repugnant to the Jews than are the Muslim *goyim*. "Everyone hates the Jews" is the explanation offered for not getting along particularly well with the other minorities. But, no doubt, the traditionally vigorous economic competition between the minorities in such professions as wine-making and music, has had a great deal to do with inter-minority tensions.

"The Bahais," reports one informant, "have religion until age eight. Until then they do not smoke or drink. Afterwards, they have no religion." In other words, the only "ritual" Bahais observe is abstinence from smoking and drinking, which they and everyone in Iran refrain from doing until adulthood. Since this is clearly *not* religious ritual, Bahaism is stereotyped as totally lacking ceremonial or cult behavior and therefore not a "religion" at all! Despite the fact that Babism began in Shiraz and successfully attracted numerous Jewish converts elsewhere in Iran, the Bahais had no success in attracting Jewish converts in Shiraz. Relations with the Bahais are excellent.

Jews often mock the other religions, but they readily concede that most people are sincere in their beliefs. It is said apocryphally that in the town of Qalat, not far from Shiraz, the bazaar was closed Friday for Muslims, Saturday for Jews, Sunday for Christians and Monday for Bahais.

The missionary efforts of European apostates such as Wolff and Stern in the nineteenth century, did not succeed in inducing Shirazi Jews to convert. In Hamadan, Teheran, Isfahan and Kerman, missionaries have met with some success in their efforts. Why then the lack of success in Shiraz? Firstly, because of Shiraz's isolation in the nineteenth century, the Protestant missionaries were unable to establish a successful school there. Alliance actually got there early enough to forestall any such development. Secondly, Shirazi Jews are known for their religious fervor, and their community organizations have not been reluctant to pressure the missionaries to stop meddling.

In about 1962, one of the missionary societies sent a converted English Jew on a mission to Shiraz. Jewish children were lured to church by food, games and picnics. Some twelve teenagers became involved in discussions with the head of the mission regarding the Tora. Otsar Hatorah appealed for help from the *Anjoman,* who in turn threatened to go to the authorities. Otsar Hatorah at the same time instituted a program to counter the missionary's and it successfully drew away most of the straying children. The missionary abandoned his efforts and left soon after.[1]

---

[1] He returned to Shiraz a few years ago and is kept under careful surveillance by concerned pietists.

The Jewish attitude towards the efforts to convert Jews was summed up by an elderly informant:

Why should we change religion? Will it enable us to live without food? Without clothes? Since it cannot, why change?

SEGREGATION OF JEWS FROM MUSLIMS

In Chapters II through III we saw that under Islam, Jews have enjoyed a special status as a "protected minority", but with the advent of Iranian Shi'a Islam, their position deteriorated to that of a pariah group. One way in which oppression was expressed was in strict segregation of the Jew.

Jewish residence in Shiraz was traditionally confined to the Mahalleh, which, except along its periphery, was completely Jewish. While the Mahalleh was not walled off, it had no room for expansion as the Muslim clergy discouraged sale of property to Jews outside the traditional boundaries of the ghetto.

Jews owning shops in the bazaar grouped together for mutual support and protection. Jews coming to shop for food in the bazaar were not permitted to handle the merchandise, since by doing so it would become contaminated. The restrictions placed on Jewish shoppers and the danger faced by them (especially by women) in leaving the Mahalleh to go to the bazaar, led to the establishment of local markets in the Mahalleh. Jews, who were excluded from selling food in the bazaar because of their *najas,* sold fruit, vegetables, spices and groceries in the Mahalleh. Jewish insistence on kosher food, necessitated having their own butcher and dairy shops. In Chapter V, it will be seen that the process of segregation provided other occupational openings for Jews.

In the political sphere, segregation of the Jew was absolute; Shirazi Jews had no access to political power outside the Jewish community. Although apostate Jews like Hajji Ibrahim gained power in local and national government, Jews who remained Jews, were able to influence the authorities only indirectly; no Jew held government office.

Social segregation was most stringent. Informants report that Jews did not often socialize with Muslims, contacts were for business purposes only. Jews visiting in Muslim homes were treated as untouchables because of their *najas.* Muslims who came to Jewish homes were treated with great respect and fear, while all valuables were hidden to prevent their confiscation by the Muslim guest. Social segregation led to a completely self-contained Jewish social order with its own institutions. The Jew was totally apart from Persian society.

Strict segregation began to break down with the advent of government supported public education in the 1920s. Jewish boys and girls, in small numbers, began to attend the public schools and compete directly with Muslim children. Informants report that at first, there was much discrimination toward Jewish children by their teachers, but as time passed, the situation gradually improved. Segregation further diminished when, in the 1940s, Jews began to leave the Mahalleh and move to areas inhabited by Muslims.

The process of integrating the Shirazi Jew into Iranian society is in its infancy. It originated among the elite and is beginning to filter down to the middle class. But Mahalleh dwellers, despite the recent influx of Muslim neighbors, have strenuously resisted this process; for them pride in ethnicity still outweighs the possible advantages of assimilation.

The young educated elite, Jew and non-Jew alike, share a desire to imitate Western values. They possess Western furniture, cars, motor scooters, phonographs and pianos. "Study for its own sake" has engendered interest in studying English, French, or Western music, while the reading of magazines, literature and scientific texts on psychology and the like, have become pleasurable pastimes. Through mutual interests, young elite Jews have made friends with non-Jews. Ritual barriers to social contact have crumbled and the young elite Jew is not at all reluctant to eat non-kosher food outside his home. Elite adult Jewish females, many of whom are unmarried and admittedly bored by sitting at home most of the day, look for opportunities to arrange coed social gatherings with Jewish and non-Jewish acquaintances. Inter-dating, though rare, is not unknown among the elite. Despite these efforts, the Jewish elite are not often included in social events of the non-Jewish elite.

Jews have made an effort to have more contact with Muslims on another level. At the Shah's coronation in 1967, the Shiraz Jewish community erected the most elaborate decorations in all of Shiraz and political dignitaries were invited for a special celebration in one of the large synagogues *tu khiyabun*. On another occasion, in this same synagogue, a public eulogy was held for a deceased Muslim clergyman attended by important Jews and non-Jews.

Jews are no longer excluded from national elections and are permitted to vote for a Jewish deputy in *Majles*, the parliament. The election of a Jewish deputy to *Majles* ensures Jewish representation there, but at the same time, by limiting Jews to voting only for ethnic candidates, their segregated minority status is perpetuated. Jews have little say in local or national politics. The Shirazi Jew is, furthermore limited even in his ethnic politics. No Shirazi Jewish candidates run for office and past elections indicate that the Shiraz votes counts very little in the selection of the Jewish deputy, who is usually Teherani.

The breakdown of strict segregation has given way to an anti-Semitic discrimination somewhat comparable to the sort known in the United States in the 1940s. Jews find it more difficult to be hired for white collar jobs, than Muslims. Once hired, they are passed over for promotions or are expected to pay bigger bribes in order to obtain advancement.

This chapter has explored various Jewish adaptations to the Shiraz social environment. Among these are: (1) a social ranking system entirely self-contained and unrelated to the social ranking of non-Jews, (2), a dual political structure whereby formal secular power was in the hands of a visible elite while day-to-day community functions were left in the hands of a non-visible "council of the pious", whose actions were shielded under the aegis of the *knisa,* and (3) an informal means of settling disputes and making decisions.

The rather ephemeral character of Jewish community organization, the abnegation of communal responsibility by many of the elite and the ambivalence towards foreign help can be attributed to a basic insecurity arising from the oppressive conditions in which Shirazi Jews dwelt. Only one institution was strong enough to compensate, in part, for the lack of access to power outside the community and the inability to establish absolute autonomy inside. That institution, the *knisa,* is more thoroughly analyzed and evaluated in Chapter X.

CHAPTER V

Subsistence, Economic Adaptation and Social Conformity

POVERTY

Travelers to Shiraz until the 1950s were agreed as to the widespread poverty within its Jewish community. A lifetime of labor would result in a minimal accumulation of property. A wine maker who died in about 1890 is reported to have left the following inheritance:

One tray, four copper pots, four plates, eight goblets, one ladle, six table spoons, one wash basin and pedestal, one strainer, one half-sized tray, one Kermani goblet, 750 small jars or casks, 300 flat bottles, 150 bottles, one silk scarf, women's veils, a linen dress or robe, one winter coat, three pair of pants, one large wrap, seven *toman* "key money", three and one-half *toman* cash and one *misqal*[1] gold flakes. (Melamed, 1951:367)

In Chapter IV I indicated that in 1968 about 11% of Shiraz's Jewish population was getting relief, while 25 to 30% more may be classified as "poor". Any household earning less than about 1500 *rial*[2] per week would be considered poor among Shirazi Jews.

The following is an approximate weekly budget of a lower-class Mahalleh family of seven, consisting of a husband, wife and five daughters aged two, four, six, eight and twelve:

Food (meat four times per week)	650 *rial*
Public Bath	20
Children's allowance	60
Utilities (electricity, oil and wood)	65
Clothing (mostly second hand)	25
Health	20
Rent (they own their own house)	—
Total	840 *rial*

---

[1] A *misqal* is equivalent to about 4.7 grams.
[2] The rate of exchange during the period of research was: 75 *rial* = $1.00.

This budget does not take into account emergency expenditures, interest on loans and so forth.

The head of household, an illiterate spinner, earns 1000 to 1500 *rial* per week, depending on the season. He can afford a few luxuries such as a radio, a fan and a large thermos bottle. He also has a certain amount of capital. Seven thousand *rial* "key money" was given to him for a room which he leases to an old man. As long as the man remains, the owner of the property has usufruct rights to the "key money", but it must be returned when the tenant leaves. Surplus cash is lent out at high interest, but some is hidden in the house for emergencies.

Poorer families have meat only twice per week and in small quantities. By eating less rice and more bread and by using more vegetables, the food budget may be cut by about one-third. On the other hand, poorer families do not usually own their own house, but pay a rent of 80 to 300 *rial* per week. The addition of children to the family does not necessarily strain the food budget substantially. Food divided seven ways can be easily redistributed for an extra child. The addition of some extra bread and a trifle more green vegetable, costing about three *rial* per day, could suffice to serve two to three more children.[1]

The chief *gabay* claims that a family must have at least 700 *rial* per week in order to subsist. Many people do not earn this much. Carters rarely earn 600 *rial* per week. The barber claimed that he earned only 500 to 600 *rial* per week. Unskilled JDC employees earn only about 420 *rial* per week. Some shopowners, mattress sewers, silversmiths, grocers and "apprentices" rarely earn the necessary 700 *rial* per week. Musicians may receive 750 *rial* for a single performance, but it is doubtful whether they earn 700 *rial* per week over the course of a year. Even Otsar Hatorah teachers, who generally earn far more than 700 *rial* per week must nevertheless be classified as poor insofar as their salaries are less than 1500 *rial* per week.

Although poverty is an inescapable fact of life in Shiraz, the chief *gabay* indicated that the situation has improved substantially. When JDC[2] came to Shiraz it gave out 700 free clothing outfits each year. Now they give only about 200, for which the recipient must pay 100

---

[1] The Shirazi food cost-cutting practice was greatly misunderstood by JDC. When it raised the cost of the school feeding program from one *rial* to four *rial* per day per child, parents had the children come home for lunch, because it was cheaper to feed them there.

[2] The indigenous charity apparatus completely disintegrated when JDC came to Shiraz, but has since been reinstituted. Traditional charity formerly met only a small fraction of the community's needs, but today the community is gradually assuming a greater share.

rial. In 1959, the annual Pesah contribution was completely provided by JDC, but today about 40% is provided by the community. This increase in the percentage of community contribution reflects an absolute increase in charitable donations as well as an improvement in the situation of the poor.

OCCUPATIONS

Until the present Pahlavi period, the Jewish role in the economic life of Shiraz was subject to numerous restrictions. International trade, largely in Jewish hands before the Mongol period, was removed from Jewish control as of the Safavid period. Herding and farming, engaged in by some Jews during the Arab period, were occupations later closed to Jews who, until recently, were permitted to own only small tracts of land, mostly within the Mahalleh. Jews of Lar may have been known for their silk farming (Tavernier, 1684:253), but, otherwise, rural as well as urban Jews were engaged in merchandising or occupations despised by, or forbidden to, the general population.

The economic position of the Jew during Qajar times was thus portrayed:

The trades open to the Jews, are brokerage, working in the precious metals, in which they are very expert; dealing in precious stones, peddling, the selling of leeches, for which there is a great demand; the making and sale on their premises of wine and arrack; music, singing and dancing (three professions only practised for hire in the East by the lowest of low); the manufacture of spurious ancient coins, the practice of midwifery by the women; and the cleaning of drains, cesspools, etc. by the men (for when any unclean or filthy job is to done, Jews are sent for to do it). (Wills, 1887:232)

The earliest survey of Jewish occupations in Shiraz (Table 1) was reported in 1903 (Alliance, 1903:108). This survey should not be considered more than a rough estimate of Shirazi occupations. The breakdown given is a crude one. Spinners, carters, leather tanners, and unemployed,[1] to list a few, are not included in the survey. Having no other statistics to work from, we nevertheless, can derive some useful data. About 70% of the listed Shirazis were employed as peddlers, masons or smiths. Only about 43% of the work force were skilled or semi-skilled, the rest were in merchandising or money lending.

In Table 2 we present an occupational breakdown of a selected sam-

---

[1] Informants report that unemployment used to be extensive but were unable to estimate how many were unemployed.

TABLE 1
Jewish Occupations in 1903

Occupation	Number	Percentage
Peddler	400	39.02
Mason	200	19.51
Goldsmith	103	10.05
Merchant	90	8.78
Liquor seller	80	7.80
Musician	60	5.85
Druggist	20	1.95
Smith	20	1.95
Butcher	15	1.46
Wine maker	10	0.98
Money changer (lender?)	10	0.98
Jeweler	5	0.49
Haberdasher	5	0.49
Doctor	5	0.49
Surgeon	2	0.20
Total	1,025	100.00

ple of persons who have lived and worked in Shiraz over the past twenty years. In the interval of sixty-five years, many new professions have been made available to Jews.[1] The number of skilled and semi-skilled has increased only slightly to about 46% of the working force. The number of shopkeepers may actually be growing, as there are over 500 Jewish men in Shiraz just selling cloth and haberdashery. The reason for a Jewish propensity towards shopkeeping will be discussed later in the chapter.

The Jews, like other minority groups in Iran, lived until recently in a symbiotic relationship with the dominant population. Although rarely "forced" into particular occupations, there was little incentive to compete with Muslims directly and so Jews sought out those professions abhorrent to Muslims. The Shirazi Jews competed with Armenians to fill otherwise empty economic niches, thereby rendering valuable service to the smooth functioning of Shiraz life.

PEDDLING

Until recently this was the most important profession among Shirazi

---

[1] Old ones have disappeared. Notice the almost total absence of Jewish masons in present-day Shiraz.

TABLE 2
Jewish Occupations in Shiraz — 1948 to 1968

Occupation	Number	Percentage
Peddler	49	12.10
Cloth store	42	10.37
Goldsmith	27	6.67
Haberdasher	25	6.17
Doctor	19	4.69
Nurse, hospital worker	17	4.17
Teacher, principal	16	3.95
Engineer	14	3.46
Musician	12	2.96
Liquor seller	12	2.96
Money lender	12	2.96
Spinner	12	2.96
Merchant of gum tragacanth	11	2.72
Druggist	9	2.22
Grocer	9	2.22
Fruit and vegetables	9	2.22
Smith	8	1.98
Mason	7	1.73
Carter	6	1.48
Office worker	6	1.48
Real estate	6	1.48
Butcher	4	0.99
Technician	4	0.99
Tailor	4	0.99
JDC worker	4	0.99
Industrial worker	4	0.99
Household goods shop	4	0.99
School janitor	4	0.99
Dentist, Cook, Carpenter, Barber, Seed merchant Laborer, Librarian, Mulla, Restaurant worker, Bath worker, Leather tanner, Photographer, Beauty parlor worker, Appliance store, Lambswool merchant Dairy store	41	10.12
Unemployed	8	1.98
Total	405	100.00

Jews. In 1903 nearly 40% of the total labor force were peddlers. Most peddlers were itinerants, servicing nearly all of the villages of Fars, where they sold cloth, clothing, carpets, utensils and such. Zarqon, a village to the north of Shiraz, once occupied exclusively by Jews, had as its main source of income the itinerant peddling of its men.

This peddling should not be confused with intercity commerce in which a handful of Jews were engaged. The itinerant peddler, alone on muleback, was involved in long trips through the rugged countryside, where he was the frequent prey of bandits in the area. This was perhaps the most dangerous of professions, the hazards of which included murder, false accusation and forced conversion. Sales were usually made on credit, and were often not paid off. Peddling was rarely very profitable and the involvement of large numbers in it was due to its accessibility to Jews – no one else would do this work.

Besides the personal danger and lack of profit, peddling was a lonely means of earning a livelihood. Most peddlers would be away the whole week, returning home only for the Sabbath. Many would be absent for weeks or even months, returning home only for Pesaḥ and Rosh Hashana. Such long absences may have contributed to a decline of paternal authority in the home, as in the father's absence someone else would have had to make decisions and accept responsibility.

Some men were engaged in intracity peddling. Women, too, peddled within the city, having easy access to Muslim women of the *anderun* (harem), to whom they sold fabrics, trinkets and perfumes.

Improved communications have decreased the necessity for peddlers. Today the inhabitants of remote villages can reach Shiraz by bus or truck. Nowadays, peddling is also somewhat easier physically and socially (though it remains financially hazardous), as peddlers traveling by bus or bicycle need not be away from home more than a few days at a time.

WINE AND LIQUOR MAKING

This profession is expressedly forbidden to Muslims. From reports by Tavernier (1684:248), Niebuhr (1778, II:170) and others, we learn that Shirazi Jews were involved in a continual struggle with the Armenians for control of this industry. Both groups, known for their heavy drinking, were relatively unscathed by a cholera epidemic in the 1820s and this was attributed to their alcohol consumption (Fraser, 1825:84).

How and why the Jews survived and thrived in Shiraz and eventually monopolized the liquor trade, while the Armenian community all but disappeared, is not known. The liquor industry itself was permitted to survive for the taxes it yielded. In 1904, for example, the Shiraz government received the equivalent of 4000 francs from Jewish liquor merchants (Alliance, 1904:33).

In that year, in an attempt to end the lawlessness of the drunks in Shiraz, the government banned the sale of liquor to Muslims. While this prohibition did not affect Jewish liquor consumption,[1] it in effect halted the profitable sale of *araq* and wine. The Jewish community strongly opposed these measures, and several Jews violated the interdict. Those caught were severely beaten and a fine was threatened against the whole community in case of future violations (Alliance, 1904:34). Nothing more is reported about these restrictions, so apparently their enforcement was relaxed.

Wine and liquor were served in the *sharab khane* (wine house), usually a room in the wine maker's house. Other "services" might have been provided for the drinker by the women of the house. Although the Pahlavis banned the sale of alcohol not bearing a government tax stamp, the *sharab khane* continued to thrive. Presently liquor is sold there only to regular customers or to members of the Jewish community, since those caught violating the law would be subject to stiff fines and jail sentences. There are about a dozen Jewish bootleggers altogether. Numerous Jews own legitimate liquor stores which are gradually driving the *sharab khane* out of existence.

SPINNING

Men and women participate in the various operations of this industry. Women often earn a few *rial* per day at home, spinning cotton thread and preparing cage spools. Men are wholly engaged in warp winding, whereby warps are "obtained by plying up to sixteen spun threads into one" by means of a thread-twisting wheel (Wulff, 1966:196). The warps are used for carpets and for the peasant shoe, *giveh*. About twenty Jewish men are full-time spinners today, but in the past there were many more. The decline in the number of spinners is attributed, in part, to hard labor and uncomfortable working conditions during the winter months, when the cellar "factories" are cold and damp.

MEDICINE

The positions of doctor and pharmacist have always been honored in Iran and Jews have long been reputed to be effective in these fields (Masse, 1954:342; Adler, E., 1905:188–190). Untrained midwives, bone-menders and folk doctors are still well attended by patients, although midwifery is fast dying out due to modern maternity facilities.

---

[1] Many households still produce their own wine and *araq* for domestic consumption.

Folk medical procedures were observed to be effective in many cases. Jewish folk doctors sometimes include a short prayer or formula at no charge, which is gratifying to Muslim and Jewish patient alike. Some reasons for the continuing popularity of the folk doctors, is their frequently successful therapy and low fee of 10 to 20 *rial* per visit.

Trained doctors who operate clinics are said to be impersonal, unconcerned, and, often incompetent. But this does not mean that the college trained physician is less respected or less well attended than the folk doctor. On the contrary, the college trained physician is one of the most esteemed members of the community and any afternoon, one may find the doctor's private clinic filled with fifty or more patients waiting to be examined.

In addition to more than thirty trained doctors, there are a number of trained Jewish pharmacists, dentists, and numerous nurses and hospital workers serving the inhabitants of greater Shiraz. About 11% of our sample in Table 2 were in the medical profession.[1]

MONEYLENDING

Moneylending is technically forbidden to Muslims so, not surprisingly, there are about fifty full-time Jewish moneylenders in Shiraz. Nearly every Jew lends money as a sideline. The poor engage in small-scale pawnbroking, while the rich lend large amounts using real estate as collateral.

Large-scale moneylending is often a family affair. Capital[2] for large loans is often supplied collectively by the kindred, with affines joining together in moneylending operations. Money loaned to Muslims fetches at least $2\frac{1}{2}$% interest per month. It was reported in the seventeenth century, that the rate often approached 10% per month (Fryer, 1912, III:109), and there is reason to believe that the real interest rate today, may also approximate this amount in cases of severe risk. Jews borrow money from each other at less than 1% interest per month.

Despite the lucrative possibilities, moneylending is decidedly risky. Often, money is lent without proper collateral and without legally binding papers. Should a Muslim borrower die, the money may be lost; should a Jewish creditor die, his heirs may be unable to collect. Frequently a debtor simply refuses to pay up. In such cases nothing can be

---

[1] This percentage in our sample is probably somewhat higher than for the population as a whole.
[2] Levi (1960, II:1011) reports that in 1949 Shirazi moneylenders had working capital of 100,000 to 1,000000 *rial* each.

done to regain the money, but this debtor is blacklisted by the entire Jewish community.

Jews working in real estate are moneylenders using property as a source of capital. In a typical transaction, a Jewish man will lease an empty lot to a Muslim tenant for a specified period of time. The lease money is "key money", which the lessor must return to the lessee at the termination of the lease. In the meantime the lessor has usufruct rights to this money, which is lent out at high interest. At the termination of the lease, the "key money" is returned to the lessee while interest on the "key money" and all improvements to the property revert to the owner. In this way, Jewish land speculators have become the owners of Shiraz's major movie theaters, office buildings and stores, though they seem to lack the power generally commensurate with such wealth.

MERCHANDISING

Merchandising in Shiraz is still conducted primarily by bargaining in the typical Middle Eastern manner (see Khuri, 1968). Marketing procedure in the cloth business is typical.

Stock is purchased by the entrepreneur during semi-annual shipping trips to Teheran. The cloth is displayed on open shelves and once the shopper sees what he wants, the bargaining begins. On cheaper grades of cloth, the merchant asks 30 to 50% over his cost on the merchandise. On expensive cloth he may ask 100 to 200% over his actual cost. The cheap cloth may be sold at as little as 5% profit per meter, while the more costly cloth brings a greater profit margin.[1] The minimum price varies from day to day, depending, in part, on the mood of the salesman. Business dealings involve personalities, and if the seller does not like the buyer, he may intentionally keep the price high. Friendship between buyer and seller is frequently invoked to exact special terms favoring the buyer, which the seller makes a great show of granting. Nevertheless, neither buyer nor seller rests the friendship on a sale/no-sale basis, and to this extent, at least, business is divorced from friendship.

Competition is keen and most merchants rely on regular customers to whom they sell on credit. In the cloth business, most of the customers are Muslim women. Jewish shopkeepers demonstrate amity to Muslim customers by displaying an Allah sign, in decorative Persian script. (Jewish customers will spot a Hebrew sign, somewhere, less prominently exhibited.) This does not, however, save Jews from slack sales during the

---

[1] Jewish merchants have deservedly earned a reputation as shrewd businessmen, *but such craftiness knows no ethnic boundaries in Iran!*

holy months of Muharram and Ramadan and occasional boycotts called by the Shi'a clergy.

The majority of Shirazi Jews are in merchandising and most of these are shopkeepers. Their shops are narrow, usually not more than 3 to 4 m wide, and not heavily stocked with merchandise; there seems to be a direct relationship between the size of the shop and its success.

OTHER TRADITIONAL OCCUPATIONS

Jews were noted fortune tellers, amulet makers (see Chapter X), musicians, dancers and actors (see Chapter VIII). Intercity commerce

PLATE 34   A sidewalk peddler holds merchandise in his hand — an imported knife and spoon set in a plastic holder case.

and import—export was limited to a few products such as gum tragacanth, silk, wine and cloth. Few Jews were occupied in large scale trade due to the serious problem of banditry in Fars. Travel time necessitated the absence from home of these merchants for up to six months at a time.

Noteworthy are those occupations ostensibly open to Jews, but not engaged in, including tailoring, shoemaking (Melamed, 1951:367) and bread baking. No one could explain why Shirazi Jews did not engage in these occupations, while Jews elsewhere in Iran did so.

FEMALE OCCUPATIONS

The traditional female occupations were: peddling, spinning cotton and silk, selling leeches, and cleaning cotton. In 1903 about fifty women were seamstresses, embroiderers and lace makers (Alliance, 1903:1909). Other women were bone-menders, midwives and prostitutes.

Bone-mending, midwifery, spinning and prostitution still survive as feminine occupations, though on a reduced scale. Most young women go into teaching, nursing, tailoring, librarianship and lab technology.

GUILDS

Some Jewish professions, best exemplified by goldsmithing, are organized into guilds. One of the elders in the profession, usually well-to-do and respected, serves as the guild leader. Formerly he was given the title of *ostad* (master) and was responsible for collecting the tax which the government levied each year on the trade. Now his chief responsibility is the settlement of disputes. The organization of the goldsmith guild is informal and there is no indication that there was ever any official apprenticeship or membership qualifications. Anyone who assists a goldsmith, be he aged fifteen or fifty-five, is termed an "apprentice". When he goes into business for himself, he is called "goldsmith".

Today, only a few Jewish goldsmiths are producing jewelry; the others only buy, sell and repair it. A single factory produces jewelry for all Jewish goldsmiths. One guild member serves as the distributor; for a small commission, he takes pure gold from the guild members to the factory and returns the finished product to the respective shops. Should a smith suffer major loss, the others lend him capital to make up the loss. Among goldsmiths there is as much cooperation as competition.

In recent years, the Jewish guild had become affiliated with the Muslim goldsmith guild. But this affiliation was curtailed upon the death

PLATE 35   One of the many Jewish goldsmith shops on Kh. Lotfali Khan-e Zand.

PLATE 36   Jewish goldsmith and apprentice greet the author. Small dark sign with white lettering reads: "*Allah*".

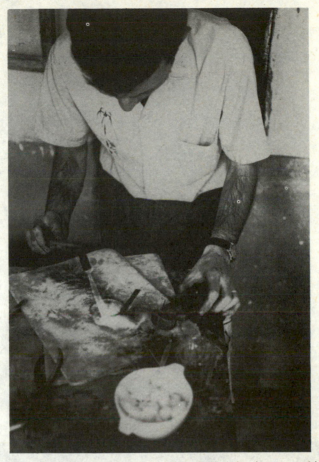

PLATE 37   Goldsmith carefully melts pure gold rod prior to working it.

of a Muslim distributor, in whose hands much Jewish gold had been entrusted; after considerable negotiation the deceased's family agreed to return the gold. By that time, however, Jewish smiths no longer wanted to risk such an association.

RANKING OF OCCUPATIONS

Perhaps in reaction to the historical necessity for Jews to engage in the most menial kinds of labor, Jews today avoid certain kinds of work, such as heavy construction, factory labor and so forth. Other oc-

PLATE 38 Shiraz' only Jewish mosaic craftsman (*hatam*) with a Muslim apprentice.

PLATE 39 An apprentice turns the wheel of a warpwinder in a basement spinning "factory".

PLATE 40   Lacking close kinsmen, these women subsist as custodians of Knisa Mulla Avraham in return for free housing in the room to the left – a minimal income is earned by spinning thread.

PLATE 41   Spinner's wife prepares yarn for husband's warpwinder.

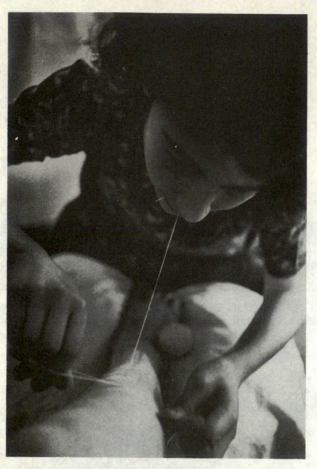

PLATE 42   Teenaged girl practices depilatory art.

cupations are not considered desirable because they require working on the Sabbath or are considered immoral. The ranking of occupations among Shirazi Jews takes these factors into account as well as the earning potential of the occupation. Notice in Tables 3 and 4, that new occupations, especially those requiring advanced education have tended to rise toward the top of the ranking, while traditional occupations with some exceptions are ranked towards the lower end. Despite his rather good earning potential, the butcher is ranked just above the beggar, near the bottom, because butchers are considered immoral and coarse.

    The ranking of occupations as determined by the author should be considered as only tentative.

PLATE 43   Sunday – washday!

PLATE 44   Woman in traditional headcovering prepares ground spices with mortar and pestle, *tu khiyabun*.

PLATE 45 Teenaged daughter plucks freshly slaughtered chicken.

PLATE 46 *Kabab* is pressed on a spit prior to roasting over charcoal.

PLATE 47   Most cooking is done over an Aladin wick burner – here, soup is boiled for *kufte,* a kind of meatball.

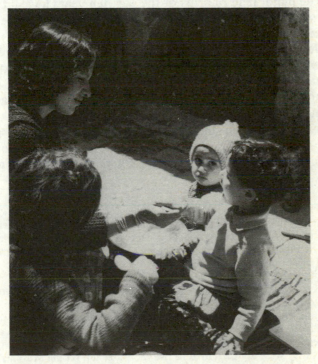

PLATE 48   Feeding of children is an important and time consuming task in a woman's daily schedule.

TABLE 3
Ranking of Jewish Women's Occupations

	(Doctor)	*(Engineer)*	
(Librarian)		*(Lab technician)*	*(Office worker)*
	(Bone-mender)	*(Folk doctor)*	
	(Midwife)		
	(Peddler)	*(Seamstress)*	
	(Spinner)	*(Maid—housework, washing)*	
	(Prostitute)		

PROPERTY

Until Pahlavi times, Shirazi Jews were unable to own land outside of the Mahalleh. During the past forty years, however, they have bought wide tracts of land within the city, gardens in the surrounding villages and even whole villages. One reason Jews have attempted to increase their land holdings is to control the production of gum tragacanth and its export.[1] The major land reforms of the past ten years have little affected the Jews, since most of their property holdings outside of the city have never been substantial.

When Jews and Muslims own property jointly, problems ensue.[2] In some cases, the Muslim co-owner has refused to allow irrigation water to reach the Jew's portion of the property, thereby severely damaging the vegetation.[3] When asked whether Jews instigate or retaliate against such behavior, informants responded that they dared not. The Muslim co-owner will not sell his share to the Jew and only offers a small fraction of the market value for the Jew's portion. Unsaleable property, such as this, is an important factor inhibiting middle class emigration to Israel.

---

[1] The commercial importance of gum tragacanth has been known for millennia. It is of critical use of pharmaceutical production and in many cottage-industry chemical processes. The extensive social and commercial contacts between elite Shirazi Jews and the Qashqai tribes of Fars were developed to secure unimpeded access to this substance and its trade.

[2] Joint ownership usually arises when a Muslim forfeits a debt to a Jew with a share of jointly owned land as collateral.

[3] He diverts the irrigation water onto someone else's property. Although this action is technically illegal, he can get away with it because Jews are reluctant to apply to the courts for legal redress. In Burujerd, Luristan, Jews sharing a house with Muslims reported that they were not permitted to use the water tap on the Muslims' property!

TABLE 4
Ranking of Jewish Men's Occupations

Secular occupations	Religious occupations[a]
(Doctor)	(Dayan)
(Pharmacist)	
(Engineer)	
(Realestate)	
(Full-time moneylender)	
(Government office worker)	
(JDC executive)	
(Auto-parts salesman)	
(School principal)	
(Technician–University worker)[b]	
(Goldsmith)	
(Carpet merchant)	
(Appliance store)[b] (Camera store)[b] (Typewriter store)[b]	
(Hotel manager) (Cloth-Haberdashery store)[b] (Government teacher)	
(Gum tragacanth merchant)[b] (Lambswool merchant) (Antique dealer)	(Shohet)
(Liquor store)[b] (Restaurateur)[b] (Otsar Hatorah teacher)	(Mohel)
(Folk doctor)	
(Housewares store)[b] (Poultry store)[b] (Village peddler)	
(Medicinal araq maker) (Mosaic maker)	
(Peddler of second-hand articles) (Silversmith) (Carpenter)	
(Wine maker) (Barber) (Grocer, Fruit, Dairy, Ice cream store)	
(Seed peddler) (Spinner) (Cook) (Apprentice)	
(Fortune teller)	
(Music store)	
(Mattress sewer) (Bath attendant) (Custodian) (Mason)	
(Carter) (Tanner) (Blacksmith)	(Mulla-prayer reader)
(Tinker) (Musician)	
(Butcher)	(Shamash)
(Beggar)	(Body washer)

[a] See Chapter X.
[b] Entrepreneurs, *only*, are ranked as shopkeepers; assistants and apprentices rank considerably lower.

TAXES

Formerly, Jews were required to pay a *jaziyeh* (poll tax). Today they are required, like all citizens, to pay income and property taxes as applicable. The poor are exempt from taxes and a bribe to the right person usually enables middle and upper class Jews to escape with minimal payment. Jewish entrepreneurs often avoid government auditing of their account books by keeping them in Judaeo-Persian. These books are further complicated by the irregularly paid-off credit sales.

In the past, Jews avoided all forms of conspicuous consumption in order to escape government confiscation of their wealth. Today, fearing heavy taxes, many Jews preserve this consumption pattern, still living in dilapidated housing, dressing poorly and having few material possessions, although they could afford better.

MONEY

Money, not property, is the most highly valued commodity. Cash is hidden away in every home for a "rainy day" even though banks pay interest and are safe from robbery.[1] Mahalleh children are taught the value of money early. *Pul* (money) is one of the first ten words learned by the infant; by age two they are given an allowance for sweets. Good behavior is sometimes rewarded by giving an extra *rial,* while bad behavior is punished by loss of allowance. The following anecdote illustrates the importance Shirazi children place upon money:

A three year old girl wanted to accompany the author's wife home. She ran ahead, out of her house into the *kuche* (alleyway). Her mother, in an effort to lure her back, shouted after her: "*do hedhar*" (two *rial*), thus implying: "come back! I have money for you!" The child stopped immediately, ran back and reached for the money ostensibly in her mother's hand. When she came close, her mother grabbed her outstretched hand and took her home. (The mother did not have any money at all in her hand!)

The mystique of money is further shown in the succeeding account from the author's fieldnotes:

One evening, in the home of a wealthy family, a rich acquaintance insisted on playing the piano. His playing was atrocious and I jokingly pulled out two *rial,* put them in his

---

[1] Shirazi Jews fear that in an emergency the government might freeze their bank accounts. Some cash is kept available in case it should become necessary to leave the country on short notice.

hand and exclaimed: "these are yours, if you will only stop playing." The young man, in his mid-twenties, a university student and the owner of a brand-new car, took the money, put it into his pocket, got up from the piano and, remaining very friendly towards me, nevertheless did not play for the rest of the evening.

The social priority of money is also exemplified by the "friend" who was devoted and loyal so long as he was paid for giving private lessons, but who never again visited when the lessons were terminated.

The Shirazi Jew is exceedingly penurious. When asked to donate money for the poor, the wealthiest pleads poverty. With the exception of some of the younger elite, every Jew lives as if he were impoverished. It is, in fact, quite difficult to differentiate among rich, middle income and poor by their style of living. Only in the last few years have wealthy Jews been persuaded that they might own automobiles and beautiful houses without their being confiscated or vandalized. Among the emerging middle "class" new clothing is still rarely purchased and despite a trend towards western furniture, in most cases only one room in the house is adequately furnished.

The Jew is constantly concerned about money. During an Otsar Hatorah teacher's strike, the plea made by strikers was that low wages caused the teachers to have "worries" and they, therefore, were unable to teach properly. Men frequently go off by themselves to think about their "worries". Their concern is historically well founded and many Jews must really struggle to subsist.

Yet, the Shirazi Jew readily admits to being lazy. Holidays are valued as excuses to take off from work. Until recently, the Shirazi Jew did not work during the intermediate days of Pesaḥ and Sukkot. No matter how great the need for money, he prefers to have the money come to him and rarely goes out looking for work. Experience has shown him that no amount of hard physical labor will guarantee his sustenance, so physical labor is shunned where possible. Jews take no pride in their work nor in their craftsmanship – work is a necessary evil, a livelihood.

As a consequence of their "protected minority" status, Jews were not permitted to compete directly with Muslims for subsistence. Like other *dhimmis,* Jews drifted into a marginal economic niche which included those occupations expressly forbidden to Muslims or so menial or insecure as to be avoided by most of the populace. Thus emerges the Jewish middleman, trader, broker and entertainer who served well the interests of Persian "power-elite" by providing critical mercantile and social services (Loeb, 1976). Not surprisingly, Jewish economic marginality reinforced social marginality so that the populace felt few compunctions about taking advantage of Jews financially whenever the opportunity presented itself. Debts could remain unpaid, segments of the community could be purchased on speculation for "tax-farming" and partnerships with Muslims must be considered as risky enterprise at best.[1]

Yet within the niche Jews occupy in conformity to the expectations of Persian society, Jews have individually and collectively managed to remain economically viable. Now, during a national effort to industrialize, Jews are in an excellent position to profit from urban expansion and the general economic prosperity. Jews in traditional merchandising occupations are finding their customers able to afford more expensive goods and in greater quantity. The college educated and technically trained are being employed in high paying esteemed positions. Even the moneylenders, perhaps not so well able to compete with the national banks, find themselves the landlords of major income-earning urban populations.

The effects of these changes on the community structure and the social fabric of Shirazi society generally is not yet clear, but it will likely lead to further dissatisfaction with the entrenched community leadership on the part of the young and force social realignments in the face of weakening kinship bonds.

---

[1] In fact, many religious Muslims would enter into far-ranging business committments with Jews, only if there is the likelihood of substantial profit. Otherwise the loss of honor suffered by such involvement is deemed unacceptable! (Thaiss, 1973:91.)

CHAPTER VI

Basic Social Relations

The most important networks of relationships among Shirazi Jews are those traced by kinship. Any relative or "*qom*" has rights and duties not extended to non-kin. Since the Shirazi Jewish community is limited in size and is largely locally endogamous, it would be no exaggeration to say that all Shirazi Jews are related either consanguinally or affinally. The means by which Shirazi Jews distinguish relatives from non-relatives will be viewed not only as an attempt to order the jumble of mutual rights and responsibilities, but as having certain adaptive value.

GENEALOGY

In examining the kinship system one is struck by the inability of Shirazi Jews to remember their genealogies. Most informants cannot recall the names of all their grandparents and less than 5% know the names of great-grandparents. Cognatic lines two or more generations distant are recognized kinsmen, but the precise relationship of kin more than five degrees distant from the informant are rarely known. Men know their patrilines better than their matrilines and vice versa for women. Occasionally single lineages are recorded in old prayer books, but these are lineages of the religious elite whose claim to influence is inherited. Otherwise, Jews make no attempt to remember their genealogy, since in general it is said: "there is no ancestor actually meriting being remembered." Jews claim, too, that the only reason the Persian Muslim remembers genealogies is because Islam stresses the chain of tradition, and thus the Persians learned to remember genealogies from the Arabs.[1]

---

[1] Alberts (1963:540) indicates that Iranian Muslims also have difficulties recalling their genealogies.

KHANEVADEH

Although the basic unit of Shirazi Jewish kinship is the nuclear family, the most important family unit is the *khanevadeh* (extended family). The *khanevadeh* is a patrilateral extended family of three generations, which, in former times, lived in one household. When the *khanevadeh* was strictly patrilocal, the corporate responsibility of its members included providing subsistence for all, and education for the young. Since inheritance was also passed patrilineally, this corporate function also belonged to the *khanevadeh*.

With the modern trend towards neo-locality, the importance of the *khanevadeh* has declined somewhat and its corporate nature has diminished. Members of the *khanevadeh* still actively cooperate in business, consider the marriage alliances of its members and share in inheritance, but most of its functions today, may be subsumed under the kindred.

KINDRED

The *famil*, (from the French "famille") or "kindred", is a more extensive kin grouping, which includes at its core, the *khanevadeh*. The kindred is bilateral and encompasses affinal as well as consanguinal kinsmen. Kindred is loosely defined, but usually includes consanguines four to five degrees distant from ego and affines no more than four degrees distant from ego. Wealthy and prestigious relatives several degrees further removed are often considered *famil*, whereas close relatives of low rank are sometimes not considered kin at all.

Kindred responsibilities are most visible at the various life-crisis rites. Ego is expected, for example, to observe certain mourning procedures for deceased kindred members (see Chapter X). When a quorum is needed by the *khanevadeh,* they call upon members of their respective kindreds. Kindred members are expected to attend the betrothal, wedding ceremony and feast, and circumcision of ego. The women of the kindred are obligated to prepare food for kindred celebrations.

The kindred is a source of capital for moneylending and provides potential business partners. Members of the kindred are favored as mates and can affect the choice of ego in mate selection; more than 98% of the endogamous marriages recorded, were within the *famil* (*cf.* Thaiss, 1973:49).

RESIDENCE PATTERNS

Formerly, patrilocality was the rule of postmarital residence. Upon marriage, the bride would be brought to the groom's house. Usually not more than ten years old at this time, she would be taken under the wing of her mother-in-law and trained in caring for her husband and family. The husband's mother was the dominant woman of the *khanevadeh,* and friction between bride and mother-in-law was common.

Patrilocality still survives in Shiraz in an attenuated form. Upon marriage, the bride moves into the groom's house for a period normally not exceeding one year or, perhaps, until the first child is born. Thereafter, they find their own house, neolocality now being more common and, among the younger generation, much preferred to patrilocality.

Shirazi Jews believe that the incidence of neolocality is inversely proportional to population density. Until twenty years ago, the Mahalleh was highly overcrowded, often more than one nuclear family sharing a room. The post-honeymoon discomfort of the newly wed couple was considerable, but if sharing was necessary, it was preferable to do so with close relatives to minimize friction. Since there was no available housing, the newly wed couple stayed with the husband's *khanevadeh.*

Today, the population density of the Mahalleh is less than one family per room. The modern bride, eighteen years old on the average, and relatively well educated, is less able to adjust to the demands of her mother-in-law, and desires a house of her own. Since housing is readily available, newlyweds move out quickly. Within the Mahalleh, neolocality is less common than *tu khiyabun.* Mahalleh inhabitants are usually poor and buying or renting a house may be beyond the means of a young husband. Also, because the population density is considerably lower than previously, the bride and groom usually have a room of their own, thereby reducing friction between wife and in-laws. Mahalleh girls marry younger and are less educated than girls outside the Mahalleh and may be better able to adjust to their in-law's demands.

Joint families are essentially of patrilocal origin. But there are cases of the families of two sisters living in the same house, and residence with a wife's unmarried maternal uncle, or with a wife's widowed mother's family.

KINSHIP TERMINOLOGY

Shirazi Jewish consanguinial kinship terminology is presented in Table

TABLE V
Kinship Terminology

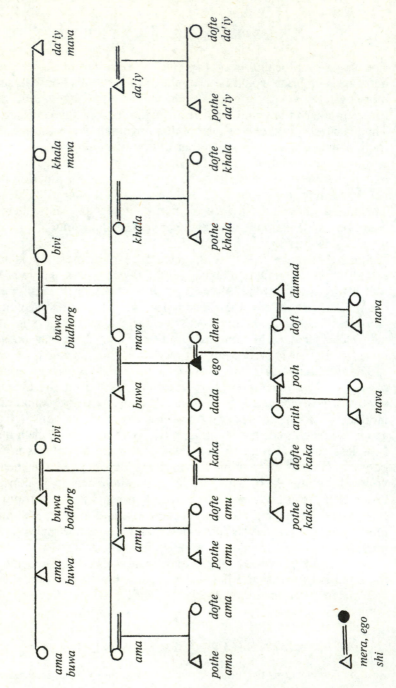

5. Except for phonetic detail, it generally conforms to the Persian system (Spooner, 1965; Alberts, 1963), occasionally making use of archaic forms. Grandparents and grandchildren are referred to by classificatory terms. The rest of the system is descriptive (and is therefore typically bifurcate-collateral), emphasizing a distinction between the respective siblings of father and mother. There are no distinctive cousin terms, nor are cousins grouped into a classificatory category. Each cousin is instead given a descriptive appellation, e.g. father's brother's daughter is called *dofte amu* (literally: daughter of my father's brother). The cousin terminology thus corresponds to Murdock's "Sudanese" cousin terminology (1949:224). Parents' uncles and aunts are referred to in classificatory terms as if they were ego's own uncles and aunts, or alternatively as father or mother's uncle or aunt. Father's mother's sister may thus be called *khala* or *khala buwa*. Classificatory kin terminology does not extend any further into the lineage, so that father's father's brother's daughter is not called *dofte amu* (fabrda) but *dofte amu buwa* (fabrda of fa). Affines are likewise referred to by descriptive terms; there is no terminology for grouping in-laws. Infrequently, where precise relationship is not significant, a person may be referred to as a member of a patrilineage: Kohan-zadeh, Berukhim-zadeh, etc. (literally: "offspring of . . .").

Terms of address are less formal than terms of reference. Many relatives more than two degrees distant are usually addressed by name unless there is considerable age difference in the speakers. Often dyadic interaction evokes terms of endearment such as *biviy jun,* or "grandmother soul", for grandmother.

Fictive terminology is used occasionally by Shirazi Jews. *Kaka,* "brother", may be used by a male in addressing another peer male or one of lower status, Jewish or non-Jewish. The Persian term, *baba,* meaning daddy or grandpa, is frequently used by a male speaker addressing a much older man. The main function of fictive kin term usage is, for purposes of etiquette, to effectuate an ostensible "kin" bond in order to bridge the social distance between actors who otherwise share little that would permit any degree of intimacy.

In general, Shirazi kin terminology operates to delineate reciprocal obligations between people and at least to identify ego's potential corporate responsibilities. The avoidance of terminology in most face-to-face interaction may even be associated with the overall Persian reluctance to be too direct — and thus offensive — in this case by reminding the other through verbal symbols of his relative rank and duties towards ego. We shall explore further the dyadic usage of kin terminology later in this chapter.

AGE AT MARRIAGE

In 1904 it was reported that a girl who is unmarried at age fourteen is considered to be devoted to celibacy (Alliance, 1904:32). Contemporary informants recall that an unmarried twelve-year old girl was said to have "gone sour".

Some claim that Shirazi girls traditionally became mothers by age twelve. It was supposedly common for a man of forty to marry a five-year old girl. It was even reported that two *mullahs* aged sixty-five to seventy, whose first wives had died, married girls of nine and ten (Alliance, 1904:32). Informants say that it used to be common among Shirazi Jews for a girl to be engaged at age six and married at eight. Scholars confirm this tendency to marry at so early an age (Melamed, 1951:367; Mizrahi, 1959:85), but this pattern is apparently peculiar to Shiraz. Elsewhere in Iran, Jewish females are reported to marry at age thirteen (Mizrahi, 1959:85).

Ta'us was seven years old when she was married fifty years ago. During the ceremony she sat playing with a doll which her husband had given her as a wedding present. Afterwards, her nineteen year-old husband brought her to his house, where they played children's games. She felt that she had become a woman, when, at age ten, her permanent teeth began coming in. The marriage was not consummated until several years later, after Ta'us experienced menarche. Raised by her husband (a first cousin) and his parents, she felt that she belonged as much to his family as to her own.[1]

Early betrothal and marriage of females has been attributed to a scarcity of women and to fear of Muslims (Melamed, 1951:367). It is questionable, however, whether there was actually ever a scarcity of women. Demographic data is too scant and unreliable to be conclusive. In support of this hypothesis one might cite the following evidence:

a) As infants, females were observed to be less carefully tended than males and to succumb more often to childhood diseases.

b) Death during childbirth is reported by informants to have been high.

c) It is also true that in present day Iran males outnumber females (Iran Almanac, 1968:495).

But an 1883 census showed a *surplus* of Jewish females in Shiraz

---

[1] Similar tales are told by Jewish women from Yemen (Johanna Spector, personal communication).

(Wilson, 1916:16), and today the number of girls of marriageable age is larger than the number of available bachelors.

Fear of abduction by Muslims had certainly been a factor in the early marriage of Jewish females (see Chapter II). Muslims today occasionally propose matches with Jewish girls; parents are then quick to marry them off to a Jew to forestall an attempted kidnapping on the part of the Muslim suitor. A similar practice for similar reasons is favored among the "new Muslims" of Mashhad (Patai, 1947:165).

Formerly, males also married early; some as early as age twelve (Melamed, 1951:367), but most were aged eighteen to twenty (Mizrahi, 1959:845; see Table 6). Males were able to marry younger then, because the burden of supporting the wife and children fell on the extended family, rather than on the individual male. The marked increase in marital age of males in recent years is probably due to two factors: (1) The disintegration of the patrilocal extended family places the burden of support directly on the prospective groom, who is forced to wait until he can afford to support a wife and family. (2) Ever increasing numbers of males

TABLE 6
Age at Marriage

			Age at marriage		
	before 1929	1929–1938	1939–1948	1949–1958	1959–1968
Females					
Sample	31	30	41	62	94
Median age	8	13	13	15	17
Mode	7	13	13	14	17
Mean	9.7	12.5	13.5	15.6	17.8
Range	(6–25)	(6–20)	(7–23)	(7–24)	(11–29)
Males					
Sample	26	26	42	58	92
Median age	20	23	21	21	26
Mode	20	25	20.5	21	25
Mean	20.6	22.4	21.9	22	26.3
Range	(13–36)	(12–38)	(13–37)	(12–33)	(17–44)
Age difference between husband and wife					
Median	10.5	10	8	7	8
Mode	12	10	10	5	10
Mean	10.8	10.6	8.6	6.7	9
Range	(1–28)	(0–25)	(0–22)	(4–15)	(0–48)

are finishing high school and even college, thereby further delaying economic self-sufficiency.

The steady increase in the marital age of females is due in part to the desire of Jewish women to complete at least nine and sometimes twelve grades before marriage. This is a less important factor among Mahalleh women who nowadays marry at a younger age then females living outside the Mahalleh.

The law permits girls aged fifteen to marry, but girls thirteen years old may marry with the court's permission. Men still prefer to marry girls in their early teens and any girl unmarried at age twenty is considered an old maid. The contention that middle aged men commonly married infants (Alliance, 1904:32) appears to have been an exaggeration; such marriages occurred rarely, and usually a large age difference between husband and wife was true only for second marriages. In Table 6, the mean average age difference between husband and wife for our sample has varied from 6.7 years to 10.8 years, over the past fifty years or so.

MARRIAGE PREFERENCES AND RESTRICTIONS

LOCAL ENDOGAMY

Whether by choice or necessity, the Shirazi Jew has generally chosen to marry with Shirazis. The necessity to do so was largely determined by communications difficulties. But Shirazis also *preferred* to marry locally, considering themselves superior to the Jews of the north. Such pretensions are no longer important, but Shirazis express pride that there are no "apostates" or "irreligious" Jews among them.[1] In Israel too, Shirazis still prefer to marry among themselves.

Prior to 1949, before large scale emigration to Israel and before reliable bus service between cities, nearly 93% of Shirazi Jews married locally. Since then, local endogamy has decreased to about 76%. In Kerman, by contrast, prior to 1949, 75% of the marriages sampled were locally endogamous and since then, the rate has declined to 50%. Shiraz maintained a higher incidence of local endogamy than most other Iranian Jewish communities, perhaps due to its large Jewish population.

Before 1949, the major reason for taking mates from other cities was that widowers and divorcees left with small children had difficulty in

---

[1] Even among the elite, those who appear to be irreligious are relatively more pious than the elite of other cities.

TABLE 7
Local Endogamy (representative sample)

Total	Shirazi mates	Other Iranians	Israeli	Non-Jewish
Married prior to 1949				
246	228	12	4	2
100%	92.7%	4.9%	1.6%	0.8%
Married since 1949				
301	229	47	21	4
100%	76.1%	15.6%	7%	1.3%

replacing their wives. During this period, nearly all of the exogamous un-ions were between Shirazi males and out-of-town females. The explana-tion given for these unions was that there was a shortage of marriageable females in Shiraz — a problem explored earlier.

Today, there is a surplus of marriageable females due to: (1) a decrease in childbirth mortality, (2) the exodus of single men to Teheran and elsewhere for schooling and vocation while single females remain sheltered and relatively immobile, and (3) the possibly anachronistic marriage preferences and restrictions. It has certainly become a "buyer's market" so to speak, and the usual dowry is said to have reached a con-siderable sum.

Restrictions on marrying non-Jews have been rigidly enforced in Shiraz. Formerly, the most frequent cause for intermarriage was family quarreling, or divorce on grounds of infidelity. In recent years, some of the elite have married American Christians while studying in the United States.

CLOSE KIN MARRIAGE

Shirazi Jews pay lip service to the concept recently introduced by JDC, that marrying kinsmen is unhealthy. Privately, Shirazis state that en-dogamous marriages are preferred and from Table 8, we learn that the practice often follows this preference.

Shirazis give the following reasons for endogamous marriage:

1) Prospective mates are known and can be quickly evaluated by the families involved.

2) The respective mates usually know each other from legitimate meetings at family gatherings.

3) In-law strain is less likely to exist in endogamous marriage.

TABLE 8
Close Kin Marriage

Relationship	Number of marriages	Percentage of sample (425 cases)
Uncle-niece	23	5.41
BrDa	7	1.65
SiDa	16	3.76
First cousin	42	9.88
parallel cousin:	28	6.59
FaBrDa	13	3.06
MoSiDa	15	3.56
cross cousin:	14	3.29
FaSiDa	6	1.41
MoBrDa	8	1.88
Other patrilateral parallel cousins	6	1.41
Other matrilateral parallel cousins	2	0.48
Other cross cousins	14	3.29
Other kin	27	6.35
Total	114	26.82

4) There is generally no loss of honor in accepting a spouse from within the kindred.

Occasionally informants would state a preference for a particular form of marriage, most often FaBrDa–FaBrSo, but there was no wide agreement as to the preference.

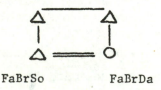

FaBrSo   FaBrDa

First cousins are the most frequent choice for an endogamous union, comprising nearly 10% of our sample. Parallel cousin marriages are twice as frequent as cross-cousin marriages and matrilateral parallel cousin marriages are at least as frequent as patrilateral. This pattern of cousin marriage was checked among the Jews of Kerman, where there is agreement that the patrilateral parallel cousin is the preferred spouse, but statistically that matrilateral parallel cousin was likewise as frequent.

Jews, unlike Muslims, permit uncle–niece marriage, though aunt–nephew marriage is prohibited. The maternal uncle is preferred to the paternal, by a ratio of about 2 : 1.

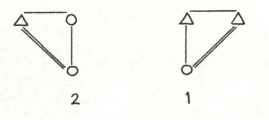

The popularity of avuncular marriage (MoBr=SiDa) is not surprising. Although one's *da'iy* (MoBr) and *amu* (FaBr) are both respected by Shirazis, the relationship with the *da'iy* is usually warmer. Shirazi women, with the children, visit daily with their mothers. A woman's unmarried brother thus has numerous opportunities to observe and become friendly with his sister's daughter. The *amu*'s contact with his brother's children is restricted to formal occasions unless brothers dwell in a joint residence, and his role is more jural than is the *da'iy*'s.

One way of looking at the pattern of endogamy is to view it as primarily involving the *khanevadeh* and, to a lesser extent, the patriline. In this explanation, the mother's *khanevadeh* and patriline provide spouses to male ego more frequently than the father's. A second approach would be to see this pattern as marriage within the *famil,* the kindred. Many of the marriages listed in Table 8 "other kin", were with affines. There are several cases of two brothers marrying two sisters, sister exchange and more complicated arrangements, such as marrying BrWiBrDa (a) or SiHuSiDa (b).

Marriage with relatives as distant as seven degrees is considered within the *qom* (literally "tribe", i.e. with a "relative"), but usually the exact relationship at such distance is blurred. Shirazis acknowledge that in some way or other, they are all related, although too distantly to merit cognizance.

FAMILY PREFERENCE

The rank and prestige of the families of the prospective bride and groom are critical factors in the successful contracting of the marriage. The prestige of a *khanevadeh* and, to a lesser extent, the kindred, measured by wealth, occupation, intellect and piety of their membership, places limitations on choice of mate. Both parties would like to marry up into a family of higher rank. The groom from a prestigious family expects a large dowry, though he may dispense with it if he is "madly" in love with the prospective bride. The groom from a family ranked lower than the bride's, is expected to agree to a large *ktuba* price, in case of divorce. The stipulations of the *ktuba* (marriage contract) are, in general, determined by the relative rank of the contracting families. Endogamy enables the parties to avoid these bottlenecks, as terms are eased considerably between relatives. The stigma of marrying down is escaped by marrying close kin or even by marrying into an affinally related *khanevadeh*.

Today, the prospective groom's rank, based largely on his education and occupation, are almost as important as family prestige. If he ranks in the top four or five occupational levels, he has an excellent chance of marrying into the elite, despite his family's rank. In exceptional cases, however, the groom's family may rank so low that the elite will under no circumstances consider the match. The groom, too, considers a girl who is a nurse or teacher, a better catch than an unemployed female of similar rank.

Frequently, differences in family rank are overlooked when marrying within the same profession. In the past, the rate of marriages within a profession was probably much higher than it is today. Of 119 marriages over the past fifty years, for which sufficient information is available, 40% of the females married men whose profession was the same as their father's or brothers'.

KOHEN MARRIAGE

Many of the elite families in Shiraz are *kohanim* (priests). *Kohanim* usually marry among themselves and are considered superior to the *levi'im* (Levites) and *yisra'el* (common Jews). In fact, there is a tradition, not universally subscribed to by Shirazis, which forbids the marriage of a *kohen* with a *yisra'el*.[1] Shirazis disagree as to how the exclusion principle is applied. One informant explained:

The primary reason why a *kohen* does not marry with a *yisra'el* is one of honor. There is no merit to be gained by a *kohen* taking a simple *bat yisra'el* (Israelite woman); on the other hand, a *bat kohen* (priestly woman) does not accept a *yisra'el* because it is not proper that a *bat kohen* should serve a common *yisra'el*.

Another informant indicates that the prohibition is one-way; the *bat kohen* cannot marry a *yisra'el*:

It is said that the *bat kohen* is sacred, and that she has *kavod* (honor). Perhaps her husband would desecrate this honor by hitting her or not allowing her to do as she likes.

Both of these informants indicate that it is the *kohen* who rejects marriage with the *yisra'el*. A third informant, an old respected *shaliaḥ ẓibbur* (precentor), indicates that it is the *yisra'el* who avoids marriage with the *kohen*:

In the past, some Shirazis had the custom that an Israelite man did not take a *bat kohen* and did not give his daughter to a *kohen* man. This was done because the *kohanim* sin grievously; should a *yisra'el* cause a *kohen* to work hard or be angered, the *kohen* recounts the misdeeds of that *yisra'el* before the Lord.

It would seem, therefore, that Israelites do not want their children marrying with *kohanim* for fear that a family squabble or, worse, a divorce might bring the curse of the offended *kohanim* upon their households.

Informants claim that the prohibition on *kohen-yisra'el* marriage is generally ignored nowadays. Yet one might surmise that a contributing factor to the large number of spinsters among the Shiraz elite, who are largely from priestly families, is the preservation of this traditional restriction.[2] It may operate to cause the *bat-kohen*'s family to reject the common *yisra'el* or simply intimidate the *yisra'el* who otherwise might contemplate such a match.

---

[1] Slouschz (1927:254–267) implies similar restrictions may have been enforced in Jerba and a Baghdadi Jew from Calcutta indicates that they have a similar custom. (*cf.* Musleah 1975:65)

[2] In one elite priestly family there were two girls of marriageable age in 1968, aged 24 and 19. Both girls had completed high school, but had not gone on to college. They were bright, attractive, well-read in Western literature and enjoyed entertaining. Neither had a profession. As of 1974 they were still unmarried!

Once the taboo is broken and someone from one *khanevadeh* marries into a family of *kohanim,* repeated exchanges of spouses between these two groups is possible. The prohibition may be relaxed for the entire kindred as reckoned from the ego when married the *kohen,* but usually it is limited to ego's *khanevadeh.*[1]

LEVIRATIC MARRIAGE

Yibbum (leviratic marriage) is said to occur in Shiraz. The law regarding such marriages is: if a woman is widowed without giving issue, her deceased husband's brother should make her his wife. The woman rarely refuses to make this marriage. A sick husband making a deathbed request for levirate marriage to be performed cannot be refused, but if he requests that it not be done, then *ḥaliza* (drawing off the shoe of the levirate; Deut. XXV:9) is performed in the presence of the *dayan* and witnesses. Informants insist that in Shiraz they follow the Sfardic rite, whereby *yibbum* is normal and *haliza* exceptional (Zimmels, 1958:172–173). However, the author was unable to confirm a single case of *yibbum* in Shiraz, although two cases of sororate marriage occurred in a sample of 533 marriages examined. The brother who marries his deceased brother's wife receives the dowry of his brother and obligates himself to fulfill the terms of the *ktuba* of his brother, unless a new *ktuba* is insisted upon (see Epstein, 1927).

BRIDE PRICE AND DOWRY

Unlike the Muslims, Iranian Jews do not give bride wealth. On occasion, such as when an old widower wishes to marry a young girl or a man strongly desires a pretty bride from a poor family, money may be given to the bride's family. More often in such cases, the groom merely forgoes the dowry.

A dowry is expected to be provided by the father of the bride. It is given in cash and in household utensils. The husband has absolute usufruct rights to the dowry cash; he may receive a part of it during *qiddushin* (the wedding ceremony), during the first week of residence in the *ḥuppa* (room set aside for consummation of the marriage), or at the birth of a son. The shortage of available bachelors is said to have raised the

---

[1] Johanna Spector reports that the Samaritans not only maintain a similar taboo, but that its violation and subsequent intermarriage patterns closely parallel the Shirazi case (personal communication).

going rate of dowry from 1000–10,000 *rial* in 1949 (Levi, 1960, III:1015) to 200,000 *rial* in 1968.

DIVORCE

A man may divorce his wife on any pretext, but a woman has no recourse to divorce and must persuade her husband to give her one. The most frequent grounds for divorce is barrenness. A Jewish bride is expected to become pregnant immediately after the wedding. If she bears no child for two or three years, she is suspected of being barren. She may be divorced soon after, although the more pious wait as long as ten years.[1] Infertility is always publicly attributed to the female, although privately it is conceded that the man is equally often at fault. At least one woman divorced on such grounds lost her entire *ktuba* money, although several years later she bore a son to her second husband. Less often, a man may divorce his wife because of incompatibility or, perhaps because he sees a "pretty face". The author knew of only two cases of divorce on the grounds of actual infidelity – one occurred nearly sixty years ago.

At first glance, it would appear that it is easy for a man to divorce his wife and extremely difficult for a woman to divorce her husband. There are, however, mitigating circumstances.

As marriage is a legal contract, *ktuba,* the husband is obligated to present his wife with another legal document, *get,* stating the terms of her divorce. If the husband cannot be present, for some reason, to present his wife with her *get,* he must designate an emissary to give it in his stead.

The bill of divorce has to be approved by the *dayan*[2] and today, a civil divorce, unrelated to the religious *get,* must be obtained. Informants claim that the *dayan* makes the enactment of a divorce difficult and tedious. He carefully examines the grounds for divorce and delays the procedure in an attempt to effect a reconciliation. Occasionally the *dayan* will try to persuade a husband to give a divorce in case of frequent wife beating or desertion, but no physical force is ever applied. Desertion is not considered a particularly reprehensible act and the absent husband cannot be forced to provide for his family. The wife may be empowered by the *dayan* to sell her husband's property in order that

---

[1] While many divorces are attributable to infertility, numerous marriages remain quite stable despite the lack of offspring.

[2] In the past, the divorce had to be approved by a court of three judges.

the family not starve, but her *khanevadeh* bears the primary responsibility for her support.

After *qiddushin,* the groom is presented with an agreed upon dowry,
by the bride's father. This dowry is returned to the bride with interest
upon her husband's death, or upon divorce.

In 1920, Azziz married Shokat. The agreed dowry was 364 *rial.* Being a relatively
poor man, this amount represented about three to four months wages. The sum was
multiplied by one and one-half, to which was added 90 *rial* more, possibly the sum of
the gifts made by the groom to the bride. The sum total of 1,000 *rial,* equivalent, then,
to about one year's wages, was the amount of money written into the *ktuba,* payable to
Shokat, should she be divorced.

The difference between the dowry received and the *ktuba* price has
grown substantially. One informant reported that he received a dowry of
30,000 *rial,* but the *ktuba* price was placed at 1,000,000 *rial,* equivalent

PLATE 49   Wedding picture taken circa 1920; bride is about 10 years old, the groom
is in his early teens.

to fourteen years wages for a married Otsar Hatorah teacher. Another informant received no dowry, but agreed to a *ktuba* price of 500,000 *rial*. In the past the *ktuba* price was rarely more than three times the dowry, whereas today amounts 10, 100 and even 1000 times the dowry are commonly agreed to.

This *ktuba* money, referred to as *mohar habbtulot* (bride price of virgins) severely limits the ability of the husband to divorce his wife. By doing so, he not only loses the usufruct rights to the dowry, but must, in addition, pay an exorbitant sum of money. On the other hand, a woman willing to forgo her *ktuba* money, can often persuade her husband to grant her a *get*.

Polygyny is an alternative to divorce for the man who can afford it, but it has never been very common among Shirazi Jews, probably due to the alleged scarcity of women or lack of wealth. The author knew of five men who had two wives simultaneously; one had had three, but one wife died. The wives are kept in separate homes and usually do not get along. In one case, a man chose a second wife to spite the family of his first wife; the two wives and their twenty-seven children have nothing to do with one another, and the man's friends choose to be seen in one household or the other, but not in both. In an exceptional case, a barren woman chose a second wife for her husband; these women live together and are warm friends.

Today, polygyny has been all but eliminated as an alternative to divorce, even though many Jews could better afford it and despite the surplus of marriageable females. This results from a government edict requiring the first wife to give her consent before her husband can take a second wife.[1]

The presence of children in a marriage is another important deterrent to divorce. Rarely does a husband want to give up his children whom he loves. On the other hand, he would find it difficult to remarry should he have children to raise – only widows and divorcees would agree to such a match. If the wife gets custody of the children upon divorce, which is often the case, she finds it even more difficult to remarry. In the past, at those periods when there may have been a shortage of women, female divorcees with children probably found it easier to find a husband than today.

Divorce is considered "ugly" and both parties are pitied. Divorce in endogamous marriages would have unfavorable consequences for the stability of the kindred, and it is thought that endogamous marriage itself

---

[1] Polygyny among Muslim men is about 4.5% (Iran Almanac, 1968:549), whereas among Jewish men it is substantially less than 1%.

eliminates some bases for friction leading to divorce. Only 2 of 114 close kin marriages (1.8%) ended in divorce, whereas 10 of 325 exogamous marriages (3.2%) ended that way.

The divorce rate among our Shirazi Jewish sample, 12 of 533 marriages (2.25%) is extremely low. Among the total population of Shiraz in 1340 A.H. (1961–1962) the ratio of divorces to marriages was more than 25% (Clarke, 1963:47).

INHERITANCE

Upon the death of a man, all of his debts are paid off. His sons equally share the *yrusha,* or "inheritance", although sometimes an unequal apportionment can be engineered by devious means. If a son is already deceased, his sons divide their father's share equally. If the deceased has daughters only, then they divide the estate equally; otherwise daughters receive no inheritance. It is explained that daughters do not normally inherit because they have already received their share as dowry.[1]

The deceased's wife inherits nothing. However, before the sons are permitted to divide the estate, she must be paid her *ktuba* money. If she remains in the house of the deceased, her sons are obligated to provide her support until she remarries or leaves the deceased's house, at which time she is paid her *ktuba* money. The sons are also obligated to support all of their unmarried sisters, provide a dowry for them and arrange their marriage.

During marriage, the only property possessed by a woman is that which she inherits or receives as a present. Any money she earns must be turned over to her husband. Often, the only valuables she possesses are the gold bracelets she wears on her wrists and her gold-capped teeth. A woman does not usually have very much property to bestow on heirs. Jewlry and light movable property such as clothing and utensils, are inherited by her daughters. If she has sons, they share equally the remainder of the estate; otherwise her daughters divide the entire *yrusha*. Should there be no children or grandchildren, her brothers, then her sisters or her nearest relatives, inherit. But if she has a husband, *her husband inherits everything*.

For many years, the "law of apostasy" wreaked havoc with the nor-

---

[1] Shi'a Muslims provide for daughters to inherit half shares and the Chief Rabbi of Israel, has tried to arrange a similar inheritance rule for Iranian Jews — without success in Shiraz.

mal pattern of inheritance. It is not known whether Jews gave away the *yrusha* before death in order to escape the consequences of this decree.

INTERPERSONAL RELATIONS AMONG KINSMEN

HUSBAND–WIFE

As we have seen earlier, the position of the Jewish woman is far better than that of the Muslim woman. She is not restricted to the *anderun,* nor forced to envelope herself completely in her *chador.* She normally eats together with her husband and children. She is present when a guest comes and may sit with her husband at social gatherings, although men more often sit alone in one room and women in another.

A wife addresses her husband "*aqa*" (sir) or, should he have a title, by that title, for example "*aqaye doktor*" (sir doctor). Usually, she speaks with him using the polite second person, "*shoma*", whereas he calls her *khanom* ("lady") and addresses her in the familiar second person "*to*". When speaking of her husband, a woman often uses his patronym without title or surname.

A wife is maid and servant to her husband. She must organize the house and maintain it, supervise the children and prepare the meals. At meal time, the Jewish wife used to be required to bring water before and after the meal for her husband's ritual ablutions, but this practice has fallen into disuse. She serves her husband first, providing him with the choice portions of food. In the past, a wife was expected to help in her husband's business, thus, if he were a peddler, she might be expected to peddle in the Muslim women's *anderun.* Today, a spinner's wife may help prepare yarn for her husband.

A Jewish wife's most important function is to bear sons. She is expected to bear them every two years or so. Lack of success in bearing male children, may lead to divorce, or, at least, discontent on the part of the husband, who suffers a loss of honor when the newborn is a girl.

A Jewish wife must not converse with strange men, nor be seen in their company, as this would lead to gossip. A wife, who misbehaves, is scolded or perhaps beaten by her husband, from whom she may escape and seek the protection of her mother. If publicly mistreated by Muslim men, a woman must defend her own honor by hitting back; her husband's intervention might lead to his being seriously injured or even killed.

A Jewish husband is obligated under the terms of the *ktuba* to: (1)

provide sustenance, (2) clothing, (3) avoid hurting her feelings, (4) take her to a doctor if she is ill, (5) ransom her if captured, (6) provide a *yrusha* for her sons, (7) return her *ktuba* money at his death or in case of divorce, (8) avoid her during her ritual uncleanliness, and (9) honor her father and mother as his own. These obligations are in accordance with Jewish law (Epstein, 1927). Violation of the first three obligations is frequent, and honoring of in-laws is far from universal.

In the Mahalleh, a Jewish husband gives his wife an allowance for food and other necessities, which she purchases herself. If they live *tu khiyabun,* he makes all of the purchases. A good husband helps his wife with any hard physical labor. Child rearing is left largely in the hands of the wife, since the husband's workday usually begins at 6.00 a.m. and ends after 8.00 p.m.; during the day he comes home only for lunch and for a nap.

Sexual intercourse between husband and wife is done in the dark, with clothes on, ideally while the children are asleep. Ritual taboo limits intercourse to two weeks during the month (see Chapter X). The major reason for intercourse is procreation, but some women claim that they enjoy the act itself and are not at all unhappy, when, at menopause, they need no longer fear pregnancy. Birth control is rare; coitus interruptus is the most frequent means used, even though it is technically one of the few methods actually forbidden by Jewish law (Feldman, 1974:152–155).

Because marriages are arranged, husband and wife rarely know each other well beforehand, unless they are close kin. A husband usually confides in his friends, rather than in his wife. A wife confides in her mother, sisters or oldest daughter. Freed from work in the evening or on the Sabbath, a husband frequently leaves his wife with the children and goes off with his friends for talk or to the movies.

Important decisions are usually left to the husband, though wives are quite strong in influencing them. Despite a public facade of subservience, many women actually manage husband, family and household with a firm hand.

PARENT–CHILD

"Dofte baden, pothe kheben" – "a daughter is bad, a son is good".

1 *Mother–child*

Mothers are quite happy to have several daughters despite the prestige of bearing sons. Daughters, however, are wanted in limited numbers, and after the third or so, the mother's interest in them tends to lessen.[1] Doting on the female infant ends at about two years, when duties and responsibilities are gradually urged upon them. Daughters are trained to help their mothers and eventually take over part of the burden of child-care, cooking and cleaning. Mother is much freer in scolding and hitting her daughters than her sons, but she nonetheless develops a close relationship with them and one or more becomes her confidante. The relationship remains close after marriage. Mother exercises a great deal of control over her adult daughters, whom she keeps tightly bound to her. A daughter's love for her mother may be used to prevent a whole family from emigrating to Israel (*cf.* Hakohen, 1970:7); a letter from mother has been known to snatch back an unmarried daughter already living in Israel.

The birth of a son brings the mother honor from everyone and love from her husband. Sons are the favored children in the Shirazi Jewish family. While very young, the son is close to the mother, but by age four or five, he is off by himself. He plays the whole day away from home, returning only to eat and sleep. Nevertheless, mother–son love is usually very strong.

Mother-love, it was observed, is quite selfish where adult children are concerned. Children are supposed to remain nearby; if the mother is poor and widowed, they are obligated to support her. She is, by contrast, free of responsibility, although she will help her daughter during child-birth and offer her advice and temporary refuge. Not able to enjoy the benefits of the formal institutions open to the men, such as the *knisa* and guild, and being illiterate and poor, the traditional Shirazi woman's sole interest and concern is her children.

2) *Father–child*

The relationship between father and daughter is at times close and warm. Perhaps because father is not at home often, thus leaving mother to discipline her, a daughter has an easy and affectionate relationship with her father. Whereas a married woman has to defend her own honor, fathers vigorously defend the honor of their daughters and have been observed to get into fist-fights with Muslim men who try to molest them, despite the obvious danger in such behavior.

However, whereas mother is referred to by terms of endearment such as *mama, mava* or *nane,* father is more often addressed by the respectful terms *buwa* and *aqa.* A father's love for his daughter is sometimes tempered by the necessity to provide her with a dowry for her wedding.

---

[1] Although there is no female infanticide, it is almost always the female child who dies through neglect.

The father exercises control over his daughter's choice of spouse, but with more attention to his daughter's wishes than her brothers might prefer.

If mother has practical need for daughters, then father has at least as great a need for sons. Mothers are largely responsible for their sons while the latter are infants. But by age three or four, fathers spend more time with their sons, taking them to *knisa* and worrying about their education. Fathers and sons spend especially long periods of time together on Shabbat, holidays and during school vacation as fathers try to enculturate them to the world and ethos of men. A son is expected to get some Hebrew training and is encouraged to finish six grades of secular school. Then he is expected to either work with his father or become an apprentice in some profession. A major part of a son's income goes to the household, thereby alleviating somewhat the financial burden of the father. Mahalleh people agree that the most important criterion of political influence, other than money, is a large number of sons. Sons not only contribute to the *khanevadeh* income and wealth, they can also effectuate valuable kin alliances through marriage, at no cost to the father.

The father–son relationship is characterized by respect and fear on the part of the sons, even after marriage.[1] Sons address their fathers formally. Fathers rarely hit their daughters, but sons are not exempt from such punishment. Fathers serve as models of masculinity for their sons, but they rarely command their sons' affection as do mothers. The disintegration of the *khanevadeh* as a residence unit means that married sons visit with their fathers only on special occasions, such as holidays. Fathers exercise less active control over their adult sons' affairs than do mothers, who constantly attempt to keep them nearby.

The child's relationship to his parents is one emphasizing formal respect for father and warm love for mother. The uterine tie is of less jural importance than the paternal, but of nearly equal overall weight. Frequently, paternal authority can be eroded by a loving mother, whereas there seems to be no equivalent reverse procedure.

SIBLING BEHAVIOR

Respect is shown toward one's older siblings, male and female. The oldest is most respected, but in any case the oldest male sibling, unless

---

[1] Father/son conflict over business matters and open commercial competition between the two were almost unknown among Shirazi Jews in contrast to the Muslim bazaar merchants of Teheran (Thaiss, 1973:87).

he is very young, commands respect second only to father. Older siblings may make and enforce decisions regarding younger ones. There is, however, no kin term to designate the difference between older and younger siblings.

Male siblings often exercise a veto over their sister's marital choice and may induce her to accept their choice. Marriage alliances are of direct concern to her brothers, since her affines become part of their kindred and are potential business partners. Brothers have no compunction about hitting their unmarried sisters. They exercise as much, or more, authority over their sisters and show more concern for their sisters' honor than they do for their own wives. At puberty, boys are no longer permitted to sleep near their sisters. They are given a separate room, or sleep at the far end of the room with the father and mother separating them from their sisters. The author never heard of any brother–sister incest.

Siblings are concerned about one another's health. Thus when Munes was ill with mastitis, Ithuf came every day to massage his sister's breast by hand, because, being somewhat *divune* or "crazy", she would not allow anyone else to do this for her. When Saltanat had congestive heart failure, her brothers and sisters visited her each day, telephoning if the visit was not possible.

Brothers often go into business together and sometimes work with their in-laws. Moneylending is a family affair; the successful moneylender will first tap his brothers and finally his brothers-in-law for capital. On the other hand, brothers have been observed to engage in cut-throat competition. Cheating a business partner, a common happening, may lead to a major disruption of the *khanevadeh* if the partner happens to be a brother. Money is the greatest cause of sibling rivalry. Jealousy over differences in siblings' living standards and strife over the *yrusha* (inheritance), are inevitable sources of friction. Siblings who marry against the wishes of the others or who do less well economically, are often ostracized. In such cases only the most minimal contact is maintained and no help is offered the unfortunate sibling, as personal success outweighs family cohesiveness.

GRANDPARENT–GRANDCHILD

The relationship of grandparent and grandchild is warm and indulgent. The grandfather may sometimes be a father-surrogate if the latter is deceased or divorced. Grandchildren visit their often old and disabled grandparents frequently. Some teenaged girls were seen to stop at their grandmothers' house daily after school.

OTHER RELATIONSHIPS

1) *Amu*

The father's brother is treated with a certain degree of respect. His relations with his brother's children are to some extent jural and authoritarian. In present day Shiraz, *amu* rarely becomes actively involved with his nieces and nephews, unless they live in the same household. One informant reported that when he misbehaved as a child he was called "*amu*", here implying "bossy".

2) *Da'iy*

The mother's brother is often considered a friend by his sister's children. His contact with them is frequent and he can often be persuaded to intervene on their behalf in family conflicts. He is a favorite marriage partner for his sister's daughter. One young man admired his *da'iy* so much, he legally adopted the latter's patronym.

3) *Ama*

The father's sister is treated with a certain degree of respect. It is difficult to generalize regarding her relations with her brother's children, but she seems to have a good deal more contact with her brother's daughters than with his sons. She may intervene with her brother on behalf of his daughters.

4) *Khala*

The mother's sister has a close relationship with her sister's daughter. Usually the relationship is friendly and warm and she has very much influence over her sister's daughter. This influence, no doubt, is of importance in the high incidence of marriage between children of sisters. But the khala's interference in her sister's daughter's affairs is sometimes resented. One informant, especially resentful of her mother's sister's meddling, claimed that the root meaning of the word *khala* is "toilet".

IN-LAWS

Mother and father-in-law are usually addressed in the manner one addresses one's parents, though perhaps more formally. Occasionally the term *amu* (father's brother) is used in a classificatory way when addressing or referring to father-in-law, a usage common to Beduin kinship, where preferential father's brother's daughter is the norm. Son-in-law is referred to as *dumad* (groom) and daughter-in-law is called *arith* (bride).

Honor and respect are due one's mother and father-in-law, but Shirazi Jews informally avoid them. Sometimes a husband will forbid his wife to allow her mother into the house, or even forbid her to visit her mother. Mothers in turn, rarely visit their daughters when their sons-in-law are home. Avoidance of parents-in-law is so extensive that special occasions occur during the year when a man is formally required to visit his in-laws. Thus during the middle of the night on Purim, he and his nuclear family are expected to go to his father-in-law's house for a Purim party and meal. During the intermediate days of Pesah, he and his wife are required to live at the house of his father-in-law.

Male dislike of the mother-in-law is by no means irrational. She exerts influence on her daughter and is, therefore, a potential source of family friction. A daughter will see her mother from as few as three times per week to as many as several times a day; her mother's advice is frequently followed. Male avoidance of the mother-in-law is sometimes extended to the father-in-law. Lack of male issue may exacerbate such a situation for the son-in-law, and the father-in-law may be resentful over the dowry he was forced to pay. Contact with one's father-in-law is limited to holiday visits and chance encounters in the street or synagogue. Sometimes relations between father and son-in-law are warm and, not infrequently, men are employed by their fathers-in-law.

Women usually get their fill of the mother-in-law during the sometimes protracted period of patrilocal residence. Formerly, when a bride came to her husband's house at age seven, it was not terribly difficult to adjust to her mother-in-law's way of doing things. Now girls marry in their late teens, and find their own well-developed behavioral patterns in conflict with their mothers-in-law. The most frequent reason

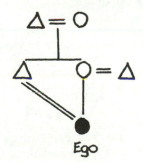

SiDa = MoBr   BrDa = FaBr

given for cessation of patrilocal residence is the inability of a woman to get along with her husband's mother. The latter is the butt of many clever songs and anecdotes. Unfortunately, a woman cannot easily escape her mother-in-law, but once she lives neolocally, she may be forced to see her only when she must accompany her husband on visits or when the husband's mother comes to visit her grandchildren. In cases of close endogamy, in-law dislike and avoidance are assumed to be less intense. Thus, when a female marrys her mother's brother or father's brother, her parents-in-law are also her grandparents, whereas the male's parents-in-law are his siblings and their spouses.

A man's relations with his sister and brother-in-law are generally good and respectful. Not infrequently they may work together or even live together. Since affines are considered to belong to the kindred, personal dislike is ideally not permitted to interfere with outward respect and proper behavior in their presence.

THE CHANGING PATTERN OF KIN OBLIGATIONS

Shirazis, like most Persian Jews, consider death a taboo subject. People go to great lengths to avoid its mention. It was noted that in many cases, first degree kinsmen of the deceased were not informed of the death for weeks or even months when they were out of the country, e.g. in Israel or the United States. Most informants expressed the opinion that this was done to spare the feelings of the kinsman, though from observation I would venture to suggest that this pattern often engendered the opposite response.

Bahram, a young college student studying the United States was informed that his sister was seriously ill. Each week he would receive notice about her grave condition. In anguish, suspecting the worst, he queried his parents about her illness as his concern mounted daily. After six or seven weeks, his mother wrote that the sister's condition was improving. As letters describing her improvement continued to be received, an older sibling, living in Israel, indirectly happened to learn the truth and wrote to Bahram that their sister had died six weeks earlier. The parents finally explained that they had wanted to wait for Bahram's return to Iran before, exposing him to the truth. This excuse was accepted without rancor, indeed, he offered a further rationale that it was too painful for them to communicate the news of this tragedy.

It is not quite clear whether the parents were trying to convey subtle hints of her passing which he should have acknowledged directly, but was perhaps too immature to properly interpret. It is also possible that this was but an expression of guilt over the death of a kinsman, or perhaps shame and/or fear over setting into motion the spirit world and the agent of death.[1]

Whatever reasons actually motivated this sequence of events, such conduct *vis-à-vis* close kinsmen who are absent from Shiraz offers a clue to the changes now being effected in kin obligations by new-found mobility.[2] Within Shiraz, the *khanevadeh* and *famil* remain fairly cohesive social groupings whose membership actively supports one-another morally and otherwise, in time of tragedy or need. The various networks of social interaction quickly spreads news of all events, enveloping those who by right or obligation ought to actively participate in the ceremonial and personal activity surrounding them. Nobody is permitted to confront tragedy by himself. So the *khanevadeh,* whose corporateness is generally rather limited, immediately extends a blanket protection to its membership abroad and therefore unable to share in solace provided by the kin group. They are alone in facing life's hardships. They should not and cannot face the ultimate crisis, the death of a close kinsman, without the warmth and security provided by the kindred. Thus, elaborate precautions are taken to shield the isolated and thus exposed members of the *khanevadeh* from any unpleasant news, a conspiracy which the entire community concurs with and participates in!

In this transitionary phase of Shiraz Jewry, in which the core of the *khanevadeh* remains intact and in place, the traditional pattern of blanket protection for exposed members remains a viable and acceptable behavior norm. But as mobility continues to increase and the local *khanevadeh* further disintegrates, this pattern will become progressively dysfunctional as the traditional kin structures find themselves fragmented and dispersed, unable to provide the necessary security to its now far-flung membership. At that point, the elaborate secrecy merely becomes lack of information, and lack of communication along the kin network will merely serve to further diminish the importance of kin groups.

---

[1] The entire complex of behavior surrounding the death of a kinsman allows this to be a real possibility (see Chapter X). Unfortunately, no projective tests, which might have offered us a greater insight into and understanding of this pattern, were administered.

[2] I am indebted to Emmanuel Marx for proposing this line of inquiry.

NON-KIN RELATIONSHIPS: UTILITARIAN FRIENDSHIP

Friendships are formed with both kin and non-kin among Shirazi Jews. Friends are of the same sex from age seven, at which time boys and girls are expected to play separately. Friends are usually peers and nowadays – classmates.

Bachelors and young married males play cards, chess and backgammon, go for walks, go to the movies, visit prostitutes and hold parties together in the gardens. Friends are often in the same profession and attend the same *knisa*. Bachelor friends spend all of their free time together. Relationships that may be characterized as strong friendships are commonly accompanied by physical displays of affection, including fondling and hand-holding.

Among young unmarried women, close friendships are formed. Here too, relationships are accompanied by display of affection, such as kissing and fondling. After marriage, the strongest ties of friendship as well as of bitter enmity are among neighbors.

Informants point out that although friends prefer to do business with each other, they should not expect too much of a "break", such as a discount, from each other. "Friendship does not enter into business" is an ethic frequently invoked in explaining this aparently contradictory behavior.

Furthermore, there must be some tangible reciprocal benefit to friends, if the relationship is to be maintained. "What more can I get out of it", an informant replied to a question regarding the dissolution of an apparently close friendship. Friendships fluctuate in intensity depending on the state of mutual moral obligations between people. A favor must be reciprocated by one of at least equal worth.[1] Informants admit that if acquaintances can be beneficial to them, they will swear undying devotion to them; but the "friendship" quickly becomes a superficial amicability at chance meetings, as soon as one can no longer profit from the other.

In sum . . . The kinship system of Shirazi Jews does not appear to be unique in this area of the world. The configuration of a bilateral kindred surrounding a patrilateral extended family core, has been described by

---

[1] This reciprocity ethic also explains why Shirazis are such ungracious recipients of unsolicited gifts.

Alberts (1963), Barth (1961), Mendelson (1964) and Thaiss (1973). But for an intimidated minority, such a pattern of kinship has certain distinct adaptive advantages.

One of the great dangers to Jewish survival in Shiraz has been "visibility". The individual who was "visible" to the authorities, was singled out for punishment or indignity. Thus Jews hid behind high walls and narrow alleys, avoided conspicuous consumption and tried to shirk social responsibility. In the Muslim Middle East, people are identified by patrilineage. Hence, short genealogies and a loosely defined bilateral kindred, preserved a certain amount of invisibility *vis-à-vis* the authorities.

A second danger was the apostate Jew. The "law of apostasy" enabled a convert to Islam to inherit from "any relative" to the seventh generation (Carmelite Chronicles, 1939:288) or at least to the fourth generation (Carmelite Chronicles, 1939:366). Since Muslim inheritance law is patrilineal, there can be little doubt that by "any relative" is meant a patrilineally traced relative. Short genealogy and the bilateral nature of the kindred served to shield may kinsmen from the claims of apostates, who could not inherit from those not patrilineally related.

The relatively weak corporate nature of both the *khanevadeh* and *famil,* complemented the passive nature of Jewish resistance to Shirazi Muslims. Certainly a clearly defined kindred, functioning in a manner similar to the Arab blood responsibility group, would have required active resistance to Muslim harassment. The consequences of such a stance would have been disastrous for the entire community.

It is possible that Shirazi Jews once had a strong patrilineal kinship system, such as is common throughout the Middle East. The survival of patrilocality, patrilineal inheritance, patronymy, preservation of the patronym by a woman after marriage, patrilateral extended family, jural role of the father's brother versus the sentimental role of mother's brother, and so forth, may be evidence that the present system evolved from a patrilineal one.

The Shirazi Jewish pattern of endogamy show some interesting variations from the Middle Eastern norm. Although parallel cousin marriage is much preferred over cross-cousin marriage, there is a statistical predominance of matrilateral parallel cousin marriage over the patrilateral form. Another pattern of endogamy not previously reported for this area, is the preference for sister's daughter over brother's daughter. In general matrikin seem to be favored over patrikin.

Finally, we note again the paucity of extensive kin obligations and the shallowness of non-kin relationships. The transient quality of these relationships seems to be characteristic of many aspects of Shirazi Jewish life.

CHAPTER VII

Formal Education

Shirazi Jews did not traditionally place a heavy emphasis upon formal education. Vocational skill was usually deemed of greater pragmatic value than esoteric knowledge so that the educational emphasis tended to focus on occupational apprenticeship. Erudite scholarship in religious matters was highly valued, but very few ever attained a high level of scholastic proficiency. In fact, the main goal of traditional education was to prepare males for participation in synagogue ritual and was, at best, only partially successful in attaining this end.

LITERACY

The literacy rate among the general population of Iran in 1968 was about 30% (Iran Almanac, 1968:519) with the literacy of males about three times that of females.

Literacy among Shirazi Jews was not very great in the past, but the improvement in the last fifty years has been far greater than amongst the general population. The change in literacy among Shirazi Jews is presented in table form (see Table 9). The sample used in compiling the statistics presented was selected in order to represent the whole spectrum of Shiraz society as it was constituted during the period of research. The age ranges selected correspond to significant periods in the history of formal education in Shiraz. Age six to nineteen includes those of present school age. Age twenty to thirty-five includes those educated after 1940, the beginning of the most effective period of government sponsored education and the commencement of Otsar Hatorah operations. Age thirty-six to fifty includes the post-Alliance community school period. Age fifty-one and above includes those who were educated in the Alliance period.

Whereas the literacy rate among Shirazi Jews nowadays is clearly much higher than among the general population, it has probably always been so. Over the past fifty years, Jewish literacy in Persian has in-

TABLE 9
Literacy among Shirazi Jews

Male

Age range	Total sample	Illiterate		Hebrew[a]		Persian	
	No.	No.	%	No.	%	No.	%
6–19	131	0	0	65	49.6	131	100
20–35	130	13	10.0	26	20.0	111	85.4
36–50	47	7	14.9	9	19.3	38	80.9
51+	34	15	44.1	15	44.1	10	29.4
Total male	342	35	10.2%	125	36.5%	290	84.8%

Female

Age range	Total sample	Illiterate		Hebrew[a]		Persian	
	No.	No.	%	No.	%	No.	%
6–9	142	4	2.8	42	29.6	138	97.2
20–35	116	27	23.3	7	6.0	89	76.7
36–50	42	30	71.4	1	2.4	11[b]	26.2
51+	21	17	80.9	4[c]	19.1	0	0
Total female	321	78	24.3%	54	16.8%	238	74.1%
Grand total	663	113	17.0%	179	27.0%	528	79.6%

[a] Hebrew literacy here refers only to ability to read; writing and comprehension are minimal in all but a few cases.
[b] 9 of the 11 are from elite families.
[c] All four are from elite families and were said to have had private tutors.

creased dramatically to the point where today's school age population is nearly 100% literate. Male and female literacy in Persian is about equal among Jews.

Most of the increase in Persian literacy occurred after 1925, the beginning of the Pahlavi era. Jews quickly grasped the potential advantages of literacy for males and by World War II more than 80% of them were literate. Illiteracy among males age fifty and less is found only among the poor; previously, illiteracy was more equitably distributed. Among females, literacy in the pre-Pahlavi and early Pahlavi periods is almost entirely associated with the elite.

Literacy in the pre-World War I period was due to the efforts of Alliance Israélite Universelle which operated a coeducational school beginning in 1903. The presence of Alliance does not seem to have affected the literacy rate of females in this sample.[1]

The oldest males in the sample studied Hebrew in the *maktab*; Alliance never emphasized Hebrew and this may have contributed to its failure in Shiraz. Low Hebrew literacy in the pre-Otsar Hatorah Pahlavi period was due to a combination of factors. The *maktab* was replaced by a community school whose curriculum followed national standards. Modern education stressed Persian at the expense of Hebrew and the severing of ties with Alliance ended supervised Hebrew education. The community school eventually became completely secular and only an occasional emissary from Baghdad giving private Hebrew lessons, ameliorated the problem to any extent. Only after 1950 when Otsar Hatorah schools began operating, did Hebrew literacy begin to improve substantially.

THE SCHOOLING SYSTEM

The *koto* or *maktab,* the traditional Jewish school was still functioning in the 1930s according to informants. Usually a *knisa* served as the school. The *mulla,* or "teacher", would sit with his back to the wall, while the students sat in a row or semi-circle facing him. Each "class" was grouped together and sometimes the more advanced students helped the others. In summer, classes were held in the cellar or otherwise out of the sun, while the rest of the year they would be in the courtyard.

A boy's education began at age four or five and continued to about age ten. Its purpose was to prepare the boy to participate in the *knisa*.

---

[1] Since the number of females attending Alliance was always relatively small, this sample chanced not have included any.

The children learned first the Hebrew alphabet and then proceeded to read from the *Siddur,* or "prayer book". Later the child learned to chant from the Tora and to recite by rote a translation of the text into Judaeo-Persian. Next in the curriculum was the learning of the *haftara* (selections from the Prophets). Finally, the student might learn some Midrash and a little Mishna, but Talmud was never studied. Any knowledge beyond this was learned informally, often by oneself. Misbehaving students were punished by bastinado.

In 1903, Alliance Israélite Universelle founded a school in Shiraz. Although little information could be obtained regarding this institution, its curriculum appears to have followed the standard Alliance pattern stressing mastery of the French language with but minimal instruction in Hebrew or Persian. One informant said that he, like many others, attended school for three years, but never became literate in Persian and could read French with only minimal comprehension.

During its operation, Alliance enrolled the following numbers of students: (Alliance Bulletin, 1905–1912). Not more than 10 to 15% of school-aged children were attending at any time.

TABLE 10
Alliance Enrollment

Year	1905	1906	1907	1908	1909	1910	1911	1912	Mean average
Males	340	310	305	258	309	252	270	250	287
Females	90	80	73	70	68	35	73	70	70
Total	430	410	378	328	377	287	343	320	357

"Le Monsieur", as the Alliance school director was known, paternalistically intervened on behalf of the Shirazi community in times of potential danger. During famine and persecution "le monsieur" called upon the British and French Consuls to aid the community and directed relief operations at the behest of Alliance.

However, "le monsieur" did not always get along with the Shirazis and complaints about him were sent directly to Paris. Melamed (1951:365) tells the following story, which was also related to me by informants regarding "le monsieur".

One of the Alliance teachers in Shiraz befriended a Muslim girl. This became known to the Imam and in his religious zeal he incited the Muslims to fall upon the Jews who desecrate the honor of Muslim girls. This was made known immediately to the Rabbi of the community who was studying *Tiqqun Leyl Shavu'ot*[1] and he hurried to the teacher and told him the news. What did the teacher do? He went that night and converted to Islam in order to save the lives of the community. Several months later, he left Persia and returned to Judaism.

At first the entire school budget was provided by Alliance. Later on taxes were levied by the community on *shḥita* (ritual slaughter) and on liquor sales. Taxes imposed to supplement the Alliance budget were apparently opposed by some Shirazis. Alliance claims that it finally left Shiraz because the community refused to pay a fair share of the budget.[2] Shirazis claim that Alliance was asked to leave by the community which charged that their curriculum was un-Jewish and their representatives irreligious. The merit of these contentions is obscured by time, but no doubt both Alliance and the community were not too unhappy at the parting of the ways.

After Alliance left Shiraz the community supported its own Jewish school known as Ibna Sina. Brawer, (1946:332–3) an emissary from Palestine who visited Shiraz in 1932, indicates that the school was financed by a tax on kosher meat. The government changed the school into a regular primary school under the direction of an "enlightened" Muslim assisted by expert teachers and at the same time agreed to provide the bulk of the school budget. Jewish studies were under the direction of old-fashioned teachers and were no better than in Alliance schools.[3] The director added a Jewish girls' school. Since the government was not willing to provide funds for the girls school, the director suggested that the community impose a tax on *araq* manufacture which would be passed on to the Muslim consumers of this liquor.[4] This would relieve the Jewish community of the sole burden of financing the school. Since there were no Jewish female teachers in Iran, the director requested that Muslim women be assigned as teachers by the Ministry of Education. Although the teachers did not want to work in the dirty ghetto, the director prevailed upon their national pride to do so.

Brawer (1936:83) reports that of the children of school age: 200 males (22.2%) attended Ibn Sina, 300 males (33.3%) studied privately

---

[1] A text read on the first evening of Shavu'ot.
[2] More recently ORT was forced to leave Shiraz for similar reasons and Otsar Hatorah is facing the same problem.
[3] Elsewhere (1936:83), Brawer implies that it was worse than in Alliance.
[4] Jews were unaffected by such a tax, since each household made its own liquor for home consumption.

and 400 males (44.4%) were not in school at all. He expressed doubt, however, that the figures given him were accurate, feeling that the number not studying was less than reported.

By 1945 Ibn Sina was failing as a Jewish-oriented school. Yishay (1950:306) reported that Hebrew was no longer studied, and children did not know how to write a single Hebrew letter. Prayers were studied in Persian characters and were garbled and mumbled in recitation.

At the instigation of Rav Yiẓḥaq Me'ir Levi, a Polish Rabbi who spent World War II in Iran, a religious school system was founded in Shiraz in about 1945. In 1947 these schools became affiliated with Otsar Hatorah, a world-wide orthodox Jewish school movement, which provided the bulk of the schools' budget. In 1950, JDC began contributing funds for the school; a free feeding program was instituted for the poor and medical care provided for all students.

The main school building, Kosar, was purchased in the late 1940s' for two million *rial,* half of which was provided by the local community. Additional money was provided by the tax on kosher meat. Four additional schools were run in Shiraz by Otsar Hatorah at that time. Initially, the main Kosar school had about 500 pupils while Ibn Sina had 300 students and served as a secondary school (Levi, 1960, III:1011).

One positive factor in Otsar Hatorah activities in Shiraz was the presence of Natan Eli. A Hamadani Jew trained in Israel, he was brought to Shiraz in 1947 by Rav Levi and spent twelve years there. He organized the school system with a missionary zeal. He also vigorously opposed many local religious practices not in accordance with general Jewish custom. He was considered a *hakham* or "sage" by the community and questions of Jewish law were referred to him. He organized the teachers and founded a small synagogue especially for them. He greatly influenced Shirazi synagogue custom, especially worship and is still revered in Shiraz as a *ẓaddiq* (righteous man).

In 1968, Otsar Hatorah schools were attended by less than one-half of the Jewish children in Shiraz. About 80% of these children were from the Mahalleh and mostly from poor families. The following schools were then serving the Shirazi Jewish community:

Sheybani, a boys' primary school, had about 200 students. This school is the only one located in the Mahalleh. The building was once a luxurious private home and, as such, has few facilities.

Kosar boys primary had about 360 pupils. This school is about ten minutes walk north of the Mahalleh. The quarters are shared with the secondary school, but each school level is in a separate wing. In addition to small classrooms, Kosar has playing fields, medical facilities, a lunch room and showers.

Kosar boys secondary, (a boys' school) caters to the seventh to ninth grades, and had 160 students. Some of its graduates go on to the Yeshiva.

Shahrom, a girls' primary school had about 230 pupils. The building, located on Khiaban-e Saadi, is owned by a Jew. The school is now run by the government; Otsar Hatorah only provides Hebrew teachers. There are several non-Jewish students in the school. It was reported that the Muslim principal suppresses the school's Hebrew-Judaica program. Furthermore, the Muslim staff has nothing to do with the Jewish teachers, nor will they touch food provided for pupils and staff by JDC, asserting that it is *najas* (unclean).

Kosar girls' school had about 220 students in the seventh through twelfth grades. The principal is Muslim, but considered very good. The average class size, about 18 students, is only one-half to two-thirds the average size class in the boys' schools. The school is located directly across the street from the Kosar boys' school and has its own athletic facilities.

The total number of male students in 1968 was about 720 and the number of female students about 450. Thus the total number of Otsar Hatorah students was less than 1200.

All children at Otsar Hatorah schools receive medical service, baths, haircuts and clothing. Formerly a feeding program provided poor Otsar Hatorah students with free lunch, but in recent years a fee has been imposed. Beginning at one *rial* per day, the fee was raised to four *rial* per day in 1968, leading to a parent-led boycott of the entire program. Collecting the normal tuition fees, (generally much lower than at secular schools) from the pupil's parents is in itself very difficult.

One of the main reasons children from poor families are sent to Otsar Hatorah schools is because of the Joint-sponsored feeding program. When this was free, many parents felt that what they perceived to be inferior education was offset by the feeding. As a cost was imposed for the feeding, some parents began to take their children out of Otsar Hatorah schools. As a result of the country-wide feeding program instituted by the Shah in 1974, it is likely that large numbers of students will be placed in secular schools and it is probable that Otsar Hatorah education will be sharply curtailed in Shiraz.

The school year extends from about September 5th to June 5th. Otsar

Hatorah schools run on a five-day week, whereas secular schools are open six days.[1] The general course of education is prescribed by the government and the shorter school week and additional parochial courses, require a longer school day. The school hours are from 8.00 to 11.30 a.m. and 2.00 to 4.30 p.m. Class periods are of forty-five minutes each and there are seven periods per day. Beginning with the first grade, each subject is taught by a different teacher. Girl students are expected to wear a uniform to school, but older girls, looking for husbands, dress more fashionably. Boys have no required dress.

General secular education in Iran stresses rote learning-memorization, rather than comprehension. Iran follows the French system of national examinations at the end of each year, which must be passed in each subject before promotion. In Otsar Hatorah schools, beginning at Purim (March) and extending some two and one-half months to the end of the school year, Jewish students learn no new material. All lessons are review for the examinations. Despite the apparently higher absenteeism during this period ostensibly for private study, it was observed that nearly all the cramming takes place during the last two weeks prior to the examinations. Tension during the pre-exam period runs extremely high. Students may be seen studying everywhere and at all hours. Late at night, older ones sit on the street under the street lamp, memorizing material. During recess, students walk around the yard memorizing from their books.

Nevertheless, the director of Otsar Hatorah in Shiraz estimated that only about 30% of the students pass all of the tests the first time they are given in the month of Khordad (May–June), and the rest must take them over at the end of the summer in Shahrivar (August–September). The make-up tests are somewhat harder, but students have the summer vacation to prepare for them. The director estimates that 5 to 6% fail the second time and must repeat the class, but from observation the author would suggest that this figure is too low; the majority of students are left back at least once during primary school.

JDC representatives attribute the large number of "slow learners" among Shirazi Jewish students to the high rate of endogamy! But the author could find no evidence confirming this hypothesis. The fault more likely lies in the home where study is not encouraged and where the constant noise and tension generated by large families living in small quarters certainly inhibit the opportunity to concentrate.

The educational system itself is at fault as well. Students are bored by

---

[1] Friday is the Government prescribed vacation and of course there can be no school on the Sabbath.

PLATE 50　First grade Kosar Hebrew class recites morning prayers.

PLATE 51　Students wearing a uniform in Shahrom Hebrew class.

PLATE 52   Kosar Assistant Principal observes student lunch program provided by Joint.

PLATE 53   Alone at home for the moment, the opportunity is seized for memorizing a lesson.

PLATE 54   During Spring exam week, the well-lit municipal circle is frequented until after midnight by panicky students unable to study at home.

the material presented and the method of teaching. Art, for example, is still learned by copying; freehand creativity is discouraged. Teachers inhibit student inquisitiveness by either not answering questions asked, or by giving totally irrelevant responses. Lecturing and class-repetition of spoken or written exercises are the most common means of passing a class period. Except in the sciences, explanations are at a minimum. American professors at Pahlavi University frequently complain that their students are unable to tackle new problems or think creatively.

Persian is the language of instruction. Judaeo-Persian is no longer used in school as it is considered substandard speech. The stick is an unfailingly utilized pedagogic device for discipline and as punishment for mistakes. Supportive motivation for students by means of positive response to fluent reading or correct answers was conspicuously absent.

Hebrew and Judaica are taught much as they were in the *maktab* sixty years ago. Fluency in *reading* Hebrew is stressed, probably at least partially in reaction to the high rate of Hebrew illiteracy thirty years ago. Reading *Siddur,* the prayer book, is the most emphasized subject, followed by the study of Tora. Pupils studying Tora are required to know the Persian translation of the text as well as to read it with facility. The translation is a standardized one, prescribed by Otsar Hatorah. It is memorized word-by-word in sequence, not sentence-by-sentence. A few words are chanted in Hebrew and then in translation; the students parrot them back. The same text is repeated day after day until the translation sinks in. The pace of learning is thus very slow; a class may spend the entire academic year on a single weekly Tora reading. Yet, pick any word out of context and the student is unable to give its meaning no matter how often it has been repeated.

An emphasis on modern Hebrew has been stressed by Israeli emissaries. Most of the textbooks, however, are from the 1940s and early 1950s and related to way of life incomprehensible to both student and teacher. The vignettes offered, describe daily events of post-World War II American Jewish culture or, more rarely, Israeli life. Neither of these is meaningful to provincial Jews in Iran. Even the text of *Hatikvah*, Israel's national anthem, as sung by the students, retains the words used before the establishment of the State in 1948.

Many of the Hebrew teachers are unable to speak correct Hebrew. Mistakes in grammar are frequent, words are often mispronounced and biblical idioms are used because teachers do not know modern usages. Question and answer sessions are nearly impossible in Hebrew and so the lessons are conducted almost entirely in Persian.

One Israeli emissary introduced special *toranit* (scholar) classes for selected bright students. In these classes everything was taught in Hebrew. He emphasized having the students question the teacher and he asked questions of the students calculated to make them think. The improvement in spoken Hebrew and comprehension among the students was impressive. By demanding more of the local Hebrew teacher, he was able to facilitate general progress in Hebrew training.

Jewish studies remain on a low level. Discussion of Jewish holidays and of philosophic problems remains restricted. Such discussion requires a dialogue between teacher and student, something unknown in Persian education and certainly lacking in the teacher's training. Most teachers are also rather ignorant with regard to Judaica, being acquainted only superficially with *Siddur,* Tora, and Midrash. During the field research, Jewish history was not taught at all because teachers know little about it. They were unable or unwilling to read texts in Hebrew and a Jewish history text in Persian had not yet been completed. As a result, a historical conception of Jewish identity was completely absent among the younger generation.

Teachers have, for the most part, received little training. Most of them have had only a summer or two of seminar study in Teheran under Otsar Hatorah auspices; a few have been on training seminars in Israel. Some of the young men are graduates of the Shiraz Yeshiva. Although hebraically well prepared, they too lack pedagogic training and, therefore, teach in the old manner, although they use more spoken

Hebrew. A recent attempt to send a group of teachers to Israel for additional study was thwarted by excluded fellow teachers.

The provision of in-service training for the teachers has been a failure. In the past, teachers have been bribed by means of a monthly increment, to study pedagogic material sent to them. The money was happily received, but few actually read the material. A course in Hebrew grammar for the teachers, begun by the Israeli emissary, failed utterly when the teachers realized that they were not going to be paid for their studies.

Otsar Hatorah authorities came from Teheran only twice during the period of research. One occasion was the annual evaluation of teacher performance. The lessons to be observed were well-rehearsed for the benefit of the Otsar Hatorah authorities. Afterwards, students were closely questioned by the evaluators to see how effective the teachers have been. Teachers rarely got positive evaluations. Most often they were publicly reprimanded, sometimes in front of their students, and threatened with loss of pay for poor performance, though the author knows of no cases where a teacher has actually been fired because of inadequacy. Improvement is rewarded by a few kind words.

In 1968, unmarried male teachers were paid 4000 *rial* per month. Female teachers earned only 3000 *rial* per month. Whereas government teachers began at 5000 *rial* per month and received annual increments to 14,000 *rial* per month plus a retirement pension, Otsar Hatorah paid no seniority or retirement benefits. Shirazi teachers complained bitterly of being short-changed by Otsar Hatorah. Raises given elsewhere and promised in Shiraz were not received, sometimes with the explanation that the teachers had not been working hard and did not deserve the increase. Allegedly, Otsar Hatorah tried to lure Shiraz's better teachers to Teheran with promises of higher wages. One female teacher has had her wages cut each year, in the hope that she could be persuaded to go to Teheran.

In January, 1968, teachers went on strike to protest the policies of Otsar Hatorah, but the strike was broken by bringing in Yeshiva students and threatening the strike leaders with the loss of their jobs. For most teachers there is no escape from Otsar Hatorah because they cannot take government positions as they would be expected to work on the Sabbath.

The students, too, take advantage of the teachers who are observed to be berated and dishonored by Otsar Hatorah authorities. Pupils show no respect for Jewish teachers and classes are often disorderly. Pupils misbehave in ways never exhibited in the presence of Muslim teachers. One despairing Yeshiva graduate was heard to remark:

It is good that they are closing the Yeshiva; all it turns out are men destined to be poor and taken advantage of.

Extracurricular activities are not much encouraged by Otsar Hatorah. Plays and skits are put on for holidays. A library of about 100 books is available in the Kosar boys' school. In 1969, reportedly, clubs were organized by a female teacher, financed entirely by student payments of ten *rial* per month. Activities of these clubs included exercise, sewing, making artificial flowers, acting, foreign dancing and studying Jewish law.

Parents and children are far more concerned with secular studies than with Jewish subjects. The school system abets this attitude by promoting children who fail in their Hebrew studies while passing secular subjects, but leaving back anyone who fails secular subjects. Secular studies at Otsar Hatorah schools are not as well taught as in government schools. Mahalleh parents usually avoid sending their daughters to Shahrom (Jewish girls' primary) school, claiming that they do not learn enough there. Public school girls entering Kosar in the seventh grade, though far behind Shahrom girls in Hebrew studies, are found to be much better in secular subjects.

THE YESHIVA

The Yeshiva was founded in 1953 by Yizḥaq Ba'al Hanes, now Shiraz's first ordained Rabbi, and two friends who wanted to continue their Judaic studies after the ninth grade. Rav Levi arranged the details with Otsar Hatorah and received government permission to establish a Yeshiva in Shiraz. The course of study was at first a six-year program, but later was reduced to five. The Yeshiva grants the graduate a secular high school diploma as well as a religious one. Graduates[1] of the Shiraz Yeshiva are found in Jewish schools all over Iran. Most serve as Hebrew teachers and some are qualified to act as ritual slaughterers.

Students enter after completing the ninth grade. JDC provides funds for renting classroom and dormitory space.[2] Students receive food, clothing and spending money; all of which serve to induce the poor to continue their high school studies at the Yeshiva. Students and teachers, living and eating together, form a very close group. Many of the

---

[1] There have been about fifty graduates altogether.
[2] A few non-Shirazis have attended the Yeshiva, but the main function of the dormitory was to enable students to concentrate on their studies without being distracted by family matters.

PLATE 55　Animated class participation by Yeshiva students.

pedagogic failings of the Otsar Hatorah schools are absent in the informal atmosphere of the Yeshiva. Jewish problems are discussed in great detail and religious attitudes in community affairs are constantly evaluated. The Judaica program includes Tora with Rashi's commentary, Bible, Mishna, Talmud and *Shulkhan 'Arukh*.

Most religious reform in Shiraz can be traced directly to the Yeshiva. Yeshiva students and graduates have actively spread the ideas of Natan Eli and others throughout the Jewish community. The students themselves often initiate reform.

Once, during a Yeshiva class on Jewish law, students objected to the Shirazi tradition of picnicking in the gardens on the last day of Pesaḥ. Not only did this practice violate the prohibition against riding on the holiday, but it necessitated the spending of money for admission to the garden. The students called for a religious reform to which the Yeshiva teachers gladly agreed. During the holiday of Pesaḥ the reform was proclaimed in all of the synagogues and people were asked to visit the gardens on the day following the conclusion of the holiday rather than on the last day of Pesaḥ. Otsar Hatorah gave the students vacation that day and many Shirazis heeded the plea of the Yeshiva students and did not picnic on the holiday.

One Sabbath afternoon, some of the boys rebelled against removing their shoes in *knisa* and despite heated opposition, their view eventually prevailed. On another occasion, the Israeli emissary, tired of the *ta'arof* in selecting a *shailiah ẓibbur* (see Chapter X), persuaded Yeshiva students to halt this practice (temporarily). The movement to halt the collection of money in the synagogues on the Sabbath was led by Yeshiva students. New melodies have been introduced in most of the synagogues by them. One Yeshiva graduate even attempted to reform ritual slaughter practice by offering his personal services as *shoḥet* to the community.

During the period of research, budgetary cuts by JDC necessitated the phasing out of the Yeshiva operation. The dormitory was closed and no new students were admitted. The demise of the Yeshiva program can be traced to the disaffection of its graduates with teaching under Otsar Hatorah auspices. As a result, recent graduates have been entering other professions or going on to the university when qualified. Superior students wishing to go to Israel for rabbinical training were hampered in their efforts by Otsar Hatorah, contributing further to the declining effectiveness of the Yeshiva. Time will tell what effect the loss of the Yeshiva will have on the effort to implement meaningful religious reform in Shiraz and on the quality of religious instruction in the schools.

VOCATIONAL EDUCATION

ORT, an international Jewish vocational school system started a school in Shiraz, but, failing to receive community financial support, it withdrew after several years. Many Shirazi students study at Teheran ORT.

Many girls go to Teheran for a two-year nursing course at the JDC hospital. They then return to Shiraz to work as nurses at the JDC clinic.

KINDERGARTEN

Organized and financed by JDC (Shiraz Ladies Committee provided 12% of the budget in 1968), the *kudakistan,* or "kindergarten", is considered quite good both by the indigenous population and by outside evaluators. During the research period, there were 280 boys and girls attending, mostly from the poorest families. Parents are expected to pay at least ten *rial* per month for the privilege of sending each child, age three to five years. The school day is from 8.00 a.m. to 3.30 p.m. Nutrition is one of the main purposes of the *kudakistan*; the children receive morning and afternoon snacks and a large lunch each day. The children nap during the afternoon. They are provided a weekly bath, a bi-weekly haircut, and everyone receives periodic medical and dental care. Clothing is distributed to the poor.

The teachers, trained in Teheran, are creative and effective. Hebrew words and songs are taught in addition to a normal kindergarten curriculum. Each child receives the warm and personal attention of the teacher, so that entering the first grade at Otsar Hatorah schools with its rigid format and cold manner, is a distinct shock to the kindergarten "graduates".

JEWS IN NON-JEWISH SCHOOLS

Beginning about 1925, Shirazi Jews began to attend government sponsored public schools and today more than one-half of the Jewish children in Shiraz do not go to Jewish schools. Usually they are able to compete successfully with non-Jewish students; the number of Jewish students at Shiraz's Pahlavi University for example, is larger than their proportion in the population. But in some schools, Jewish students are sometimes harassed by their teachers, leading, in at least one case, to a nervous breakdown.

Jewish education for students going to non-Jewish schools is minimal. During the past few years, Yeshiva students have been holding summer

PLATE 56   Joint/Otsar Hatorah Day Camp provides supervised play and informal learning in a cool shaded garden during the hot summer months.

classes for some of these children, attracting a number of them from the wealthier families. The summer course stresses Hebrew reading. The classes meet for three hours per day to study *Siddur,* Tora and vocabulary. In 1968 there were 120 summer students. The Youth Committee offers Hebrew lessons two evenings per week during the academic year. Although these classes are attended primarily by adults, perhaps thirty high school and college age youths are also present. Here the emphasis is on spoken Hebrew. In addition to the above-mentioned, there were about thirty to forty children studying Hebrew privately.

Fewer than 1400 Jewish children were studying Hebrew in 1968. Under the present circumstances, it is most unlikely that more than one-half of the younger generation will ever study Hebrew or any Judaic subject. This is a particularly irksome problem for Otsar Hatorah and the community's pious leadership.

THE LEARNING ETHIC

The widespread Jewish norm, "study for its own sake," is not an accepted principle in Shiraz. The very pious occasionally study Tora or Midrash, but few Shirazi Jews ever read for pleasure or engage in self-study. "Non-technical, non-rational (non-functional) education," may, as Jacobs (1966:157) claims, be the ideal of Iran's elite, but this value is not shared to an appreciable degree by Shirazi Jews.

Children are not strongly encouraged by parents to study. Many parents are illiterate and cannot help the child. Parents do see the value, especially for boys, of learning reading, writing, and arithmetic, since this will enable them to run a business. Most parents are content, therefore, that their children finish six grades, since they assume that at that point these disciplines have been mastered for all practical purposes. Perhaps 50% of the children stop at this point – the boys to start working and the girls to prepare for marriage.

The attitude towards higher education is slowly changing. One factor in this change is the realization that professionals such as doctors, engineers, and technicians enjoy a higher standard of living. Vocational education, still not common in Iran, is seen as a means of assuring adequate income and providing a useful vocation perhaps, in Israel.

A second factor encouraging higher education is prestige. "Study for its own sake" may not be part of the traditional ideology, but religious knowledge nevertheless enhances prestige and helps improve one's social position. Titles such as *dayan, darshan, shaliah ẓibbur* and *ḥakham,* usually handed down from father to son, are highly revered. But few strive to achieve religious knowledge in imitation of this learned "elite," perhaps, because doing so provides little *financial* reward.

In the past, secular learning was neither prestigious nor especially pecuniarily advantageous to Shirazi Jews. Today, however, anyone who finishes college, particularly if he has studied in America, is accepted among the elite whether or not he is wealthy. This newly acquired esteem is shared by the entire nuclear family and, to a lesser extent, the bilateral kindred, serving increasingly as an important incentive to higher education.

We have seen that the relatively high literacy rate among Shirazi Jews, as compared with the general Iranian population, is due, in part, to the efforts of Jewish aid organizations from abroad. Shirazi Jews have been aware since the commencement of Pahlavi rule that one effective way of escaping traditionally imposed economic limitations is by moving into newly created occupations. As literacy is an important means in attaining this goal, they have actively sought to become literate. Unfortunately, Shirazi Jews have been hindered in their attempts to reap the benefits of education by the traditional rote-learning method of teaching which stultifies initiative and by their own learning ethic which discourages "study for its own sake".

The Jewish school system, financed and organized from outside the community, exploitative of its teachers and offering an inferior education, has nevertheless promoted its goal of Hebrew literacy while encouraging religious reform. The majority of Shirazi Jews, however, never come under the direct influence of this system, which, by catering mainly to the poor, may unintentionally drive a wedge between the pious poor and the non-observant rich.

CHAPTER VIII

Arts, Amusements and Leisure Time

AMUSEMENTS

Music, acting, secular and religious poetry and storytelling are some of the creative amusements which the Shirazi Jews have traditionally enjoyed. But the most popular family amusement and group experience has been the *bagh* or "garden".

Even in the worst circumstances, Jews have had access to Muslim-owned gardens – for a fee. These gardens are the only place the Jew can go to escape the monotony of the dirty drab Mahalleh. In summer, the garden, with its trees and running water, is cool and pleasant. On Shabbat and holidays people often spend the day there. The eighth day of Pesaḥ used to be the favorite occasion for family picnics in the gardens. Many marriages were arranged on the basis of a few words or glances shared on that day. Not infrequently, wedding ceremonies, too, are held in a garden, far away from the city, so that rejected suitors be unable to subject the couple to acts of sorcery. Nowadays, Friday is a favorite day for university students, nurses and other youth, to picnic in the gardens. But any day, men of leisure may be found gambling, playing cards and carousing in the *bagh*.

THE ARTS

There is no record of Jewish participation in the plastic or graphic arts. The Muslims, despite Islamic prohibitions, continued their artistic traditions. Armenians too, are known for their painting and metal craft. There are occasionally excellent miniatures found in Judaeo-Persian manuscripts (Fischel, 1960: 1164–5), but there is no indication as to whether these were painted by Jews. The paintings the author viewed in Jewish manuscripts and in synagogues in present day Shiraz are not comparable to good Persian work. Favorite colors are soft reds, yellows and blues. Synagogue decoration and painting is rather sparse.

151

In Shiraz, one of the Jewish fortune tellers serves as the local artist. He carves tombstones, writes a decorative Hebrew script called "Ashkenazi", i.e., the script of German Jews, and paints the kabbalistic "Name of God" and Psalm 67 in the mystical seven branched candelabrum pattern.

There are about seventy-five Jewish gold and silver smiths in Shiraz. Most of them are entrepreneurs who merely touch up, adjust and occasionally repair finished objects. The few Jewish silver artisans, produce crude imitations of the Persepolis design on silver or copper for the tourist trade. Local informants indicate that the smiths of some fifty years ago were more creative than nowadays. Today, however, even the silver Tora decorations are made by non-Jews, although previously this was done by Jewish craftsmen.

Carpet and silk weaving were not done by Shirazi Jews. There is one Jewish ḥatam (mosaic) craftsman. Although his work is good, he does not rank among Shiraz's best.

DANCING

There is no folk dancing among Jews today, nor are there any indications that there had been any in the past. Jewish males, did dance professionally, although it was not a well-paid occupation (Descos, 1908:232). Dancing was considered the most degrading of arts in Iran. There is good evidence that it was the sort of exhibitionism that would be absolutely forbidden to Jewish women:

The most beautiful women in Persia are devoted to the profession of dancing; the transparency of their shift, which is the only covering they use to conceal their persons, the exquisite symmetry of their forms, their apparent agitation, and the licentiousness of their verses, are so many incentives to a passion, which requires more philosophy than the Persians possess to restrain. (Waring, 1807:55)

To this day, Jewish women do not dance in public, although young girls have learned to do so in school.

The Jewish dancing boys were young, pre-pubescent, possibly so that they would be mistaken for females. Homosexuality is constantly implied in discussing the role of the male dancer. Jewish dancers were described in the following terms:

The dancing boy cannot have been more than 10 or 11 years old. When performing he wore such raiments as is usual with the addition of a small close fitting cap, from beneath which his black hair streamed in long locks, a tunic reaching half-way to the knees, and a mass of trinkets which jingled at every movement. His evolutions were characterized by agility and suppleness rather than grace. (Brown, 1950:320)

The Jewish dancers were known too, for their acrobatic stunts:

Having filled the wine-glass, he took the edge of the circular foot on which it stands firmly in his teeth, and, approaching each guest in turn, leaned slowly down so as to bring the wine within reach of the drinker, continually bending his body more and more forward as the level of the liquid sank lower. One or two of the guests appeared particularly delighted with this manoeuvre, and strove to imprint a kiss on the boy's cheek as he quickly withdrew the empty glass. (Browne, 1950:321)

There were reportedly numerous Jewish dancers in 1903. Alliance representatives made strenuous efforts to reduce their number, opposing the participation of Jewish boys in "a life of idleness and of debauchery" (Alliance, 1905:94). Musical evenings in which the dancers participated, often degenerated into orgies.

Dancers who were favored by the Muslim elite could be very successful. A 19th century traveler tells of a Jewish dancer from Isfahan named Yekuti'el, who was so beloved by the Shah that the latter eventually made him prime minister. In 1850, this same Yekuti'el led the Shah's forces in crushing a rebellion in Isfahan (Benjamin, 1859:238–9).

But dancers could also be a source of conflict. In 1905, an imagined insult to a Muslim *akhond* by a dancing boy, almost led to a full-scale pogrom against the Jews of Shiraz (Alliance, 1905:94–6).

Why and when Jewish dancers disappeared cannot be precisely ascertained. Today's professional dancers are all non-Jewish women. Dancing is featured at special occasions such as weddings. Young and old enjoy the sensuous dancing style, and reward good control of bodily movement with shouts of approval and clapping. The dancer who attracted most attention and approval during the author's period of study was endowed with an extremely large torso and belly, which she controlled perfectly. She and other dancers are generally considered prostitutes or at best "loose" women.

ACTORS

Most of the acting troups, numbering eight to ten performers, are entirely Muslim; only a few Jewish males are actors nowadays. Numerous non-professional actors, especially the musicians, are mimics or participate otherwise in the performances. Many are extremely adept at making facial distortions. Browne (1950:320) reported having observed one Jewish mimic applauded for his skill in imitating Browne, and his audacity in imitating the Muslim clergy. The Muslim actors who perform at Jewish celebrations are adept at using the Jewish dialect and knowledgeable about Jewish customs. Most of the skits performed, depict daily Persian life, with village scenes being especially popular. The professional actors of today are in all likelihood the "spiritual" heirs of the *lutis*,[1] whose position at one time paralleled that of the court entertainer in Europe.

The telling of a joke, joking behavior and practical jokes were not commonly observed by the author. Uncontrollable or guffaw types of laughter were only observed in the audience of playskits and movies. Happiness is otherwise rarely expressed, except by smiling. Sorrow, is a more easily expressed emotion which has been ritually formalized. Individual sorrow is kept under control and Shirazis claim that bad news is not spread.

Repression of spontaneous emotional expression suggests "shallow affect", to some degree. Among Shirazi Jews, there seems to be a general reticence on the part of the individual to freely, deeply and uninhibitedly express an emotion, be it one of joy or of grief. Only when an individual can assume the identity of another — either by portraying a character in a play, or by completely identifying with a character being portrayed on stage — can he release strong emotions which are otherwise concealed under the guise of "shallow affect". It is not surprising, therefore, that young adolescents performing in school plays, often have more "stage presence" than professional actors in the West. In plays, they can express many feelings, such as love, wrath, exhilaration, which in real life, they are constrained to suppress.

---

[1] The *lutis* were a sodality of men having a characteristic raiment, speaking a distinctive dialect and primarily engaged in recreational activity. Some had distinctive skills, such as animal trainer, clown or acrobat. They were active participants in the *zurkhane* "house of strength" and in the religious observances during Ramadan and Muharram. Arasteh (1964:25–9) feels that they made positive contributions to Persian life and have been misunderstood in the West. They were active in communal affairs and worked in conjunction with the guilds. Waring (1807:55) presents them as "a kind of buffoon. . . ." Haas sums up the rather unfavorable view that most historians have, describing a *luti* as,

"Mountebank, brawler, and rowdy, he dressed and posed as a dandy and a beau . . . A jovial merrymaker, he was a man of the moment and ever ready to exploit present events to his advantage. . . . A skilled troublemaker. . . ." (1946:107).

Ella Sykes (1910:128) claimed that Jews too were *lutis,* but this is rather unlikely. The *lutis* were among the worst instigators of anti-Jewish harassment (Wills, 1887:231; Stern, 1854:123).

MUSIC

THE PROFESSIONAL MUSICIAN

There is only a minimal amount of historical information with regard to Jewish professional musicians. Almost none of it refers to the period prior to the Safavid era. Under Islam, music-making by believers was discouraged, but when Shi'a Islam was proclaimed the state religion, Muslims were strictly forbidden to perform. From this time, Persian music, as such, is thought to have ceased developing and to have almost died out (Levi, 1960, III:357). For the past 300 to 400 years, Iranian music has been left in the hands of professionals from the minority groups: Jews, Armenians, Nestorians and Zoroastrians. Of these, the Jews were the most widely dispersed and perhaps the largest in number; professional music-making became identified with the Jew.

In all of Iran, the Shirazi Jews were considered the finest musicians. They were the ones who best preserved and transmitted the classical Persian music tradition (Levi, 1960, III:435–6). Folk music continued to be performed by non-Jewish musicians throughout Iran. Each area has its own style heavily influenced by the tribes of the region, who were unconcerned with the Islamic restrictions.

Besides the sporadic income and peculiar working hours, the musician had to contend with extraordinary hardships. Jewish musicians were frequent intercity travelers despite the many dangers *en route*. Frequently while traveling, they were forced to entertain their fellow travelers (Browne, 1950:243). At unpleasant events, such as the execution of a faithless Muslim woman in Shiraz, Jewish musicians were "forced to play upon their instruments and join in the procession" (Wills, 1883:377). Musicians were at the beck and call of the Shah and other government officials who made outrageous demands on their time and talents (Morier, 1812:225).

At the turn of the century, music and dance in Iran were centrally controlled from Teheran. One of the palace staff members was appointed chief of the arts by the Shah. He, in turn, appointed someone in each city to be head of the local *nakara khane*.[1] The official purpose of this institution was to provide music for royal occasions, especially for saluting the king. The musicians performed at royal *salams* (salute) and

---

[1] Descos (1908) does not define this term, which seems to refer to a music guild. The term is probably an inaccurate transliteration of *naggara khane* (house of the kettle drum), or *nagar khane* (house of the arts).

at *ta'aziyeh* plays during Muharram. For their service, the musicians received a government stipend. It is not clear whether Jews too belonged to the *nakara khane*. In Shiraz, where the best musicians were Jews, it is likely that Jews participated in the *nakara khane*. The chief of the *nakara khane* in Teheran and perhaps the provincial chiefs too, exercised control over all the musician troups of the district. There are no indications that Jews ever served as local *nakara khane* chiefs.

At the beginning of this century, being a musician might have been degrading but it was also a very lucrative profession (Alliance, 1903:108). The ordinary dancer earned twenty to forty *toman* per year; an exceptional one earned 100 *toman* (Descos, 1908:232). But musicians in Shiraz probably earned considerably more than this, as the dancer generally was not as well paid as the musician.[1]

THE MOTREB

The *motreb* (professional musician) was, in the popular mind, nearly synonymous with the Shirazi Jew. In 1903, there were sixty professional Jewish musicians in Shiraz, far more than in any other city (Alliance, 1903:108). Teheran might have had about forty Jewish musicians (Descos, 1908:233), but elsewhere there were only three or four in any locale. Informants report that by 1949 there were at least 150–200 Jewish musicians in Shiraz. Habib Levi (1960, III:1011) confirms that in that year 10% of the Jewish men, i.e. at least 250, were musicians. Since then, most of these have emigrated to Israel or moved to Teheran, while some have found other employment. Today there are approximately thirty-five Jewish *motreb* in Shiraz.

The majority and the most accomplished of Shiraz's musicians today are Jews. Some of them are outstanding and are frequently commanded to perform for the Shah. Near-dynasties of musicians exist, from whose ranks musicians have been drawn for generations. Such families, when forced to adopt surnames during the reign of Reza Shah, chose names such as *Shirakhun* (*shira*–Hebrew, for "song", *khun* – Persian, for "sing"), *Qanuni* (the musical instrument *qanun*), *Zamir* (Hebrew, for "nightingale"), and *Managen* (Hebrew *mnagen* – "play an instrument"). Musicians tend to marry within the profession, further reinforcing these musical "dynasties".

In the 1870s, it was reported that Shirazi Jews were playing the *da'ira* (round frame drum), *zarb* or *dombak* (single headed hand drum), *tar* or

---

[1] The average income for Jews in those days, according to informants was two *toman* per week.

setar (fretted long necked lutes) (Wills, 1887:165). At all times, Jewish singers were found in large numbers. In 1903 the *kemanje,* (spiked fiddle), *tar* and *setar* were the favored Jewish instruments (Alliance, 1903:108). Today there are nine violinists (the *kemanje* is no longer played), thirteen *tar* players, fourteen *zarb* player–singers, and one *qanun* (trapezoidal zither) player.

Jews have generally not been solo instrumentalists, and the *santur* (dulcimer), the Persian solo instrument *par excellence,* is not generally played by Jews. Musical performances have usually been given by all-Jewish music troupes. In the past these troupes would consist of six to nine *motreb*[1] as follows: one to two *tar* players, one to two *kemanje* players, one to two *zarb* players, one *dohol* (drum) player, one *da'ira* player, a singer and perhaps either a *setar* or a *nay* player. Many musicians double-up by playing more than one instrument. Today the music ensemble usually consists of three or four musicians: one to two violinists, one *tar* player and one *zarb* player who doubles as a singer. At large affairs additional musicians are called for, but occasionally only two *motreb* are hired: one violinist or *tar* player and one *zarb* player–singer. The instruments most identified with Shirazi Jews are the *tar,* violin and *zarb.* The *qanun,* a solo instrument, was imported into Iran from Iraq by the present player's father. Very few in Iran can play this instrument, and this man, the *qanun*'s acknowledged master, is a favorite performer for the Shah.

Although Jewish musicians used to belong to an informal guild, its organization has disintegrated, over the years. Today, the musicians merely congregate to socialize near one of the three Jewish-owned music stores outside the Mahalleh. During the day, having nothing else to do, the musicians sit around discussing their experiences, occasionally offering opinions on philosophical concepts such as "skill versus feeling" in music. Usually however, the discussions are more mundane and concern renumeration and the like.

On holidays and special occasions, musicians may give up their free time to entertain the children in school. Evenings, when they have no work, musicians visit and entertain friends, who are obligated to provide a festive meal and an abundance of *araq* to drink. Otherwise, the musicians expect to be paid.

Most *motreb* cannot be considered dedicated artists; they are merely earning a living in the way they know best. Many with whom the author spoke are not particularly interested in music, and their performances are mediocre by local standards. Few ever practice on their instruments;

---

[1] Descos (1908:231) says that the musician groups had nine to twelve members.

the performances rely on improvization and thus serve as practice sessions, in themselves.

One musician, aged twenty-seven, whom we shall call Mussa, is a well-known singer and *dombak* player. His deceased father was a *tar* and *kemanje* player. His brother in Teheran, plays the violin. Mussa supports a wife, two young children, his mother, his wife's siblings and her mother. He usually works with Shiraz's best violinist, Keramat, often as a duo. In this arrangement he gets three-eighths of the fee, while Keramat, more famous and respected, receives five-eighths. A fee for the two of them is usually 500 *rial,* but it may range from 300 to 2000 *rial* for an evening. Summer is the busiest season; Mussa averages two to three performances per week from June to September when the number of Muslim and Jewish weddings is at a peak. The winter months are slack due to the cold, and then he does not perform more than once per week, or once every two weeks. During the months of Ramadan and Muharram and for other short stretches during the year, Muslims do not permit music. Jews too, avoid celebrations during these periods. On Shabbat, holidays, during the seven weeks of *sfira* and for three weeks preceding Tisha B'av, Jews do not permit any music.

Mussa's earning period is thus very restricted. During peak months, he gets from 100 to 750 *rial* per performance, a mean average of about 425 *rial.* During these months he may earn between 950 and 1400 *rial* per week, wages approximating those of an Otsar Hatorah teacher. During the rest of the year his earnings are much lower and there are periods when he earns nothing at all. A few musicians do better than this, but many do worse.

Rank

The musician ranks very low on the occupational prestige index. Only the butcher, beggar and body washer rank below him. The following factors contribute to the musicians's low prestige among Shirazi Jews:

1) The occupation is considered among the lowest ranked by Muslims, and Jews have apparently accepted this evaluation.

2) The musician's financial situation is considered very insecure, as we have shown. When I inquired why one gifted musician remains a bachelor, I was asked: "What will he do when he loses his good looks?", i.e. how will he then support a family?

3) The musician works peculiar hours and is never home at night with his wife and children. He is said to be exceptionally lazy, because during the day he is seen sitting around and talking, but never working or practicing.

4) He allegedly eats non-kosher food at Muslim affairs, something which in traditional Shiraz is abhored.

5) He allegedly performs on the Sabbath and holidays.

6) He is too friendly with the dancers, many of whom are known to be prostitutes. In the past, musicians were suspected of participating in orgies, both heterosexual and homosexual.

7) Years ago, the various troupes had to compete for jobs. When they would learn of an affair, they would come, stand outside the walls of the house and play. After some time, they would be invited inside to continue or were paid to leave. Such behaviour was extremely impolite and was considered equivalent to begging, a behavior pattern repugnant to Jews (Alliance, 1903:107). Although this pattern of job-seeking no longer exists, the criticism for such behavior is still directed against the musician.

Instrument making, a reputable craft, usually done by musicians in their spare time, was once a Jewish profession also. The last Jewish *tar* maker died several years ago, and only two Jews in Shiraz still know how to repair violin bows and *tar* frets.[1] Shiraz's three musical instrument shops are owned by Jews.[2]

THE DECLINE OF "LIVE" MUSIC

The disappearance of the professional musician in Shiraz is directly related to the improvement in the condition of Jewish life and to modernization. Improved educational opportunities and vocational possibilities have enabled potential musicians to escape from this low-ranked profession into more lucrative ones. Improved communications have enabled many musicians to emigrate to Teheran and many more to go to Israel. But changing social patterns and the advent of the radio are the most important factors in the decline of the *motreb*.

Until radio became widely available in Shiraz about twenty-five years ago, live music was the most important form of entertainment. No Persian could entertain guests, whether at home or in a garden, without a musical performance. No celebration, Jewish or non-Jewish, was complete without music. To the Persian elite, music and poetry were intellectual stimuli which turned thoughts from the mundane to the philosophic.

---

[1] New instruments are brought to Shiraz from Teheran.
[2] In Teheran nearly all of the 35–40 music stores in the vicinity of the *Majles* are owned by Jews.

PLATE 57   Ḥanukka concert by Jewish musicians at kindergarten. The instruments
displayed from left to right are: *dombak,* violin and *tar.*

Music, accompanied by dance, frequently acted as a sexual stimulus,
and private gatherings were known to have become orgies.

For the Jewish audience, music represented a true refuge from the
problems of survival. Religion focused the individual's attention on his
personal troubles, while providing him with means to actively participate
in a communal catharsis through prayer and ritual. Through religion the
Jew could be made to understand his sufferings and to hope for eventual
deliverance. Through music, however, he could escape from thinking
about his problems, and simply enjoy the experience.

Fine renditions of the folk music of Fars as well as Persian classical
music have been the epitome of Jewish performance. But radio has
largely ended the dependence on musicians and on live music. Most of
the poor have radios and many members of the middle and upper classes
have phonographs as well. The best musicians, Jewish and non-Jewish,
have been recorded and can be heard all day long. The novelty and
special nature of being able to hear good music has disappeared. Now
the *motreb* is reduced to performing at weddings, circumcisions, occasional parties and gatherings. A new institution, the summer
"nightclub" which, in Shiraz, features out-of-doors eating, drinking and
music making, discriminates against Jewish entertainers. Declining income has forced the *motreb* to seek other employment, and many who
remain musicians, do so because they are unable to do anything else.

AMATEUR MUSICIANS

There are a large number of amateur Jewish musicians in Shiraz. Many men can play *tar, kemanje* or violin and *zarb*. Some younger men play *setar, nay* and even *santur*. Among the elite, females are now permitted to learn music; piano and Western music being the usual choice.

People no longer sing or play so much for their own entertainment. Women still sing lullabies and songs of love and longing to entertain their children. Wedding songs too are popular, and men sing local or "*mahalli*" songs at work, synagogue, or on special occasions. Young people learn songs in school and compose songs about favorite characters. Most people, however, turn on the radio. The elite prefer Persian classical music; the poor listen mostly to "*mahalli*" music of Fars. The young enjoy popular Persian music, Israeli songs, and Western pop. The horizons of music-making have greatly expanded to the detriment of traditional music, as is commonly the case. On the other hand the musical experience is becoming progressively more passive.

Secular music performed by amateurs consists largely of folk song, whereas the classical Persian music played by the *motreb* included many completely instrumental pieces. The folk song of the Jew is sung mainly in Persian, usually in the local Jewish dialect; semi-sacred songs are sung in Hebrew.

Muslims and Jews in Shiraz share the same folk music. In all probability the Jews adopted the music of the majority population as is the case, for example, in Europe. However, Jews have been the professional preservers and performers of the local folk music for hundreds of years. Informants report that Jewish musicians make a conscious effort to use "Jewish" sacred and semi-sacred melody in public performance. Certainly then, non-conscious use of "Jewish" melody in secular music is to be expected. The following anecdote was told by an informant:

Izḥaq, one of the great musicians during the reign of Nasser-ad-din-Shah (1848–1896), was called away from the synagogue one Yom Kippur eve to play for the Shah, who was in an especially melancholy mood. Obliged to serve the Shah, Izḥaq played his tar and sang, but the melodies were those he had heard all evening in the synagogue. When the Shah asked why such exceedingly delightful melodies were being performed that evening, Izḥaq replied that they were from the most sacred of Jewish prayers, from which he had been forced to separate by order of the Shah. He was then swiftly returned to the synagogue amidst great praise and with a present of much fine gold.

It is not inconceivable that music of Fars is greatly influenced by Jewish motifs, introduced by the Jewish musicians. The determination of the similarity of folk music of Fars with Jewish sacred and semi-sacred song must await detailed analysis of large corpuses of this music. Suffice it to say, the folk music of Fars is identified in the public mind with the Jewish musician. The popular song: *Eshq Yahude Shiraz* "Love of the Shirazi Jews" (Teheran Records, No. 1713; Montajam Shirazi), for example, relies on this identification to ridicule the Shirazi Jews and their peculiarities.

While there are significant style differences between men's and women's songs among the Jews of Yemen (Katz, 1969), these differences are substantially smaller among Iranian Jews. In Yemen, in the absence of Jewish professional musicians, men who sing for pleasure or ritual, do so in Hebrew and in Aramaic. The Yemenite women, on the other hand, sing in Arabic only. In Iran, traditionally, the Jewish men rarely sang other than ritual songs in Hebrew and in Judaeo-Persian, in the confines of his synagogue, for he feared hostile Muslims in the bazaar or in the villages in which he peddled. Jewish women, in the safety of their homes, frequently sang, primarily in Persian. In recent years, however, Jewish men feeling somewhat safer among the Muslims, have become less reluctant to sing secular songs in Persian. Thus the difference in style and language between Jewish men's and women's songs is gradually narrowing.

SONG CREATIVITY

Jewish professional and amateur singers are known for their ability to create topical songs. Most of these songs are rather innocuous, sung, for example, to congratulate a newlywed couple or the parents of a newborn child. Others, though, can be very biting. After the Six Day War, many songs were created in honor of Moshe Dayan and Israel's victory. The author recorded several versions, but the one reputed to be the best could not be recorded because the singer feared that he might be identified by it and thence punished by the authorities.

In most cases of song creation, a popular melody is selected and a new text improvised on the spot. Most Jews are adept at this and it is most entertaining to see who can be the most original, while keeping the melody and rhythm going.

SHALLOWNESS IN JEWISH FOLKSONG

Despite numerous enquiries, the author never heard traditional folk songs on a Jewish theme, divorced from ceremony or religious activity.[1]

---

[1] In Yazd the author recorded a number of traditional Zionist songs.

Songs celebrating happy events are most frequent; songs of mourning are non-existent — they tend to be sublimated into prayer. All of the songs are of an unspecific nature; one rarely sings of real events of circumstances that have occurred to individuals known personally.

Strangely, despite all of the past persecutions, I could not find a single song about these happenings. Nor do any songs bewail the fate of Shirazi or Iranian Jews generally. No one could explain why this was so.

Jewish participation in the arts, as musicians, dancers and actors has been important economically and emotionally to the Shiraz community. The declining participation by Shirazi Jews in music, dance and acting is due to improved economic opportunity, and the availability of recorded music. For almost 400 years, Shirazi folk and classical music was largely in the hands of Jews who preserved the tradition while they themselves became identified with this music.

LEISURE TIME

It is readily apparent that Shirazi Jews have considerable leisure time. Besides the Sabbath, many have part or the entire day off on Friday. During weekdays, there are extended lunch breaks for a leisurely dinner and for napping and the evening hours everyday are a period for relaxation. Women often find extended periods during the day in which there is no pressing work to be done.

The gardens, music and performing obviously take up only a small portion of this available time. Most of it is rather taken up in visiting relatives and friends, attending synagogue, eating and sleeping. Recently, attendance at movies, and nightclubs have become routine leisure activities. Generally males and females engage in separate activity even when leisure times overlap. Thus, a husband may attend synagogue while a wife and daughter visit her mother and sons play *gerdu baazi,* "the nut game", in the *kuche.* Frequently in the evening the men of the family go off visiting or strolling or for a *minyan* while women remain at home, or perhaps huddled with some neighbors near the front door.

The favored social activity is visiting of one sort or other. Much visiting behavior is quite formal, associated with ritual or life-cycle events, or perhaps prescribed by local custom. But whether the circumstances are formal or informal, guests are ushered into the best room in the house where they engage in the elaborate *ta'arof* process described in Chapter IX. Although the "guest room" is not institutionalized among Shirazi Jews in the sense that regular and frequent interaction recurs in the same place with the same participants, kinsmen and friends, with implications for aligning community political structures (as alluded to in the many Middle Eastern village studies), visiting behavior is never the less more than a mere manifestation of gregariousness. For many it serves as an opportunity to assess sentiments with respect to controversial issues of familial or communal interest, for others it provides a learning opportunity by means of the sermon and story.

FOLK TALES

Storytelling is a favorite Iranian leisure-time activity. I was therefore a bit astonished to find a very limited corpus of traditional oral literature. Most of what there was focused on religious themes — the Shirazis have a well-developed local exegesis on biblical subjects. But traditional stories about the Jewish experience in Iran were far more limited. Most of these date to the seventeenth century Safavid period with lesser numbers associated with Zand and Qajar times. While there is some variety of theme, many of the tales deal with miraculous deliverance from persecution usually associated with some kind of blood libel. No methodic attempt was made to collect these stories and I must assume from comparison with archival collections that numerous such stories do indeed exist. Why did I not hear them? When are they told? This remains a source of puzzlement to the present day, and needs further investigation and clarification.

Most stories not told as a response to my prompting were recounted as a part of sermonizing in synagogue or at a house of mourning. Shirazi men spend up to several hours on Shabbat and festivals listening to this most creative of Judaeo-Persian literary forms. The tellers are accorded great religious merit for their efforts, though as religious functionaries, *darshanim* (preachers) receive no renumeration (see Chapter X). Secular storytelling is of little importance, though quite extensive.

Shirazis deserve their reputation as pursuers of leisure and pleasure. Jews make an effort to savor blocs of time through religious and secular means. Whether leisure time is utilized to be entertained, to appreciate nature, to visit, to imbibe or to smoke the *water pipe,* it is hardly less important to Shirazis than the time devoted to productive labor or to obligatory family interaction.

CHAPTER IX

Shirazi Jewish Ethics and Attitudes: A "Little Tradition"

The values shared by Shirazi Jews are not, for the most part, "Jewish" values *per se*. The local Jewish world-view tends to reflect the ethos of the Persian urbanite masses admixed and often in harmony with tenets of the Jewish "great tradition". But it also responds to the particular vicissitudes of the Jewish experience in and around Shiraz.

QESMAT (DESTINY)

Fatalism is an essential component of the value system of Shirazi Jews, as it is among Iranians generally. The Iranian masses have been exploited, intimidated and repressed at the hands of the elite and due, in part, to their impoverishment and lack of political power, many suffer calamitous personal misfortune. But the Jew, who often serves as a scapegoat for the frustrated populace, is aware that he is even less able to determine his circumstances than others.

Tragedies are taken in stride — they are Heaven sent. Initiative is no virtue since *dast-e khoda* (the hand of God) will provide, no matter the effort made, if such be His will. No form of labor, no amount of effort will bring prosperity, unless it be God's will. Physical labor, especially if it is strenuous, is rejected as unworthy, whereas menial work was and still is acceptable, provided the exertion is minimal. "Why work hard to accumulate wealth, when tomorrow the Muslims may come and take it away?" ... is a most common explanation given by informants when asked why shopkeeping, peddling, moneylending and cottage industry are favored professions.

TIME

Time is not viewed as important except with regard to ritual. As is common throughout the Middle East, time is tentative, an abstraction. Fixed times for appointments, awaking, opening business and fulfilling contracts are a relatively new innovation in Shiraz life and rarely adhered to. The Shirazi Jew is concerned with the present and the immediate future; the past is infrequently recalled except at religious festivals. The future, beyond two or three months, is not even considered. People rarely plan ahead. The chief *gabay* complained that the biggest problem faced by the Mahalleh poor is their inability to properly budget money – a complaint often leveled at the urban poor of industrial countries. Military service, marriage and other potential crises are of little concern until they are at hand. *'Aliya,* emigration to Israel, is in the back of everyone's mind – *someday*; purchases and repairs may be delayed in its anticipation, but no one really plans for *'aliya* far in advance.

Shirazi Jews tend to act somewhat impulsively. Often, after months of indecision, a wedding may be arranged and consummated within two weeks time, including betrothal party and wedding feast. Disputes often begin with an impetuous comment regarding some incident or other, simmer for a time, and are then quickly settled. This impulsiveness characterizes the verbal interaction of the entire Jewish population and, not surprisingly, opinions and positions vacillate with great frequency and explosive suddenness.

For months, a reputable goldsmith had been rejecting everyone's advice about remodeling his store. He argued that every Jew must settle in Israel and his proposed *'aliya* was imminent. One day, he returned home for lunch and informed everyone that he had contracted for and, in fact, had commenced that very morning to make the necessary improvements. He proffered no reason for this sudden change of heart.

Such spontaneity and the singular disregard for the merits of hard work have earned the Shirazi Jew a special reputation among his co-religionists elsewhere in Iran for being lazy and shiftless.

EDUCATION

Earlier, it was indicated that education is thought to be beneficial, but only literacy is considered a necessity. Education is a means to greater prosperity and prestige, but knowledge is not considered an end in itself. Not only is this pragmatic attitude *vis-à-vis* education contrary to the Jewish "great tradition" ethic: *tora lshma'* ("study for its own sake"), but it is also in opposition to a similar moral among the Persian elite. The Jew instead joins his non-elite Muslim fellow-urbanite in rejecting the personal efficacy of such wasteful behavior in view of his social and economic deprivation. But unable to completely disregard the Jewish "great tradition", the ambivalent Shirazi Jew sees such non-vocation-oriented learning as playing at least some limited role in his life, if only to strengthen religious and ethnic identity.

HONESTY

In order to accomplish some task whose successful and profitable completion is out of his hands anyway, the Shirazi Jew will employ whatever shortcuts are at his disposal. Lying, cheating and deceit, whether in business, school or social relations are not generally considered unethical. Cheating a customer, be he your best friend, is considered an acceptable business practice.[1] While honesty is demanded of high community officials such as the chief *gabay* and its absence is loudly condemned, there is otherwise little merit ascribed to the truth. Shrewdness and chicanery bring their own reward.

Not much attention is paid to the consequences of less than truthful statements and their morality is not an issue:

One day, during Sukkot, I wanted to go shopping with a Yeshiva student. As we walked into the yard from my apartment, a neighbor asked us to join in a quorum for *mishmara*, the vigil for the dead. My companion begged off telling them that he had to go to school for a class. (He was actually on vacation.) When I asked him later why he had lied, as it appeared to me that our shopping excursion was an adequate excuse, especially as they had had a quorum without us, he explained: "One has to lie in such circumstances; this is the way we do things in Shiraz".

Little lies or telling fibs may well be a necessary convention in a society emphasizing formal polite behavior. Frankness, insofar as it may hurt someone's feelings, is a behavioral trait normally discouraged. The lame excuse does not suffice where an imaginative airtight alibi can be concocted.

ẒDAQA (CHARITY)

Philanthropy, held in high esteem by Jews the world over, is comparatively uncommon in Shiraz. The stinginess of most Shirazi Jews is, indeed, almost proverbial among the various foreign Jewish organizations working there.

In 1930 one foreigner observed: "There is no organized charity in Persia, nor any institution for social welfare" (Kopellowitz, 1930:46).

---

[1] One is careful not to cheat the *goyim* too much, for fear they might retaliate violently.

While Kopellowitz was apparently overstating the case, it is true that Shirazi Jews are most reluctant to extend help to their neighbors and unwillingly give *ẓdaqa*. One man, well known for his piety and learning, even refused to aid his elderly, destitute mother. During the many persecutions, expulsions, famines and epidemics, there were few instances of intercommunal assistance beyond the sheltering of refugees (Loeb, 1970:265).

Nevertheless, the Jews of Shiraz are not wholly unconcerned about the poor. Kopellowitz briefly described the indigenous "poorhouse" in the following terms:

It is a dilapidated structure, containing eight low, tiny rooms, in each of which lives a family of six to eight people. (1930:46)

These quarters were available to the poor until about 1963, when the JDC was permitted to build its health clinic on the site.

The community also reserves the position of *shamash* (beadle, caretaker) of the synagogue for the indigent. In one *knisa* there lives a poor blind woman from Nahawand, who had hoped to have her eyes operated on in Shiraz. The Shirazi community was even willing to raise the money for this surgery, but the doctors considered the case hopeless, so she settled into this meager though undemanding mode of subsistence. In a second *knisa* live three old spinsters; a third *knisa* houses the sickly family of an old retired musician and a fourth was given to a mentally retarded newcomer from Teheran, who had left his family behind and had volunteered his services as community body-washer. Each resident family or individual residing in the *knisa* must be approved of by the synagogue membership. The *shamash* and family occupy a single room in the *knisa* in return for such services as cleaning the synagogue, guarding it and taking care of the lights. It is considered shameful to live in such circumstances and those who do so, avoid mention of it. The poor living in their own homes are welcomed to use the synagogue tap for their water needs.

The *gabay* has the primary responsibility for the collection and distribution of funds for the poor, but the *ḥazzan* (overseer) of each *knisa* also collects money for the needy on Purim, the evening of Yom Kippur and on Tish'a B'av. The *ḥazzan* or *gabay* used to collect money for widows and orphans to provide for their subsistence and accumulate dowries. Sometimes it was necessary to send the destitute themselves to one of the tightfisted rich to "awaken his mercy" and thus contribute his pledge (Melamed, 1951:366).[1]

For the non-Jew, the Iranian Jew is stereotyped as niggardly. One who haggles tenaciously over the price of an item is said to be engaged in *jud baazi* (the Jew game). This characterization, however unfortunate its implications, seems to be well deserved. Direct contributions to the poor rarely exceed two or three rial except on special occasions such as weddings when several hundred rial may be publicly donated.[1] The Muslim rich are also known to be miserly, contributing large sums for the poor only under pressure (Avery, 1965:229). Any relationship between the Jewish and non-Jewish attitude with respect to charity is not easily unraveled. Muslims, however, do seem to be somewhat freer with their petty charity.

The middle class and elite Jews do not hesitate to state the reasons for their parsimony:

Were it not for JDC contributions to the poor, the poor would all emigrate ... Israel needs such people badly! The poor are lazy (many so-accused readily admit to this charge!) and as long as they are not starving, they are content to just get by. Some of the poor are only pretending; they are accomplished actors.

The elite, in fact, have not always been well-to-do. They had to struggle to earn their money; to defend it, they were forced to hide it and feign poverty themselves. This perhaps explains their resentment and indignation at being asked to contribute to the poor.

All levels of the community do give *ẓdaqa,* but many do so only when they are formally expected to. Donations to the *knisa* for its maintenance through the purchase of *kvodot* (ritual honors) is probably the least painful means of philanthropy. Most of the contributions for relief purposes are made by the pious poor themselves. Thus the once lofty Jewish "great tradition" principle of *ẓdaqa* emerges in twentieth century Shiraz radically transformed: *ẓdaqa* is the redistribution of the wealth of the *poor* among themselves!

Shirazi Jews make no pretense of being motivated to give charity for humanitarian considerations. They believe that the Almighty will, by Himself, sustain the poor if they are pious.[2] The principal motivation for giving charity is a selfish one. "The Holy One, Blessed be He, accepts bribes!", I was assured by the chief *gabay.* "*Ẓdaqa* given to the poor is

---

[1] Jews generally give large sums to Israel with minimal coaxing.
[2] The belief in Divine intervention on behalf of the poor is an old concept among Persian Jews. Shirazi Jews used to reiterate this thrice daily during the very important *'amida* prayer – according to a sixteenth century manuscript (Adler, E., 1898:606).

---

[1] Upon one occasion, when the Joint director in Shiraz wished to coerce the Anjoman into contributing a substantial subsidy to finance the school feeding program, she intimated that when the poor received word of the Anjoman's refusal to cooperate, they would descend *en masse* to protest at the gate of the *ra'is.* To her disappointment this did not transpire.

the way we bribe Him to be good to us." The merit in giving may be defined in formal economic terms as generalized reciprocity. Something approaching sympathetic magic is intended; by giving *ẓdaqa,* one assures God's reciprocating a similar kindness, should the need arise. The largest donations of all types were given in times of crises, e.g. during mourning, at weddings and circumcisions and on Yom Kippur – as an atonement offering.[1]

VIRTUES

The following qualities are considered important virtues for Shirazi men: education, piety, virility, shrewdness, having a prestigious occupation and being a good provider.

Womanly virtues include: physical strength, white skin (the most important criterion of beauty), fecundity, bearing male children, warm love of children, acquiescence, a quiet tongue, shrewdness and proficiency at housekeeping.

ABERU (HONOR)

Honor is understood to be a *value* associated with relative prestige which may be exchanged in face-to-face situations. It is also a *valuation* composed of two factors: (1) an individual's self-estimation (pride), namely, his *claim* to rank, (2) society's acknowledgement of this claim by deference and respect confirming his *right* to rank.

As throughout the Middle East and Circum-Mediterranean, *aberu,* "honor", is *the* critical factor in Iranian social relations. It has been shown that the Jew, forced to submit to public insult and suffer numerous indignities at the hands of the Muslim population, was traditionally considered devoid of honor. Nevertheless, within the Jewish community, *aberu* became an essential complex in the Jewish value system.[2] Despite the Shirazi Jew's preoccupation with physical survival – perhaps because real wealth and security were unattainable goals – honor became as much sought after as wealth.

Honor can be acquired, added to, saved, exchanged and even spent, i.e., in exchange for economic or political considerations. In essence, honor functions as if it were a special-purpose, albeit intangible, money! Shirazis often attempt to manipulate and accumulate honor in hope of increasing their prestige and ultimately their status within the communal rank order.

---

[1] Some such motivation often underlies the religious act of giving charity (see Tylor 1958:461–2; Weber, 1964:26–7).

[2] Jews usually use the Hebrew term *kavod* to denote "honor" in ritual contexts.

The loss of honor (shame), no matter how slight, is a most serious matter. He who is offended withdraws, becomes sullen and sulks by himself. The offender is avoided at all costs. If amends are not made, the offended individual attempts to enlist support and may spread rumors about the offender. Defense of one's honor is almost always verbal; outright anger is always contained before it reaches the point of violence. There are no blood feuds such as are found among the *goyim*.

Unlike his Muslim counterpart, the Shirazi Jew considers personal honor more important than family honor. The latter assumes importance at betrothal or in cases of premarital or extra-marital intercourse by a female from one's *khanevadeh*. Shameful family circumstances are concealed and conversation about it is avoided. Family members victimized by misfortune or whose honor is otherwise compromised suffer the added indignity of social ostracism by their kinsmen. Positive steps to improve family honor include: bettering the occupational, educational and religious prestige and ranking of its members, increasing the family's wealth and marrying up. Such steps benefit all members of the *khanevadeh* and, to a lesser extent, the entire kindred.

Ta'arof, variously defined as "compliment, ceremony, offer, present...", refers to the Persian system of polite formal behavior, verbal and non-verbal, by which means honor exchanges are transacted in face-to-face situations.[1] Traditionally, *ta'arof* was most strictly adhered to by the elite who found it an effective mechanism for reinforcing rank differentiation. It was the model of proper public behavior, much imitated by the rest of the population, including the Jews. In its pristine form, *ta'arof* is best preserved today by society's more conservative elements: the aged, religious and poor. Not surprisingly, it remains a prime example of culture-lag in modern Shiraz; the elite now tries to affect western manners and initiates *ta'arof* exchange only infrequently, although they expect to be recipients of *ta'arof* from others. As of 1968, Shiraz had maintained *ta'arof* to a degree rarely observed elsewhere in Iran.

The fundamental core meaning of *ta'arof,* "offer", gives a clue to its most important process. An "offer" may be made on the street when acquaintances meet; "*befarmayid*" ... (lit. "at your command") is the expression used by which the speaker indicates that the other should accompany him. Often this general offer is immediately followed by a specific request to visit the speaker's home. Such offers are never accepted; nor are they intended to be!

---

[1] The transactional analysis of honor exchange developed here and in Chapter X follows Barth (1966), with the reservations expressed by Paine (1974).

A variety of offers are made in guest situations.[1] The guest is offered a seat of honour *bala* or "up front", away from the entrance. He may then be offered several or all of the following; the water pipe, tea, nuts, raisins, fruit and a meal. Should a meal be served, the guest is offered the choicest portions. The host will press his guest to eat to the point of satiation and beyond, for he may finally resort to placing the food in the mouth of his protesting guest. The guest, on the other hand, no matter how hungry he may be and no matter how little food he is given, must leave food on the plate to demonstrate that his host has been overly generous. Should a chance remark slip from the guest's mouth that some item belonging to the host pleases him, the latter will press the guest to accept it as a gift, saying; "*manzele man, khodetun*" – "my house is your own."

The target of offers is expected politely to refuse them. Repeated offers are declined firmly and great powers of persuasion may have to be employed to force their acceptance. If more than one guest is present, the initial target of an offer must attempt to defer the honor of acceptance to the others. It is expected that each person present will accept the offer in rank order, from highest to lowest. Should someone accept out of turn, the others, who consider themselves to have been slighted, adamantly refuse to accept at all.

This ideal model is not always adhered to. Because *ta'arof* acts as a mechanism of exchange, honor may be bestowed and accepted out of turn for strategic reasons. Furthermore, the educated Shirazi, rebelling against this institution, may refuse to participate by requesting those present "not to make *ta'arof*".

Pre-school age children are well trained in *ta'arof*. They are told, for example, that their acceptance of an offer the first time it is made is "ugly", but that they must repeatedly insist that a guest accept *their* offer. Polite forms of address and self-effacing terms of reference are also learned as concomitants of *ta'arof*.

Suffice it to say, that *ta'arof* functions not only as a means of protecting one's honor but often serves to hide one's true emotions behind the facade of formal polite behavior. This dovetails nicely with the general restraint placed on emotional expression outside the formal ritual channels established for it. *Ta'arof* is maintained during crisis situations, such as death, as a means of linking those emotionally and spiritually removed from the community with the whole membership.

---

[1] Among Shirazi Jews, the guest-house or guest-room is not a formal structure. Guests are invited or come for a particular purpose or at a specific occasion. The best room in the house is selected for entertaining the guest.

PRIVACY

"Honor and Shame" cultures make conspicuous use of mechanisms for maintaining personal and familial privacy. The veiling of women, the walling-in of property, and the avoidance of conspicuous consumption are widespread in Iranian life. Maintenance of social distance, however, is effected not only through manipulation of the environment but (as previously indicated) also through formal polite behavior. In effect, the various patterns of formality used tend to maintain considerable social distance among the members of society except within the *khanevadeh* and among close friends. There, a compensatory intimacy and intensity of interaction is observable, although overall, it would appear to this observer that Iranians tend to be more exclusive about their feelings than do Americans.

The attitude of Shirazi Jews with regard to personal and family privacy parallels that of Iranians generally. However, as was indicated previously, Jews do not appear to have any formal institution equivalent to the *anderun* (harem), nor is there the same measure of insistence on the veiling of their women in public or in private. In fact there seems to be a distinctive stylistic difference in the manner in which Jewish women wear the *chador*; they rarely cover any part of their face. Women living *tu khiyabun* must be classed among Iran's most emancipated with respect to veiling.

When troubled or offended, most adult males tend to avoid the company of others while they internalize their concerns. But communal social pressure for gregarious interaction does not allow for extended withdrawal. Due to family obligations, women do not generally have recourse to a withdrawal option and instead make extensive use of a confidante when troubled.

In sum, privacy is given high valuation by Shirazi Jews both for defense against an external threat and to balance interpersonal relations within the community.

"ALL ISRAEL ARE RESPONSIBLE FOR ONE ANOTHER" (San. 27b)

When an Iranian Jew is asked by another what he is, he replies that he is "*yisra'el*". The term, *yisra'el,* is an exclusively Jewish appellation for self-identification. The *goyim* refer to the Jew as "*kalimi*", or, should they wish to be derogatory, "*jud*".

The Shirazi Jew is proud of being Jewish. He considers himself superior in every way to non-Jews. His apparent amiability towards *goyim* is for the sake of peace and to ensure a means of livelihood. Jews respond to the many years of persecution totally united in a smoldering, repressed hatred for their tormentors.[1] In the privacy of their homes and in public, through the mediation of a language not understood by others, Jews mockingly point out the flaws in the life-style of the *goyim*. For the Shirazi Jew, Islam and the Arab nations are synonymous with all that is evil.

The Shirazi Jew considers himself superior to the Jews of the north. He bases this contention on his scrupulous adherence to religious tradition and resistance to conversion, especially to the efforts of the Bahais and Protestants. Only the Yazdis and Mashhadis can claim to be as strictly observant as the Shirazis.

Jewish visitors from out-of-town are treated very well in Shiraz. Emissaries from Israel are given a near royal welcome and receive numerous invitations to dinner and even to reside. But there exists a certain degree of xenophobia with regard to Jews from elsewhere:

One Sabbath evening, Bashi returned home late from buying bread for the Sabbath meal as was his wont following the evening prayers. He explained his delay as resulting from a strange experience occuring after the service in his *knisa*. A man claiming to be a Jew from Hamadan had asked a group of Jews where he might stay for the night and have a meal. They were a bit suspicious of him, but Bashi, a good host, tentatively considered inviting him to his house. First though, it was necessary to test his Jewishness. They asked him to recite the *shma'* (the central belief in the uniqueness and unity of God.) – this he could not do. Next they requested that he recite the blessings on the Tora; these he claimed not to have learned. (In Shiraz, every male, even the illiterate, know these prayers.) Finally they asked him to tell them about the Sabbath. When he was unable to do that, they concluded that he must be a Muslim trying to masquerade as a Jew, to gain entrance to a Jewish home, in order to rob and perhaps kill its inhabitants.

---

[1] Stern indicates that from time to time, Jews would revenge themselves on their oppressors:

Now and then, the smothered feeling of revenge and vindictiveness which has long been rankling in the heart, will burst forth and vent itself on the first Moslem whom he encounters in a narrow and dark lane. Sometimes such assaults attract people from a neighboring street, and the Jew, in order to avoid the punishment which his temerity would draw upon him, immediately raises the most pitiable cries and, to avoid suspicion, inflicts a serious wound on himself; and then covered with blood and dirt, excites either ridicule or compassion as the gazers are disposed towards him, and escapes the consequences in which so grave an offence might involve him and his people. (1854:194)

Identification with Jews all over the world and particularly with those in Israel is very strong. Terrorism against Israel, the hanging of Jewish citizens of Iraq, the show trials of would-be emigrants from the Soviet Union are tragedies personally felt and deeply mourned in Shiraz. Prayers and fasts are offered on the behalf of Jews no matter where they are endangered. Jewish solidarity is felt deeply and expressed in many ways. Informants simply refuse to believe that there are "liberal" Jews in the U.S. who smoke on Shabbat in Synagogue or participate in ritual without a head-covering. This should not be misconstrued as mere naivete, for as Mashallah put it:

There are only good Jews in the world and even if one does not follow all of the minutiae of Jewish law then at least he gives *zdaqa*.

Ethnic survival is second only to personal survival in the hierarchy of Shirazi Jewish values.

"IF I AM NOT FOR MYSELF, WHO WILL BE FOR ME?" (Avot 1:14)

Despite the strong sentiments for ethnic unity, there appears to be a powerful undercurrent ethic for communal fragmentation we may summarize as: "every man for himself".

Apostate Jews, and even seemingly loyal Jews, have in the past spied on the Jewish community for the government. Bacher (1906, 51:93) reports that one, Ovadya of Isfahan, was murdered by coreligionists in Safavid times. A number of Jews today are suspected (some with justification) of working for SAVAK, the Iranian Secret Police.

Some of the more appropriate examples of individualism, informing and group disloyalty involve the Otsar Hatorah teachers:

a) The teachers' strike, January 14, 1968, was broken almost immediately because someone told the school authorities who was on the secret strike committee, despite oath-taking that this would remain in confidence. The informer in this case hoped for a personal reward for his "good behavior" though it appears that this was a vain hope. Yeshiva students, studying to be teachers, were willingly employed as strike breakers, despite the fact that they were hurting their own long-run possibility of obtaining better wages.

b) A teacher once wrote to the Otsar Hatorah authorities that a fellow-teacher, who was receiving a bonus for studying additional pedagogic material, was not actually doing the required study. Without further inquiry, the bonus was taken from the offender and given to the informer.

c) A project to send several teachers to Israel for a summer seminar had to be cancelled when fellow teachers threatened to make representations to the government over such "Zionist" activities, unless they too were sent.

FEAR

No discussion of values, ethics and attitudes would be complete without some reference to the importance of fear as a motivator of diverse forms the behavior. Underlying so many of the patterns of avoidance activity including the lack of conspicuous consumption, niggardliness, privacy, general maintenance of low visibility, etc. is the fear of what fate has in store for the Jew. He fears his neighbor, the authorities, the mob, the thief, the stranger, the evil eye, bad spirits and, most especially, the wrath of the Holy One manifested as *dast-e khoda,* "the hand of God"! Fear acts to evoke both unity and discord, commonality and individualism, it activates kinship networks, the locking and barring of doors, religious ritual and sorcery. Jews fear for themselves, their families, their community and their nation. Fear — in various guises — permeates every aspect of Shirazi life. Fear most certainly plays an important part in the lifestyle of many Iranians (Black, 1972:624). But for outcaste groups such as the Jews, who perceive themselves as the passive victims of circumstances, the pervasiveness and impact is especially visible.

The ethos of the Shirazi Jew is in many ways at variance with prevailing "great tradition" attitudes. "Little tradition" principles with respect to honesty, work, fate, time, honor and learning are with minor discrepancies, those of the general populace of the region. Since ideology evolves as a response to social conditions, posturings from fear and uncertainty are understandable matters of Shirazi Jewish life. Thus personality characterizations and labels; "dishonest", "lazy", "impulsive", "shiftless" and "stingy" may be seen as reflections of adaptive responses to the economic and social oppression to which the Shirazi Jew has been exposed. Ethnocentrism likewise remains strong in the face of overt hostility.

The "little tradition" ethos corresponds most with the Jewish "great tradition" where ethnic identity is aroused. It would seem that ethnicity is the most important theme in the Shirazi Jewish world-view — and probably throughout the traditional Jewish diaspora.

CHAPTER X

Local Religious Practice and the Jewish "Great Tradition"

> Judaism is a *religion of time* aiming at the *sanctification of time* . . .
> Jewish ritual may be characterized as the art of significant forms in
> time, as the *architecture of time.*
>
> (Heschel 1952:8)

Heschel's view that Judaism is a time-centered religion is relevant to
the present case study. We shall endeavor to show that Shirazi Judaism
is indeed time-oriented. The meshing cycles and periodicities of daily living, by being given ritual significance, create an impervious and stable
non-material structure into which the Shirazi Jew can escape from the
mundane and often hostile everyday world.

SHABBAT

"More than Israel has kept the Sabbath, the Sabbath has kept Israel"
(Ahad Ha'am, cited in Millgram, 1959:253). One of the important
stabilizing elements in all Jewish society has been the Shabbat (Sabbath).
As a weekly day of total rest, it is an escape from the daily subsistence
cycle, and for Shirazi Jews it is completely unlike the other days of the
week. Shabbat begins some minutes before sundown on Friday and lasts
until about one-half hour after sunset Saturday. The entire week is
oriented about that day and the days of the week are reckoned from it.

Men have little to do to prepare for Shabbat, other than to take their
weekly bath. Additionally, men living outside the Mahalleh are also
responsible for purchasing the groceries for Sabbath meals. Meat is
purchased on Thursday, the peak slaughtering day; during the cool
months fish too is purchased and usually smoked for the Friday evening
meal.

Mahalleh women do their own marketing, mostly on Friday morning
when the peddlers crowd into the main Mahalleh alleys. Friday is spent

in preparing food for Shabbat since making fire and cooking are forbidden on the Sabbath. Foods are cooked beforehand and kept warm on charcoal in a special Shabbat kitchen. This room is separated from the main rooms of the house, so that the heat will not be bothersome to the family during the hot weather.

Prior to sundown, women light Sabbath candles and men go to *knisa*. The real focus of Shabbat is *knisa*. Attendance there is quite high; even those who must work or go to school attend. Friday evening worship begins at sundown, and lasts about forty minutes, so that men can get home for dinner. Latecomers can catch a quorum until about one hour after sunset. The time for Saturday morning services, which last from one and one-half to two and one-quarter hours, varies with the season of the year. In the cold winter it begins late, while in summer, in order to escape the heat of day it begins early. During morning worship congregational business is conducted followed by a period of active socialization. *Minḥa,* the afternoon worship, is held after 12.30 p.m., but not in all synagogues. In the Mahalleh there are continual quorums until sunset. *Minḥa* is well attended and those present have the opportunity to hear a *drasha* (sermon). Shabbat ends with the simultaneous, but unsynchronized recitation of the *havdala* prayer by several persons, scattered about the *knisa*. In winter, nearly half of the Shabbat daylight hours are spent in *knisa*.

Shabbat is an occasion for visiting kinsmen, going on family outings and getting sleep. Men drift away from the house and go for a walk sometimes taking a child with them, or they seek out their friends to talk or play cards with; women sit in the *kuche* gossiping.

Sabbath meals, as contrasted with the other days of the week, are multi-coursed, served with an abundance of utensils and eaten from a table cloth spread on the carpet. *Qiddush* is recited over wine before the meal; the poor usually make do with hot water poured over raisins and allowed to stand a few hours. Even the illiterate recite *qiddush,* though with numerous errors.[1] An extended blessing is made over the bread. The custom of a special bread or portion (*ḥalla*) known in Yemen (Kafih, 1963:207–9), Kurdistan (Brauer, 1947:219) and most Ashkenazic and Sfardic communities, is unknown in Shiraz.[2] Shirazis buy their bread from their regular bakery, Friday evening after worship. The three large Sabbath meals, reflect the special nature of the day, as

---

[1] Shirazis conclude the *qiddush* saying: "*barukh adonay asher natan mnuha l'amo yisra'el bayyom shabbat qodesh,*" (Praised is the Lord, who gave rest to his people Israel on the holy Sabbath day).
[2] Jews reportedly baked a special bread and set aside a special *ḥalla* portion in Kashan, in the pre-Pahlavi period.

they are eaten leisurely, with obvious enjoyment and considerable con-versation. The meals are all meat-meals, usually some form of *khoresh* (stew) or chicken with rice. One dish eaten in winter on Saturday mor-nings and peculiar to Shirazi Jews is called *khalebibi*; it is made from beef, turnips, leek, cabbage, beans, lentils and rice. Since cooking on the Sabbath is absolutely forbidden, this mixture is pre-cooked and then left on the heat all night until it is eaten. The resulting porridge is not unlike the East European *chulent,* the product of a similar Sabbath cooking restriction. The knowledgeable recite grace after each Shabbat meal.

The Shirazi observance of the Sabbath may be summarized, as follows:

1) Smoking, cooking and the use of fire is avoided by all, in accor-dance with the "great tradition".

2) Electric lights, radio and other electrical appliances are used by all but the most pious.

3) Except for Yeshiva students and graduates, everyone permits carrying on Shabbat, in violation of Talmudic restrictions.

4) Everyone travels by car, bus or taxi, except for the most pious.

5) Most Jews spend money on the Sabbath, although this is clearly in violation of all of the law codes.

6) Work is forbidden, including business, housework and sewing, but these prohibitions are no longer strictly observed.

Druggists, doctors, dentists, government employees, white collar workers, students at secular schools and university, work as usual on Shabbat. The commencement of Shabbat is rather loosely defined and should housework or business be pending, the Sabbath is postponed un-til the job at hand is finished. Some people open shops before the Sab-bath is concluded. Informants report that Sabbath observance was more strict and consistent in the past, but that use of money, traveling and carrying were permitted then too.

THE CYCLE OF HOLIDAYS

PESAH (*MO'ED* – "FESTIVAL")

Without doubt, Pesaḥ, or "*mo'ed*", is the most complex and all-inclusive of the various holidays. Unlike the other festivals, it is unmistakeably

TABLE 11
Shirazi Jewish Feasts and Festivals

Name	Occurrence[a]	Distinctive features
Shabbbat	From Friday before sundown to Saturday after sundown.	Special prayers, elaborate meals, no work is permitted and the use of fire is prohibited: it is day of complete rest.
Rosh Ḥodesh (New Moon)	The beginning of each month.	Special prayers are said and a feast prepared in a house of mourning. Community *kappara*.
Pesaḥ *"mo'ed"*	15th to 22nd of Nisan (March/April)	Commemorates the exodus from Egypt. No leaven is eaten. First two days are complete holidays. The first two nights a special meal is eaten following the reading of the *'aggada*.
Yom Ha'aẓma'ut (Israel Independence Day)	5th of 'Iyyar (April/May)	Commemorates Israel's independence. A day of picnicking in the gardens.
Lag Ba'omer	33rd day of counting the *'omer* (May)	Special songs about Shim'on Bar Yoḥay. A *drasha* is given in *knisa*. Commemorates the cessation of a plague on the students of Rabbi Akiva (2nd cent. C.E.)
Shavu'ot *"mo'ed–e gol"*	6th–7th of Sivan (May–June)	Commemorates the giving of the Tora and the offering of the first fruits. All night study marks the first evening; dairy foods are eaten. Complete holiday.
Shiv'a 'Asar Btammuz	17th of Tammuz (July)	Fast commemorating the breaching of Jerusalem's walls by the Romans. Beginning of three weeks period of mourning.
—	5th of 'Av (July/August)	Prayers commemorating the death of the "Ari" (Isaac Luria) – a new innovation.

cont.

[a] All festivals extend from sundown of the previous evening to shortly after sunset.

TABLE 11 – *cont.*

Name	Occurrence	Distinctive features
Tish'a B'av *"zaqarun"*	9th of 'Av (July/August)	Commemorates the destruction of the Temple in Jerusalem. Full day fast. Mourning behavior and garb are observed. Special prayers are recited throughout the day; *kappara* is performed.
Slihot	First of 'Elul to 10th of Tishre (Aug.–Sept.)	Penitential prayers are receited each morning from 3.00 to 6.00 a.m.
Rosh Hashana	First and Second of Tishre (September)	Commencement of New Year and heightened period of penitence. Full festival. Special prayers, blowing of the shofar, special foods and pilgrimage to the shrine of Serah bat Asher.
Zum Gdalya *"barabar kippur"*	Third of Tishre	Fast in memory of death of governor of Judea in 6th century B.C.E. Shirazis believe it is a practice fast for Yom Kippur.
Yom Kippur *"adir, kippur"*	Tenth of Tishre Sept./Oct.)	The Day of Atonement. A complete fast. Jews spend the entire day in synagogue, and are especially responsive responsive during worship. More ritual restrictions than on Shabbat.
Sukkot *"mo'ed-e sukka"*	15th to 21st of Tishre (Sept./Oct.)	Full holiday the first two days. Special booths are constructed and lived in; prayers are said over the palm and citron. All-night prayer vigil and the beating of willows takes place on the seventh day.
Shmini 'Azeret/ Simhat Tora	22nd and 23rd of Tishre	The Eighth Day of Assembly and Rejoicing of the Tora; full festival. On second day, Tora-reading cycle is begun again.
"Medak/ mo'ed qatan"	2nd (3rd?) of Heshvan (Oct./Nov.)	Indigenous Shirazi Jewish holiday commemorating community's deliverance from its enemies. No special observance.

(cont.)

TABLE 11 – *cont.*

Name	Occurrence	Distinctive features
Ḥanukka	25th of Kislev to 3rd of Tevet (Dec./Jan.)	The lighting of holiday lamps in commemoration of the victory of the Maccabees over the Syrians in the 2nd century B.C.E.
'Asara Btevet	10th of Tevet (January)	Fast recalling the siege of Jerusalem.
Tu Bshvat	15th of Shvat (Jan./Feb.)	New Year of Trees. Special fruits are eaten.
—	7th of 'Adar (Feb./March)	Commemorates death of Moses; special prayers are read. This is a new innovation.
Ta'anit Esther	13th of 'Adar (Feb./March)	Fast commemorating the fast of Queen Esther (Esther 4:16).
Purim	14th of 'Adar (Feb. March)	Recalls the victory of Persian Jews over Haman. Reading of the *mgilla* feasting at 2.00 a.m. in the house of one's wife's father, burning effigies of Haman, noisemaking, special foods.

home-oriented. After Purim, women begin their preparations. Rice is carefully cleaned and sorted; every wheat grain must be removed. Utensils to be used for Pesaḥ are taken out of storage. Daily utensils, to be used also for Pesaḥ, must be carefully scrubbed with coarse gravel, then dipped in boiling water and thereby made fit for Pesaḥ use. The ignorant do this for all utensils, while the knowledgeable discard wooden and plastic objects entirely. Spits to be used for *kebab* are heated red hot; mortars and pestles are placed in boiling water with hot stones, and glass is immersed in water for three days. Some metal objects are tinned for Pesaḥ.

Khamis (soured) foods, not fit for Pesaḥ, are finished before the holiday. Shirazis do not observe the widely practiced Ashkenazic custom of selling *khamis* to the *goyim*. After inspecting the house for *khamis* the evening preceding the holiday, the remaining *khamis* was customarily thrown into the water and not burned, as burning is said to antagonize the *goyim*.[1]

Shirazis follow the Sfardic-oriental tradition with respect to permitted Pesaḥ foods, allowing such questionable items as rice and white beans.

Foods permitted on Pesaḥ vary according to the informant asked:

Permitted:
by all: rice, meat, fruit, closed nuts, imported-packaged sugar (dates used to substitute for sugar), oil (Israeli or home-made from animal fat), tea, salt, eggs, fish, white beans, vegetables, home-prepared spices, wine, *araq*, specially collected milk.

Not permitted
by all: peas, chick peas, bread, red beans, lentils, barley, milk, yoghurt (*maast*), butter, soda, cheese, spaghetti, candy, ice cream, figs, drugs, oil.

by some: flour

by some: dates, corn, cauliflower, turnips, olives, coffee, fish, carrots, dried fruit.

Nevertheless, the strictures on Pesaḥ food consumption are quite rigorous when compared with normal dietary restrictions. Note the confusion among some informants, especially the illiterate, who forbid such "great tradition" acceptable foodstuffs as fish, carrots, olives, cauliflower and turnips, while permitting flour, the archetype exemplar of leaven.

Maẓẓa (unleavened bread) baking begins about two weeks before Pesaḥ. In the past, Shirazis strictly observed the prohibition on preparing more than $1\frac{1}{2}$ kilo of dough at one time, but now they are lax about this restriction. Seven grams of salt in 300 kilo of flour makes it unfit for use. Wheat for *maẓẓot* is purchased just after Sukkot and carefully stored until several weeks before Pesaḥ, when it is ground separately at the commercial mill. *Maẓẓot* are baked at one of three "factories", or at home on a tray of gravel over a primus stove. In the factories, everyone supervises his own baking. Each factory employs about eight people, two preparing dough, four forming the flat round dough cakes and two handling the baking. The *maẓẓa* cakes are not baked on trays, but are placed against the inside wall of the oven, to which they adhere. When the baker thinks they are ready, he hauls them out with a hooked stick. There is no set baking time, but the whole batch takes about twenty minutes. Nearly 10% of the *maẓẓot* are likely to be considered unfit, usually for being underbaked. The finished *maẓẓot* are roughly round, about $\frac{1}{2}$ m in diameter and of varying thickness. Most families prepare at least 13 kilo of *maẓẓot* for the eight-day holiday. The *maẓẓot* are taken

---

[1] Why the burning of leaven should be offensive to Muslims is not at all clear. Perhaps this custom also has its roots in Zoroastrianism where fire is pure, uncontaminated, sacred, while water is used for purging the polluted, the unfit. Nowadays, *khamis is* burned by many Shirazis.

PLATE 58   "*Agala*", ritual purification of metal utensils in boiling water for Pesaḥ.

PLATE 59   Kneading dough for *maẓẓa*.

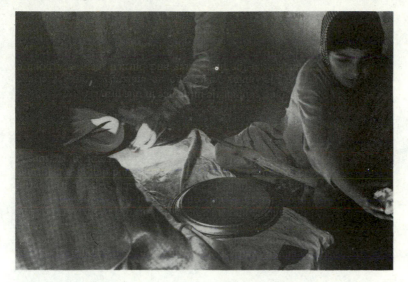

PLATE 60   Rolling out *mazza* flat cakes.

PLATE 61   An Israeli emissary chats with a Yeshiva teacher as they wait for their order to be baked at one of three privately owned Shirazi *mazza* "factories".

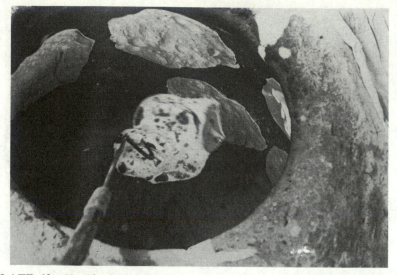

PLATE 62   Hooking the finished *maẓẓa*, the baker pulls it off the oven wall.

home and stored in cloth bags until use; by that time they are so hard, that many Shirazis place a damp rag on top of the ones to be used for the Pesaḥ meal.

The day before Pesaḥ is a fast day for the first born son (*ge'ulat bkhor*). If the child is too young to fast, his father or mother fasts for him.

The preparations for Pesaḥ are long and tedious and involve the entire family. The holiday, too, differs from other holidays, in that the whole family is involved in its various rituals. The first two evenings, of Pesaḥ, the *khanevadeh* eats together as it is desirable to have a minimum of three males present for a quorum.[1] The *seder* (order), as Ashkenazim call it, is referred to as "*aggada*", meaning "legend". In the past, during the reading of the *aggada* text, the story of the exodus from Egypt was acted out in detail by the members of the family. Remnants of this practice are still extant: at the recitation of "this is the bread of affliction", every member of the family, including women, recite the verses and hold a tray on their shoulders like slaves; at the *dayyenu* prayer, everyone beats each other with leeks in memory of the lashes received by the slaves. The *afiqoman* (dessert) *maẓẓa* is twice the size of regular *maẓẓot* and is eaten at the conclusion of the meal amidst merriment and clow-

---

[1] The full quorum, *minyan* requires ten males to be present, but for some ritual purposes, a *mzuman* of three constitutes a secondary level of "community" sanctity.

ning contortions.[1] Instead of a sweet *ḥaroset* condiment, such as the Ashkenazim eat, Shirazis have a sour mixture of nut, green almonds, pomegranate juice, vinegar, cinnamon, sugar, raisins and wine called: *'alaqiye*. No bitters are available in Shiraz, so lettuce which is at least slightly bitter is consumed instead.

The second evening of *mo'ed*, before *aggada*, the synagogues are packed as everyone comes to hear the *sfira* (counting) blessing. The biblical commandment to count 49 days by sheaves (*'omer*) to the festival of Shavu'ot (Lev. 23 : 15) on the fiftieth day, has long been a focus of Jewish mystical practice. Shirazis faithfully throng the synagogues each evening of the counting period, which is further observed by prohibiting weddings and by not shaving (a stricture widely observed in the past, but not very common nowadays).

During the intermediate days of Pesaḥ, many men are on vacation. The entire family goes then to live with the wife's parents. On the eighth day, Shirazis go picnicking in the gardens and the opportunity is seized by young adults to prospect for potential mates.

YOM HA'AẒMA'UT

Israel Independence Day, is sometimes celebrated by taking a holiday and picnicking in the gardens.

LAG BA'OMER

Lag Ba'omer, the thirty-third day of counting the *'omer* is celebrated by singing about the sainted rabbi, Bar Yoḥay, and having a special *drasha* (sermon) at *knisa* in honor of the occasion.

SHAVU'OT (*MO'EDE GOL* – "FESTIVAL OF FLOWERS")

Nothing very special happens on Shavu'ot; indeed the only thing festive about it is that no mundane work is done and time is spent in *knisa*. The

---

[1] Bash-e Khan, the chief *gabay*, ate the *afiqoman* with his right hand placed in back of his head so that he reached up over his *left* shoulder to bite at it. No reason was forthcoming in explanation of this practice. For many Jewish communities, the *afiqoman* is an object of ritual joking. Among Ashkenazim it is customary for a young child to steal this *maẓẓa* and retain it until ransomed by the *seder* leader. The *afiqoman* is often attributed magical powers: in medieval Europe, it was hung to keep away the evil eye; in Kurdistan, it was kept with stored grain and salt to ensure sustenance; and in Morocco, it was believed capable of restoring stormy seas to calm when tossed overboard (Goodman, 1962:379).

first evening is devoted to all-night study, usually in a house of mourning; these sessions are not particularly well attended and the illiterate do not go at all. At morning services, a special prayer called *ktuba* (wedding contract) is read. At the first day Tora reading of the Ten Commandments, the *knisa* is packed. Shavu'ot is the occasion when a Tora may be donated to the synagogue, an event which occasions singing and great joy as the procession winds through the Mahalleh. It is customary to eat dairy foods, but no great fuss is made and the meals are much like on weekdays. The use of fire is permitted on holidays and few ritual restrictions are observed.

TISH'A B'AV (*ZAQARUN* – "MEMORIAL DAY")

From the minor fast of the 17th of Tammuz until the 9th of 'Av, a three week period of mourning is observed for the destruction of the Temple. Like *sfira*, these three weeks are without weddings or festive events and many men refrain from shaving. From the first of 'Av, no meat is slaughtered except in honor of the Sabbath.

Zaqarun is a full day fast, but not everyone observes it strictly anymore. People gather for *'arvit* in the courtyard of the *knisa*. In the past the synagogues were draped in black as were the Tora scrolls (Mizrahi, 1957 : 369–372), possibly in imitation of Muslim Ashura practice. The Book of Lamentations is read in translation and dirges (*qinot*) are chanted; there is much crying. Afterwards, the lights are turned off and a funeral oration (*misped*) given. This usually lasts more than forty minutes and the preacher harangues the congregation, blaming the destruction of the Temple and the harsh *galut* on the Jews themselves and Shirazi Jews in particular. One *shaliah zibbur*, for example, lambasted his congregants for using money on the Sabbath, complaining that such violation of the Shabbat would be reason enough for the people of Israel's misfortunes.

In the morning, worship is held sitting on the floor of the *knisa*. In most synagogues, prayer shawl (*zizit*) and phylacteries (*tfillin*) are not worn, but Otsar Hatorah teachers have instituted a new custom of wearing them, explaining that not everyone comes to *minha* worship and thus would miss the opportunity to do so. Lamentations and *qinot* are recited again and later in the day, *haft baradaran* (Seven Brothers), the story of Hannah and her seven sons, is recited in Judaeo-Persian. Some older men also read Job. Jewish beggars do much begging on *zaqarun* and the people are more generous than usual. In the afternoon, there are *kapparot* (animal sacrifices as sin offerings) in the various synagogues after *minha*; many animals are sacrificed and their meat is given to the poor.

PLATE 63 The recitation of *qinot* (dirges) on Tish'a B'av night in the courtyard of Knisa Kohanim evokes weeping and remorse from the assembled worshippers.

SLIḤOT (PENITENTIAL SEASON) – FROM THE FIRST OF 'ELLUL TO YOM KIPPUR

Beginning the first day of 'Ellul, people gather in *knisa* every weekday morning between 3.00 and 4.00 a.m. for penitential prayers. Only about 10% of the men and just a handful of women attend regularly. Many prayers are translated into Judaeo-Persian by the *shaliaḥ ẓibbur* and there is considerable self-searching and wailing over sins and the punishment suffered for them.

ROSH HASHANA

It is traditional to make the pilgrimage to the shrine of Seraḥ bat Asher on this occasion. Those remaining home, enjoy Rosh Hashana as a time of feasting. A special order of blessings on various kinds of food is required on both the first and second night. The foods include: dates, black-eyed peas, leeks, beets or sugar beets, squash, pomegranates, apples and honey, and the lungs and heads of sheep, fowl or fish. These blessings are in accordance with the Baghdadi liturgical rite. Morning worship includes numerous additional prayers and lasts as much as $5\frac{1}{2}$ hours. The highlight of the worship is the blowing of the shofar (ram's horn) at which time the *knisa* is filled to capacity. The shofar is blown frequently and, in accordance with the Sfardic tradition, during the silent *'amida* prayer and at the final *qaddish*. Although the *'avinu malkenu* prayer was not traditionally said on the Sabbath in Shiraz, Shirazis adopted the Baghdadi custom of saying it about ten years ago. On the afternoon of the first day, *tashlikh*[1] prayers are said by the pool in the courtyard of the *knisa*.

ZUM GDALYA (FAST OF GDALYA)

The day following Rosh Hashana is called: "*barabar kippur*", or "opposite Kippur". Shirazi Jews believe that this is a practice-fast for Yom Kippur and only the learned know its true meaning (see Table 11).

YOM KIPPUR (*KIPPUR* – "ATONEMENT", *ADIR* – "MIGHTY")

The evening prceding Yom Kippur, a *shoḥet* goes from house to house to perform *kappara*. A rooster or hen for each male or female respectively, is slaughtered, after first being passed over the heads of each member of the household with the appropriate verses of the atonement sacrifice. The pious take blood from the *kappara* which has dripped onto the earth and this is mixed with ashes and the blessing *kissuy haddam b'afar* is recited (Manzur, 1951 : 4). The pious perform *kappara* at about 3.00 a.m., just prior to *sliḥot*.

After *shaḥarit* (morning worship), men take turns sitting in "courts" of three "judges", to free each other from vows, curses, and the evil eye as they recite *hattarat ndarim* and *hattarat qlalot* according to the Sfardic rite. Then each male in turn removes his shirt, faces the wall and leans against it with his right hand over left as the *shaliaḥ zibbur* lightly[2] bestows on each man's back thirty-nine lashes with a leather strap. These *makkot* represent the forty lashes minus one, which were actually given out by the courts in ancient Israel for violations of religious law;

---

[1] This custom of symbolically casting one's sins into water is first noted in medieval Europe and probably entered the Shirazi rite in the last 150 years.

[2] In Kurdistan, these lashes are applied heavily (Brauer, 1947:259).

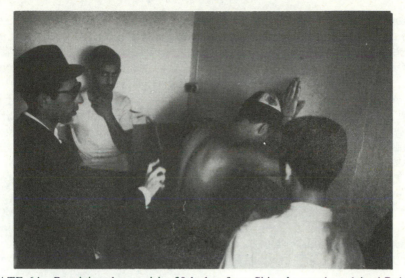

PLATE 64   Receiving the requisite 39 lashes from Shiraz' recently ordained Rabbi, on Erev Yom Kippur.

every Jew is presumed guilty of sins meriting such punishment. At the conclusion of these ceremonies, many people go to the cemetery.

Minḥa is said at about 3.00 p.m. and then the men go to the *maqve*, immersing themselves three times. Everyone eats chicken as the final meal before the fast. This fast is strictly observed by all males and females over the age of thirteen.

At *'arvit*, the evening service, all of the Tora scrolls to be held during the recitation of the *kol nidre* prayer are auctioned. Many individual prayers, ritual honors for the whole year to come, and parts of the *knisa* are auctioned; large sums are pledged on this day. The reciting of the *sheheḥeyanu* [1] blessing is the greatest honor auctioned. At its recitation, the author was struck by a communally shared emotion of great fear; several times during the day, there were several such ecstatic moments when emotions wavering between fear and awe were manifest. This deep emotional response, which was explained as fear of retribution for sins committed, occurs only on Yom Kippur. Customarily, silent prayers are recited out loud on Yom Kippur to enable the illiterate to participate in the worship.

In addition to fasting, one is forbidden to drink, wash, wear leather

---

[1] "Blessed are You, Lord our God, King of the universe who has given us life and sustenance, and brought us to this occasion."

shoes or sleep in a bed. The pious sleep in the *knisa* and the more careful among them do not sleep at all, but read psalms all night. The very pious also dress in white as a sign of purity. In the past, the *shaliaḥ ẓibbur* used to wear a white turban at *musaf*, the additional service, as, according to Shirazi tradition, did Aaron the High Priest.

At night, *'arvit* lasts about four hours; the daytime worship begins at 6.00 a.m. and lasts until sundown. Most people remain in the *knisa* all day, and toward mid-afternoon, many men take a siesta in their places. The synagogues rent extra chairs to handle the large crowds. At dusk the fast is proclaimed at an end by the sounding of the shofar.

During the period from Rosh Hashana to Yom Kippur one greets his neighbors with the expression *tizku lshanim rabot, tovot vn'imot* (may you merit many good and pleasant years). At the end of the Yom Kippur fast one says: *ta'anit vtshuva mqubbal* (may your fast and repentance be accepted).

SUKKOT (*MO'EDE SUKKA* – "THE HOLIDAY OF THE TABERNACLE")

The day following Yom Kippur everyone begins to construct a *sukka* (tabernacle) in his yard. The frames of wood, saved from year to year, are taken out of storage and set up. Nowadays, the *shakh*, or special roof greens, are also saved because the government forbids the cutting of public trees for this purpose. The walls of the *sukka* are of cloth or sometimes Qashqai woven mats (*gelims*). Furniture consists of some chairs, wooden benches, a carpet and perhaps a table. The *sukka* is decorated with hanging fruit, onion mobiles and pictures of Moshe Dayan and of Moses. Families eat all their meals in the *sukka*; *mishmara* (vigil) for the dead is held there and children also do their homework there. One curious aspect of *sukka* construction is that sticks and logs are tied together with string or cloth, because Shirazis believe that just as nails were forbidden in the construction of the ancient Temple in Jerusalem, so, too, they are forbidden in *sukka* construction.

Few Shirazi Jews own a *lulav* (palm branch) or *'etrog* (citron). The citron is imported from Israel or comes from Bam in eastern Iran; there are rarely more than two or three dozen in the whole city of Shiraz. Since it is proper for everyone to make the appropriate blessing over the *lulav* and *'etrog* on Sukkot, those fortunate enough to own them are motivated by the acquisition of the religious merit and personal prestige to conspicuously place them in the centre of the *knisa* so that everyone might make this blessing. *Lulav* construction lacks the elaborately woven palm receptacles for the willow and myrtle such as are found in the United States and in Israel. The three branches of willow and two of

PLATE 65   The *sukka* of the chief *gabay*.

PLATE 66   The *lulav* is prepared prior to eating dinner, on the first night of Sukkot.

PLATE 67   Hosha'na Rabba all-night study vigil in the *sukka*.

myrtle are arranged alternately and tied to the *lulav* by three strips of palm leaf.

In the past, Jews used to close their businesses throughout the holiday, but very few do this today. During the seven days of Sukkot it is customary to read the whole Tora at home, privately.

Hosha'na Rabba, or "*arava*" (willow), is celebrated on the seventh day of Sukkot. As on Shavu'ot, there is an all-night prayer vigil; psalms, penitential prayers and the Tora are read. *Ptirat Moshe*, a poem on the death of Moses, is read in Judaeo-Persian amidst great weeping. This *yeshuva*, or "sitting", all night, is supposed to be concluded with the blowing of a shofar, but most Shirazis refrain for fear of disturbing their Muslim neighbors. Morning attendance at *knisa* is good and everyone participates in the *hosha'not* (salvation prayers) procession around the *knisa*. *Ta'arof* deferral is discarded and the loudest singer leads each circuit of the synagogue. The beating of the willows usually takes place outside of the *knisa*, but not many participate in this ritual.

Mizraḥi (1959:54) describes a nightly celebration held during the Sukkot holiday called *simḥat bet hasho'eva* (the joy of the house of the water-drawing). This celebration included feasting, singing and dancing. Shirazis claim that they have not observed this celebration for several hundred years.

Shmini 'Aẓeret and Simhat Tora follow immediately after Sukkot. On these two days, attendance at *knisa* is low and many people spend the day picnicking in the gardens. On Simḥat Tora, boys march around the *knisa* with torches made from a candle placed at the end of a long stick. A time of great joy, Simḥat Tora processions are accompanied by singing and merry-making. Every male present in *knisa* is called to the Tora on Simḥat Tora.

MEDAK OR *MO'ED QATAN* "LITTLE FESTIVAL"

This is a minor holiday celebrating the deliverance of Shirazi Jews from their enemies. The following stories are offered by way of explaining this indigenous holiday.

About 200 to 250 years ago, an important Jew, insulted by his fellow Jews, decided to revenge himself on them. A dog's head was placed in a Tora container with a sign saying "Husseyn" and put in the *knisa* of the important religious leaders. This Jew then reported to the Muslims that on Ashura, Jews place the head of a dog in a Tora case and call it Husseyn. That night the caretaker of the *knisa* repeatedly dreamt that the ark was on fire and that a Tora was burning. He finally investigated and found the planted evidence. He ran to Mulla Rahim,[1] the chief *dayan*, and together they burned the sign and disposed of the head. The next morning, during *shaḥarit*, hundreds of Muslims descended on the *knisa* threatening death to all Jews if the information they had received proved correct. The Jews called them fools and asked them to inspect the Tora scrolls themselves. When the scrolls were found intact with no sign of the planted evidence, the Muslims left angrily. The once proud Jew tried to convert to Islam, but was refused and he fled to Baghdad.

Binning (1857, I : 271) reports that the incident described above by informants occurred one year before his visit to Shiraz in 1851. According to another tradition.:

About 150 (sic!) years ago, a *sayyid*, the chief *akhond* of Shiraz, produced a book written thirty to forty years earlier by a converted Jew, which proved that the Tora predicted the coming of Muhammad. The Jews were given thirty days to decide whether to convert or be exiled from the city. The Jews were worried, but their *dayan* told them everything would be all right. The *sayyid* meanwhile became more and more self-righteous, even lambasting the Shah by calling him a dog. The day before the decree of the *sayyid* was to be enacted, 3,000 agents of the Shah surrounded his house and took him, bound and gagged, to Teheran. Nasser ad-Din Shah was going to have him hung, but a vizier pleaded that the *akhond* would be willing to repent for his misdeeds. He was returned to Shiraz, where he is said to have behaved very well towards the Jews from that day on.

The third account deals with the persecutions under the aegis of Abul Hassan Lari. According to the reference, this apostate Jew died under

---

[1] Mulla Rahim Dayar was one of the addressees in a letter from Calcutta, June 11, 1848. (Musleah 1975:66)

mysterious circumstances in Bushehr on the 2nd of Heshvan (Alliance, 1903:107).[1]　Shirazis were said to have greeted one another: *"mo'ed qatan! abul hassan"* (Alliance, 1903:106).

While *medak* is no longer observed by most Shirazi Jews and although most Jews have no idea what it is all about, it is unique in Iran as the only reported indigenously evolved Jewish holiday.

HANUKKA

This is not a very significant holiday. The only ritual is the lighting of the candles each night at home and in the *knisa*. Many families still use oil lamps for Hanukka. The first night, one light plus the serving *shamash* is lit. Each night thereafter, one additional lamp is lit. In addition, one lamp for each male member of the household is lit every night, so that in one family of nine sons and the father, a total of nineteen lamps were burning on the final night of the festival.

SHOVAVIM

The letters of this word are the initials of the Hebrew names of the first six weekly Tora readings from Exodus. During these six weeks, men are supposed to fast on the first day of the first week, the second day of the second week and so forth. The second and fifth week are special, and on those weeks one is expected to fast both the second and fifth days. The reason given for the *shovavim* fast is the sin of *qeri*, or thinking lewd thoughts about pretty women. Shirazis say: *"shovavim tiq'u vateze'u"* (The wild you shall strike and cast out).[2]

On Tu Bshvat (15th of Shvat) everyone eats many kinds of fruit.

PURIM

The Sabbath preceding Purim is called *zakhor* (remember). Besides the special Tora and Prophetical readings, the highlight of the day is a special dramatic reading in Judaeo-Persian of a poem, *mi kamokha, v'en kamokha* (Who is like unto You, and there are none like unto You). Many songs are distributed throughout the text.

On Purim eve, everyone goes to the *mgilla* (scroll of Esther) reading,

---

[1] The chronicle source of this story reports that Abul Hassan was actually killed in Farahabad on the Caspian (Bacher, 1906, 52:241–242).

[2] *Shovavim* is of medieval Austrian origin (Zimmels, 1958:194) and was probably introduced to Shirazis in the past 100 years, through kabbalistic works.

PLATE 68   Lighting the Ḥanukka candles in Knisa Shokr.

often in someone's home. During the reading, when the name of Haman is mentioned, boys strike the walls or floors with a homemade device, the end of which contains an explosive cap which goes off like a cherry bomb. The *mgilla* is read like a letter and allowed to trail on the floor.

At about 2.00 a.m., a son-in-law and his family are expected to visit his wife's father for a Purim feast. This is supposed to be the time of night Esther went in to speak with Aḥashverosh (Esther V). A full meal is served, with special Purim sweets. At about 5.00 a.m., children sneak out of the house into the *kuche* with a homemade effigy of Haman which they burn with great joy.[1] Later everyone again goes to hear the *mgilla* reading. On the 15th of 'Adar, or Shushan Purim, only the recitation of Psalm 60 sets it apart from other days. While many Shirazis expressed a desire to go to Hamadan on Purim to the tomb of Esther and

---

[1] Muslim children, identifying Haman with Omar, sometimes join in the fun.

Mordekhay, the weather is usually prohibitively cold and wet to undertake such an extensive trip in winter.

There are numerous other ritual occasions during the year: each New Moon, the 10th of Tevet fast, the Fast of Esther preceding Purim and *Birkat 'Ilanot* (the blessing of the trees) during the month of Nisan. New fast days such as the 7th of 'Adar (the death of Moses) and the 5th of 'Av (death of the 'Ari) have been added to the calendar in recent years. There is at least one special sacred day each month of the year and most months have more.

RITES DE PASSAGE

In Shiraz, as elsewhere, ritual is closely connected with the various stages of life passage.

MILA

Jewish males undergo *mila*, or "circumcision", just as the Muslims do. *Mila* for Jews occurs on the eighth day after birth. The rite may be postponed only if the child is sickly or if a parent is not well. Boys are named at circumcision and girls are named the Sabbath after their birth, in *knisa*. Boys are rarely named for living relatives, but name chains could probably be derived for Shirazi Jews, such as Peters notes for the Cyrenican Beduin (1960:33), if only people could recall their genealogies. Today, most children have a Persian civil name and a Hebrew ritual name. The two names are often related by the same first letters as is common among American Jews.

Mila takes place during the daylight hours, either at home or in the *knisa*. At home, among the wealthy, it is accompanied by a big party with entertainment by professional musicians. In *knisa* it is a more modest affair; only wine and candy are served; later a meal is prepared at home for close kin.

On weekdays, the *abu'aben* (father of the son) puts on *ẓiẓit* (prayer shawl) and *tfillin* (phylacteries) for the ceremony. This is done so that the boy will be brought up to the study of Tora and the worship of God. A *sandaq* (godfather) is chosen from among one's kinsmen by the father, with an eye toward an expected reciprocation from the one so honored.

The child is brought to the site of circumcision amidst singing. He is carried on a white pillow and is swaddled in green.[1] The baby's head is

---

[1] Green is a symbol of luck and fertility.

covered by a green or white hood, to which is attached a gold-encased cube of salt, to ward off the evil eye. Covering the child is an imported old white mesh silk shawl embroidered with silver. Near his feet lies a sprig of green leaf. Tucked under the swaddling straps is a piece of bread sprinkled with salt to keep away the evil eye and the *nshamot* (spirits).

The child is placed on the lap of the *sandaq*, on a white cloth, and the *sandaq* firmly grasps his legs to keep them apart. The preparations completed and the blessings said, the *mohel* (circumcisor) rubs some ash on the penis. No clamps are used to hold the foreskin. Rather, the foreskin is grasped between thumb and forefinger, pulled out and severed with a straight cut made with a razor, scalpel or, the sort of knife used by the *shohet* to slaughter chickens. The foreskin is then thrown into a basket of ash. The skin remaining is pushed back over the penis, to which powdered penicillin is applied. The penis is bandaged in white gauze and then often covered with a green bandage. The child is then reswaddled. During the entire procedure, one of the older men takes some *araq* on his middle finger and places it in the child's mouth to suck on.

The operation is no more bloody than similar circumcisions in the United States and it is far quicker, since no clamps are used to retract the foreskin. In Kurdistan, according to Brauer (1947:140), the *mohel* shows everyone his bloody fingers and the *sandaq* proclaims "behold the blood', but no such custom was observed in Shiraz.

The foreskin is usually buried in the courtyard. A woman sometimes grabs it when no one is looking and swallows it, believing that by doing so she guarantees that her next child will be a male. Similar customs are reported among Jews in Kurdistan (Brauer, 1947:140) and in North Africa (Briggs and Guede, 1964:26).

BEN MIZVA

Although very important in many parts of the Jewish dispersion, *ben mizva* (Bar Mizvah) is of little significance in Shiraz. The occasion has nothing to do with a boy's first *'aliya* (literally "going up") to the Tora, which may occur at age seven or eight. Rather, the occasion marks the first time a boy puts on *tfillin* (phylacteries). Often, a boy may not receive his *tfillin* until age fifteen or sixteen, and sometimes not at all. *Ben mizva* is usually held on a Monday or Thursday, so that the boy can be called to the Tora

The author knows of no parties for *ben mizva* in Shiraz, although they were observed in Yazd and Kerman. Otsar Hatorah has been encouraging the revitalization of this ceremony, but so far the celebration consists of throwing candy, and cheers (*kelele*) of the women. Until the

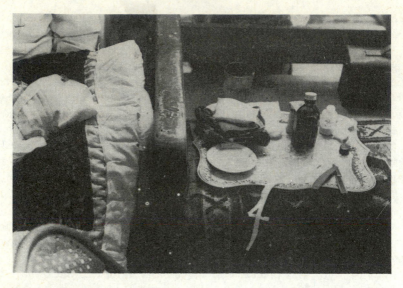

PLATE 69   *Mila*: baby is brought into the room on a green velvet pillow (left) as circumcision utensils are spread out – note the salt crystal amulet on baby's hood.

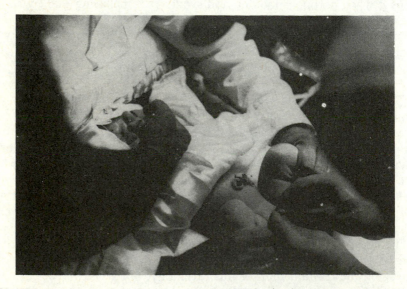

PLATE 70   As the foreskin is stretched, the baby is given some *araq* to suck.

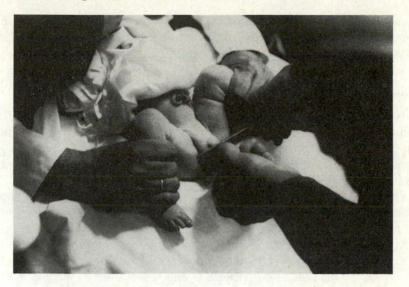

PLATE 71   The *mohel* cuts the foreskin without benefit of clamps.

PLATE 72   After *mila*, the chief *gabay* and leading *darshan* (preacher) get into a friendly dispute with the *abu 'aben* dressed in *tallit* and *tfillin*.

present, *ben mizva* is insignificant to the Shirazi because it has little meaning as a rite of passage. It brings no prestige, religious stature, duties or privileges.

MARRIAGE

It is not the author's intention to present a complete account here of the steps involved in betrothal and marriage, but to consider its ceremonial aspects.[1] The betrothal customs and most of the marriage customs are common to Jews all over Iran and Kurdistan (Brauer, 1947; Mizraḥi, 1959; Patai, 1947).

In Shiraz, the prospective groom takes the initiative in obtaining a wife. He may have someone specific in mind or he, or a kinsman, may go to a *daleleh*, a professional matchmaker. When the prospective bride is chosen, representatives of the groom's family are sent to discuss the match. If it is acceptable to the bride's family, a flower is given to the family of the groom. The betrothal is announced and a party is held at the bride's house, where sweets are presented to the future bride by the groom.

A few days before the wedding, henna is applied to the palms and soles of the bride. The following day, a party is given for the bride at the bath, and the next day for the groom; both parties are at the groom's expense. The day before the wedding, the bride goes to the *maqve* for ritual immersion; some women do this at the spring near the tomb of Sa'adi, as Muslims do.

The wedding party, at the expense of the bride's father, is peculiar to Shiraz; the groom pays only for the musicians. In the past men and women used to celebrate in separate rooms (Mizraḥi, 1959:89), but today, they sit together at Shiraz wedding parties which are held out-of-doors in the courtyard. In the past, the wedding ceremony itself used to take place after the feast, but because heavy drinking sometimes led to arguments over contract terms, the ceremony is nowadays held before the party.

The wedding day is most commonly a Thursday, since for many Friday is a day off from work. For ritual reasons weddings are not held during *Sfira* (7 weeks), the three weeks preceding Tish'a B'av, and rarely during Sliḥot or until after Sukkot.[2] Few weddings ever take place

---

[1] See Loeb, 1974.

[2] An Isfahani informant reported that weddings are not performed there in the Hebrew month of Marheshvan (October–November), because that was the time of the *Flood* in the days of Noah.

December to February because of the cold. No weddings occur during Ramadan or Muharram out of respect for the Muslims. Opportunities for weddings are thus severely restricted.

The *qiddushin* (sanctification) ceremony is much like that of other Jews. First the bride and groom sign the government registration and then, the *ktuba*. The latter contract must be witnessed and is binding with regard to money exchanged, obligation of the groom in case of divorce and any additional stipulations agreed upon by the parties. The bride and groom sit during the ceremony. The bride is veiled in green. The groom empowers the *dayan* to act in his behalf and recite the marriage blessings. Traditionally, there is no *huppa*, or "canopy", over the couple. A new custom among the elite is to hold a *ẓiẓit* over the couple, but this has not yet fully caught on.

After the *'erusin* (betrothal) blessings over the wine, the bride and groom share wine from one cup, the groom drinking first, while the *dayan* drinks from a second cup in accordance with the Sfardic tradition (Zimmels, 1958:180). The groom then gives the bride a silver coin[1] and recites after the *dayan*, word by word:

> *hare at maqqudeshet li bmatbe'a zo kesef, bifne ile sade gubrin ya'udayi kasheri kadat moshe vyisra'el.*
>
> Behold, you are sanctified to me, with this silver coin, before these assembled witnesses (who are) fit Jewish men, according to the custom of Moses and Israel.

The statement is then translated into Persian. The bride, in response, may give the groom a sugar cone, as a symbol of a sweet life together. The groom then takes the glass and smashes it against the wall above the head of the bride, or throws it at the floor.

The *dayan* gives a short explanation of the ten duties of the husband to his wife. Then the *dayan* proclaims: "may the mouths of all enemies of the bride and groom who wish them ill be shut up forever". At that moment the mother of the groom closes a lock, symbolically locking out the "enemy" while sealing the bond between her son and daughter-in-law. If a rejected suitor is present and can lock his own lock before the groom's mother can close her's, he will symbolically lock the groom out of the bride, thereby preventing consummation, while cementing the bond between himself and the bride. He then throws the key into a pit to prevent this extra-marital "bond" from dissolving. To avoid such magic,

---

[1] The coin usually used is a two *rial* piece of the Reza Shah period. The coin may be made into a ring for the bride or she may save the coin and give it to her daughter.

the *qiddushin* is unannounced and is often held in the morning in some far-off garden.

The *sheva' brakhot* (seven benedictions) are then recited over wine; the bride and groom again drink from one cup, while the *dayan* drinks from a second.

The *dayan* presents the bride with the *ktuba* and the groom says:

> *Qabali keteboykhi vidoykhi base li la'intu bifne ile sade qubrin yahudayi kasheri kadat moshe vyisra'el.*[1]

> "I accept your contract and with this in your hands you (become) my wife before these assembled witnesses (who are) fit Jewish men, according to the custom of Moses and Israel."

This, too, is translated into Persian. The bride may then give the sugar cone to the groom if she had not done so before. The bride and groom kiss and then the groom kisses the *dayan*. Finally, a cock is passed over the head of the groom and a hen over the head of the bride, while the appropriate *kappara* verses are said as on the day before Yom Kippur. The chickens are slaughtered and the meat given to the poor.

After the *qiddushin* and feast, the groom brings the bride to his house. Today, the custom is to drive to the tomb of Saadi first, as do the Muslims. Previously, when the Jews lived together in the Mahalleh, the bride was led through the streets, to the accompaniment of music, to the groom's house. On occasion, Muslims annoyed the small procession. Today, Jews are afraid to be so conspicuous.

As the bride enters the house, she is supposed to knock her head against the doorpost while entering the bridal chamber, to indicate her submission to her husband. Jews refer to the bridal chamber as the *ḥuppa*. The room is decorated with streamers, and the bedding is especially embroidered for the occasion. Next door, the musicians and guests play music, sing, and feast until dawn. The bride's father recites the *shirat hayyam* (Song of the Sea) (Ex. XV), before the couple retires for the night.

It is generally agreed that the bride and groom do not consummate the marriage on the first night. Formerly, the morning after the wedding, the mother of the groom would invite a *mama* (midwife) to inspect her daughter-in-law's hymen. Later a bowl of *nogle* (white rice candy) covered by a white handkerchief was placed in the room with the understanding that the bride was to make use of the handkerchief at consummation. The handkerchief was later placed back over the candy, and

---

[1] This text is similar to one found in an old Persian prayer book manuscript (see Adler, 1898:618).

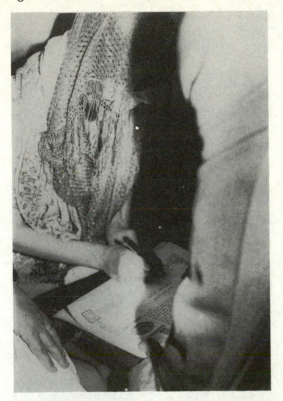

PLATE 73   The bride, wearing a green veil, signs the *ktuba*.

the mother of the groom would display the blood stained candy to her mother and then to the *dayan*. Today, the doctor sometimes examines the bride before the wedding, but proof of virginity is no longer always insisted upon. The initial delay in consummating the marriage, some explain, is because the groom needs a day to work up his courage. If there is blood after the first intercourse, the couple must refrain for a week, and after the bride's ritual immersion, on the eighth day, they can resume.

During the week following the wedding the bride and groom are not permitted to leave the house unaccompanied. Each day there are guests at the house, who bring presents and feast and celebrate with music. On Shabbat morning, a delegation from the *knisa* comes to escort the groom. He, his family and his wife's family receive the chief honors of the day in *knisa*, to the accompaniment of singing, *keleles* of the women and throwing of candy. *Sheva' brakhot* (the Seven Blessings) are recited

PLATE 74 The bride accepts a coin from the groom who recites the betrothal verse.

over wine, as the bride and groom stand together at the cessation of worship; the only time they will every do so in *knisa*. The groom, who is presented with a suitcase.or tray-full of clothing at the wedding, wears a new suit for this occasion. Formerly he was also escorted to *knisa* with singing on Friday night, but, with the disperal of Jewish settlement in Shiraz, this custom has been abandoned.

DEATH

Until the old cemetery southwest of the city was sequestered by the army around 1940, the dead were washed at home to the accompaniement of lamenting and wailing. The dead were then carried in open coffins to the cemetery with dirges and weeping and, if an especially beloved son had died, sorrowful Persian poetry was sung to the accompani-

PLATE 75 The groom's mother seals the marriage bond by closing a padlock. (Note: her neck tattoo was probably an intended goiter cure.)

ment of the *kemanje* (spiked fiddle). The funeral was held in the evening because Muslims would harass the procession during the day. Nowadays this is no longer neccesary.

When someone dies, word spreads more slowly than it did in the past. If the deceased is from outside the Mahalleh, the procession stops at the Mahalleh first and then proceeds to the cemetery. In this way the Mahalleh people receive the news and often spontaneously charter a bus to take them to the cemetery. Burial is usually on the day following death, during the morning. No burials are permitted on Sabbaths or on the first day of holidays. Those who die on these occasions, are often buried at night, at the conclusion of these special days.

The present Shiraz cemetery is located southeast of the city. Unlike the old cemetery, this one is walled and the graves are clearly identified, because the Muslims no longer deface the Jewish graves. Men are buried

PLATE 76   The groom holds a sugar cone given him by his bride as a symbol of sweet marital bliss.

PLATE 77   A *shoḥet* performs a *kappara* over the groom so that married life will begin in purity.

separately from women and those dying a violent death are sometimes buried apart from the others.

While the mourners sit in a chapel chanting dirges and wailing, the body is prepared for burial in a room next door. At the cemetery there may be violent disagreement regarding the thankless task of washing the body. Usually, someone in the family must do it, unless a *morde shur* (body washer) is available. Women wash a female and men wash a male. The underlying hostility to the performance of a "great tradition" positive duty, i.e., attending the dead, indicates that beneath the veneer of Jewish funerary practice lies a fundamental and intensive fear of death. Yet, as Malinowski puts it:

The testimony of the senses, the gruesome decomposition of the corpse, the visible disappearance of the personality – certain apparently instinctive suggestions of fear and horror seem to threaten man at all stages of culture with some idea of annihilation, with some hidden fears and forebodings. And here into this play of emotional forces, into this supreme dilemma of life and final death, religion steps in, selecting the positive creed, the comforting view, the culturally valuable belief in immortality, in the spirit independent of the body, and in the continuance of life after death. In the various ceremonies at death . . . religion gives body and form to the saving beliefs. (1954:51)

The body is unwrapped and laid out on a stone in the special room for the purpose. Before the ritual washing of the body, it is generally soaped and rinsed several times. Women and younger men are rinsed with a single large jug of water, after the washing pronounces the proper blessing. While the water is poured over a deceased male, the *morde shur* recites the names of the patriarchs: Abraham, Isaac, Jacob, Moses and others; if the deceased is female, then the names of the matriarchs are recited.

For a *zaddiq* (righteous man), usually a man over seventy, a special *rhiza gdola*, or "great washing", is performed. Many prayers are recited, and, before the large pitcher of water is poured over the body, cups of soapy water, salsola soda solution, water with myrtle leaves and pure water are alternately poured over the body. Altogether forty cups are used, symbolizing the forty lashes due for violating various religious commandments. Each cup is shattered, after use, as is the pitcher, since vessels coming in contact with the dead are impure, and there is danger that someone might drink from them.

The burial shrouds are usually prepared by one *shohet* who is adept at it. These are made from coarse white linen and include, for males, a special *tallit* and *zizit*. The deceased is formally dressed with pants, shirt, booties, mittens, turban, veil and finally in a cape with hood, all fabricated from the same white linen. Women's garments are less elaborate.

When the body is prepared, it is lifted onto an open coffin. The men carry it to the excavated grave, reciting psalms, while the women remain behind. The corpse is lowered from the coffin and placed face upward in the grave, which is nearly two meters deep. The grave is dug in such a way that narrow shelves line it a few inches above the body. Across the shelves are placed large stones.[1] Both head and feet extend into a hollowed out area so that neither are directly below the stones. Everyone present then throws dirt into the grave, while chanting *vhu raḥum* ("and He, being merciful . . ." Psalm 78:38). A *qaddish drabbanan*[2] (scholars' *qaddish*) is recited, and, as the procession retreats from the filled in grave, a second *qaddish* is recited in the presence of the women. The deceased's son recites *qaddish* at home, but not in the cemetery. Just prior to burial, those kinsmen one degree distant from the deceased, tear their outer clothing.

Mourning customs among Shirazi Jews are similar to those of Kurdish (Brauer, 1947) and Baghdadi (Sassoon, 1955:206) Jews. The mourners go immediately to the house of the deceased. Here they remain for *shiv'a*, "seven" days and nights. They are permitted to leave only on the Sabbath and on holidays, when they go to the former *knisa* of the deceased. In the house of mourning, men and women sit in separate rooms. Mourners sit on the floor, in the place of least honor, while nowadays, the others sit on chairs. Mourners eat, sleep and live in this room during the seven days. Mourning males wear a *shal* (shawl) around their shoulders. The *shal* is an old, elaborately embroidered Kerman or Kashmir wool-scarf. One explanation for this custom, known only in Shiraz, Yazd, and perhaps in Isfahan, is that the mourner is like a prisoner; he thus wears a chain around his neck. Others say that it represents sackcloth and ashes. The Muslims were once reported to have had a similar custom (Thevenot, 1687, II:93), but it is not known whether they maintain this tradition. In Baghdad, Jewish sons used to tie a kerchief around their necks (Sassoon, 1955:206).

During *shiv'a*, friends and acquaintances, Jew and gentile alike, pay their respects to the mourners. Jews time their visits to coincide with the three services of the day, in order to provide a quorum for the mourners to recite *qaddish*. One or more *mullas* are present to read the complete

---

[1] Such is also the case in Kurdistan (Brauer, 1947:166).

[2] The *qaddish* is a doxology, recited universally by Jewish mourners. The text, in the once vernacular Aramaic, is an affirmation of faith in God and serves as an important structural element in all Jewish worship (see Millgram, 1971:153–157).

Tora in the course of the seven days. Selections from the Prophets and Psalms are also read.

Mourning women do not cook and others must prepare the meals for them. Meat and liquor are not consumed by the mourners. Guests are served fruit, raisins, chickpeas and tea; the mourners do not eat nuts, which are a symbol of joy.

When *shiv'a* is over, mourners go to the cemetery and then return to their own homes, which have been especially cleaned to welcome them back. Mourners wash and change their clothing.

A secondary period of mourning, *shloshim* (thirty), continues until the thirtieth day. Mourners do not shave during this period and members of their kindred shave only in honor of the Sabbath. Mourners continue to abstain from meat and liquor during the thirty days. Women are permitted to cook during *shloshim*, but do not apply their eye make-up or henna. Mourners do not engage in sexual intercourse during *shloshim*. Men cannot work a full day as they must return to the house of the deceased each day for *minḥa* and *'arvit* services. At the conclusion of *shloshim*, mourners go to the cemetery, work themselves into an ecstasy of grief and then recite *qaddish*. Before returning home, they stop at the *knisa* to view the Tora and thereby rid themselves of the pollution of the dead. The kindred gathers in the house of the deceased and a large feast is served. Meat is consumed by the mourners for the first time, other than on Shabbat, when they are permitted to eat it even during *shloshim*. Mourners continue to refrain from participating in celebrations or going to the movies for a full year.

During the year of mourning, *qaddish* is recited by male mourners at every possible opportunity. Each mourner recites it as loudly and as quickly as he is able. During the first seven days of the twelfth month, the mourner ceases the recitation of *qaddish*, but then resumes it to the completion of the year.[1] For the entire span it is customary for the mourners to wear an amulet to ward off death. Mourners are thought to be especially vulnerable to a revisit.

A candle is donated to the *knisa* of the deceased to be lit there very evening. At home, an electric light burns all year and an oil lamp is lit on holidays in memory of the deceased. The blessings of the "fruit of the tree" and the "fruit of the earth" must be recited daily in the house of mourning. On Tu Bshvat, thirty-five kinds of fruit must be eaten there.

---

[1] The deceased is considered to be under divine judgement for a full twelve months. However, the full-year duration of this judgement is thought to apply only to the wicked. Since the mourner presumes that his kinsman does not fall into that category, the *qaddish* is recited for less than the full period. (Lamm, 1927:163).

Each week, on the day of death of the parent, a *mulla* is paid to read Tora during the whole day, in the house of the deceased. If the deceased was a *ẓaddiq*, a *mulla* comes and reads the book of Deuteronomy in the presence of a *minyan*, each New Moon. *Qaddish* is recited and a feast served.

Each Friday evening during *shloshim* and each Saturday morning throughout the first year, a *minyan* of kinsmen gathers in the house of the deceased for *mishmara* (the vigil). Special study texts, e.g. *ḥoq lyisra'el*, are read and prayers for the deceased are said. The *hashkava*, memorial prayer is also recited in *knisa* whenever a mourner receives a ritual honor. On Saturday evenings, *mishmara* is again held, and frequently a *drasha* (sermon) is given.

All-night study sessions on Hosha'na Rabba, Shavu'ot, and the evening *mgilla* reading on Purim, are observed in the house of the deceased as a *neder* (vow) of the mourners. This gathering, called a *yeshuva* (lit. "sitting") includes the consumption of food, which women kinsmen of the deceased prepare in their honor. Several times during the Hosha'na Rabba and Shavu'ot *yeshuva* the assembly goes through a ritual meal. The order begins with the smelling of a sweet fruit such as a citron, some flowers and myrtle and finally some grasses, each with a designated special blessing. Thence follows the consumption of some sort of halva, raisins, chickpeas or melon seeds, and finally liquor, each with its own blessing. This little ceremony is completed by recitation of the *hashkava* (Mizrahi, 1959:36-37).

If someone below the age of twenty dies, *shiv'a* and *shloshim* are kept, but *qaddish* and *mishmara* are not usually said. A stillborn child or one who dies within thirty days or so, is mourned only one day. The funeral is attended only by the nuclear family.

Yerẓe'it [1] ("memorial day") is observed in the following manner: On each anniversary of the death of the deceased, a *mulla* spends the day reading Tora in the deceased's former house. The kindred comes and feasts at lunch time. On the Sabbath nearest *yerẓe'it*, *mishmara* is observed. At *yerẓe'it*, mourners in *knisa* are permitted to remove an additional Tora, which is read simultaneously with the main Tora; *'aliyot* are distributed among the kin of the deceased. The first *yerẓe'it* signifies the end of mourning and mourners can return to their normal activities.

---

[1] The term is of Judaeo-German origin (Jahrzeit) and may be of fairly recent import. It is, however, found in medieval law codes and kabbalistic writings of the seventeenth century and thus may have been diffused hundreds of years ago and adapted in Judaeo-Persian usage.

SORCERY, MAGIC AND THE SPIRIT WORLD

Although dabbling in magic is expressly forbidden in the Jewish "great tradition", Old World Jewish communities have often had numbers of ostensibly pious people employed as sorcerers, amulet makers and fortune-tellers. In most cases this magic was made to serve the ends of the gentile rather than the Jewish world and we shall indicate that this was also the case in Iran. The prestige of the Jewish "sorcerer" was doubtlessly enhanced by his literacy, which, in the semi-literate medieval world was identified with mystery and secretiveness, a pattern of belief maintained since it was foistered upon the middle eastern public by the priests of ancient Sumer. But there may be authentically Jewish roots for some magical practice: the *kohanim*, who are given special ritual status (and perhaps social status) because of their powers of blessing, are also believed to have the power of curse! Furthermore, there are widespread Jewish "little traditions" about the spirit world and the necessity for coping with its assumed hostile intent towards humankind (see Trachtenberg, 1939).

In the popular mind, the importance and even the stereotyping of the Persian Jewish sorcerer was already well established in the first millennium C.E. One such magician is described in Ferdosi's tenth century epic "*Shahnameh*". For a while he is held in esteem for the magic he performs for Zuran, but eventually he is executed for his evil mindedness.

The Jewish magician can be classified in economic terms as amateur or professional, but there seem to be little difference between the two in actual practice. The professional, relying on his practice as a major source of income, usually has greater recourse to literature and generally being literate is to be depended upon for more important fortune-telling and for the manufacture of amulets.

PREVENTATIVE OR AVOIDANCE MAGIC

The pattern of behaviour associated with "*ayin hara*" or *cheshm-e bad*, "the evil eye", is the primary example of this form of magic. The evil eye belief is akin to Evans-Pritchard's Zande concept of witchcraft (1937). While it is thought that malevolence is intended, there is no suggestion that the giver of the evil eye actually can control the power. In fact, all people are potential givers of the evil eye, so that certain precautions are routinely taken to avoid untoward hostility. Verbal statements are couched in negative terms: the mother of the beautiful child is told that he/she is ugly; if one slips, and says, for example: "my son is very smart", the blessing "*masha'alla*", i.e. "may God preserve him (from the evil eye)" is immediately added. Since manifestation of the evil eye can only be observed with hindsight, ceremonies are performed for anyone who may have been subject to exposure. The following procedures generally take place Saturday night:

A whole raw egg is passed over the hands, feet and the back of the head of the subject. The following formula is recited:

> "*cheshm-e in ke midune*
> *cheshm-e in ke nemidune*
> *cheshm-e in ke bade*
> *cheshm-e in ke as darvaze ke birun mire*
> *cheshm-e in ke darvaze dakhel mishe*"

Loosely translated, this formula means:

> For the bestower of the evil eye who knows of it
> For the bestower of the evil eye who does not know
> For the wicked bestower of the evil eye
> For the bestower of the evil eye who leaves town
> For the bestower of the evil eye who has just arrived ...

The egg is thrown at the eastern wall [1] (that is where God listens best) outside of the house, or is given as *ẓdaqa* to the poor.

A second ceremony requires the taking of wild rue, powdered salt and a crystal of alum. The rue is mashed between the fingers as the previous formula is recited. The crushed rue, salt and alum crystal are mixed and passed over the head of the apparent victim in a circular manner, while the practitioner recited:

cheshm-e yek shambe zaa	the eye of Sunday born ...
cheshm-e do shambe zaa	the eye of Monday born ...
. . .	. . .
cheshm-e adine zaa. . .	the eye of Friday born ...

The entire mixture is thrown into the fire as everyone witnesses the melting of the alum crystal which resembles a bubbling eye. When the center core of the "eye" dissolves it stares vacantly like a blind eye, symbolizing the blinding of the evil eye. The practitioner asserted that this practice is written in the Tora!!!

Other measures taken against the evil eye include the wearing of a salt

---

[1] The designation should be the *western* wall in all probability, since the eastern wall does not seem to be of any importance in any other context, whereas the western wall faces Jerusalem.

crystal around the neck, the wearing of various types of amulet and the insistence on placing a *mzuza* on the doorpost. The fear of the evil eye and the steps taken to ward off its presence are similar to the attitude towards spirits and will be commented on further.

A second set of preventative measures are taken against the bizarre, unpredictable eccentricities of the spirit world. In this instance the origin of the evil is non-human and defense consists of prayer and the donning of special Hebrew talismans. The two most efficacious talisman sources are elderly ostensibly pious *shliḥe ẓibbur*, who specialize in the occult. The Jews of Western Asia, especially the Persian speakers have long been renowned for the variety and quality of their amulets, whose texts refer to the ancient widespread "little tradition" demonology and more recently, kabbalistic formulae (*cf*. Schrire, 1966). The use of amulets is widespread within the Jewish community despite the consensus of the more knowledgeable that their use is not really condoned by the "great tradition".

FORTUNE TELLING

The two men who serve as amulet makers are also the most successful fortune tellers. A majority of clients are Muslim, but Jews too, especially women, come to the *falgir* to have their fortune told.

Morad serves as *shaliaḥ ẓibbur* at *knisa* Mulla Mishi in Zire Takh. As a young man he was a *mulla* and he directed a *koto* traditional school in one of the synagogues. Being a rather talented artist and calligrapher, he is often asked to write the *ktuba* and *get*. A major source of income is tombstone carving and the Hebrew carving over the portals of Mulla Mishi synagogue and Knisa Ḥadash are his work. His most regular source of income is obtained through fortune telling, an art learned from his father and developed in a personal way since the late 1930s. He generally receives a nominal 5 to 10 *rial* for his services and handles about 15 clients per day. When clients ask questions he searches for the answer in a book called Ḥokhmat Aḥitofel published in Jerusalem in 1866.[1] The book is filled with mystical formulae and the client chooses a page at random from whence the fortune should be read. The questions usually concern specific matters, e.g. when to hold a wedding or build a house. For Muslim clients, Morad reads fortunes from the Koran. When people who suspect the evil eye seem to be suffering from a physical malady, he sends them to a medical doctor is a physical malady seems

---

[1] This is one of many mystic books used by Jews for "magic". Sefer Razim was allegedly used by Isfahani Jews in a magical plot against Abbas I (Fischel, 1937a:282).

likely. Otherwise he designs an amulet on paper, usually containing the text *'ana bkoaḥ*, of mystical kabbalistic origin, and gives it to a Muslim artisan to execute in metal. Morad's delving into the occult makes him a respected and feared individual to much of the population. The pious suspect him of indulging in sorcery and as a result refuse him all social contact and ritual honor. His granddaughter is considered "strange", perhaps having received the "power" as well.

AGGRESSIVE MAGIC – SORCERY

The use of magic to gain specific ends is well known but not often spoken about. While magic exists in the form of love potions [1] and charms to arouse desire or to ensure the birth of male, most of the aggressive magic is directed against enemies to cause them pain. The most common technique is to effectuate the dissolution of family ties, as in the following account given by Ithuf Limud-e Tora:

It is believed by many that the Pesaḥ *seder* has special ritual merit. The wine spilled out during the recital of the ten plagues, together with the water used for handwashing (*urḥaz* and *raḥza*), if saved, can be used to punish enemies. It is collected and thrown at the door of his house and causes the family to split up.

In describing the powers of one Jewish sorcerer it was said that one neighbor was so scared that he made plans to move to another house. When Hajji Masha'alla learned of the impending move he told them that he would take measures to insure that the entire household would die. He is also said to be capable of throwing an egg at someone's house causing the inhabitants to grow apart.

As is frequently the case in societies manifesting sorcery, witchcraft *accusations* are far more common than witnessed *acts*. In a society where considerable lip-service is given to social cohesiveness, accusations of witchcraft and sorcery are a means of relieving the anxieties produced by behavior manifestly contradicting the ideal pattern (cf. Nadel 1952).

NSHAMOT: "SOULS" AND OTHER DENIZENS OF THE SPIRIT WORLD

There are *nshamot*, "souls", which float in the heavens. They are *nim omre* (lit. "half-lived") and have not lived their full term. Each of them is "good" for a set time

---

[1] Special *sharbat* drinks are consumed under the sorcerer's direction which causes a straying husband to love his wife more. An object is given a woman to place near her threshold, so that when a man comes in the room, he will fall in love with her. *Kase chehel klid,* a bowl in the bottom of which are glued 40 keys is filled with water from the spring at the base of Sa'adi's tomb. It is spilled over the heads of women whose marriage has gone sour. This last is supposedly of Muslim origin and thus uncommon among pious Jewish women.

PLATE 78   A respected member of the "council of the pious" who is reputedly a successful fortune teller. He is clothed here in the traditional holyday dress of the early 1900s.

limit, e.g. a month or two, or even a year or more. God sometimes puts these souls, which have not completed their life span in the body of a child. When the life span of this soul runs out, the child dies. My daughter, Shahla, had only a two-month soul, and so she died. . . .(fieldnotes: 28 year old female informant)

The soul of the deceased returns home for a year after death. The kinsmen of the deceased often prepare wine for Friday-night *qiddush* on a specially set table and close the door. It is believed that the *nshama* returns to recite a *brakha* (blessing) and leaves. Sultanat was frightened whenever she set that table and when she came to get the wine, she often found a dead moth in it.[1]

---

[1] The moth frequently emerges as the symbol of the wandering soul: One day a *ẓaddiq* ("righteous" elder) died in Shiraz. The Levi-Ẓedeq family held a small memorial feast in memory of their close recently departed friend. Throughout the meal a moth flew around and everyone swatted at it trying to kill it, but it would not die. Since then the family does not kill moths fearing that they may carry the soul of some dear one.

Souls that died at an inopportune time or those of sinners wander aimlessly trying to find a body to enter, so that they may be given another chance at living. Souls wander at night and near bodies of water. Women are particularly vulnerable to them and should not go to a cemetery alone, walk alone at night or sleep alone. A woman is most susceptible during ritual uncleanliness and after giving birth. During these periods she is not permitted to be by herself. An onion is placed on a spit in the house and the woman's garments are marked with a purple dye to ward off the *nshama*. When a woman exits from the cemetery the men accompanying her recite psalm 91 seven times and toss weeds over their shoulder as they symbolically leave the *nshamot* behind.

The soul is thought to communicate with the living:

Munes Raḥmin's brother died shortly after his wife gave birth to their first child. A *mulla* who came to their house during mourning was served a breakfast of bread, butter and jam. He complained that the soul of the dead man liked food with aroma, i.e. from fried oinions, etc. Munes's mother arose early the next morning in the pre--dawn cold and made *shaami* (pancake usually of carrot, onion and flour) and *kabab* (broiled ground beef) for the *mulla* as a means of pacifying the dead man's soul. Sometime later, Munes dreamt that her dead brother appeared, wearing a long white robe. He told her not to allow his wife to take his daughter to Israel. One day when Munes and his wife were at the cemetery they sat on his grave and cried the whole morning. Finally the caretaker told them it was time to leave. He left them while they continued to grieve. Finally Munes heard a voice say "*baste*" ("enough") – she believed it was her dead brother speaking.

Informants were not easily able to differentiate among the *nshamot* and other spirits. Eliyahu Hannavi (Elijah the prophet), the symbol of Jewish redemption, often appears in the visionary experience of Shirazi Jews. Clearly, he represents more than a wandering soul and is considered friendly. His being encountered is seen as a positive omen:

Six months after her wedding, while Bejat and her husband Namaki were forced by poverty to live in back of *Knisa* Kazerunian, she entered the *knisa* during the day when no one should have been there. As she came in, she spotted an old man with a long beard, dressed in a white cloak, sitting near the ark. Frightened, she ran out and finding her sister-in-law at home, related her experience. She told Bejat that the old man was undoubtedly Eliyahu Hannavi and had she asked anything of him, it would have been granted. Bejat rushed back, but the old man had disappeared.

Many of the Jewish beliefs about the spirit world parallel those of Iranians generally. Shirazi Jews believe in *gazand*, "harmful" spirits who dwell near the ground and wherever there is water. One shouts "*parhiz*" before spilling boiling water on the ground, so that the spirits will be warned to watch out. One does not throw stones in water for fear of frightening the spirits resting there. Many of the steps taken to protect against *nshamot*, also ward off *gazand*. At least one of these spirits, which lives underground, seems to be a "broker" for soul-exchange. As one informant explained:

It is dangerous to leave a child under forty days old alone, because Asuna may take a liking to it and try to exchange its soul with the soul of his own child, while leaving the body intact. To prevent the child from being harmed when no one is with it, one must place nearby a Tora or piece of bread (both symbols of life and sustenance). People sitting *shiva* for the dead are not permitted any kind of labor, because this would require banging and otherwise disturbing the ground. The angered Azuna might be sufficiently provoked to cause harm to the vulnerable mourner. Postpartum mothers are also quite vulnerable. The Azuna is a friend of the cat. One day, a boy who cared for pigeons, found one of his charges being eaten by a cat. Angered, he swore that if their paths should ever cross again, he would kill the cat. Sometime later the cat returned and was slain by the boy. The Azuna caused the boy to faint and after awakening he said "meeow!".[1]

These spirits are sometimes even *seen* in deserted places:

When Junjun was a little girl, her mother sent her to the often deserted bath in Zire Takh to see if there was hot water. She always did this with some trepidation because the place was empty. Once, she entered the bath and saw a woman, with white skin and soft breasts washing her baby who was also pale white. Their faces and trunk were human, but their hands and legs were like those of a chicken. Junjun shrieked and ran out. The bath keeper soon returned with her, but the creatures were gone. Junjun believes that spirits often come to bathe when the bath house is empty.

The belief in souls and spirits, the defensive measures taken to avoid them and the harm they cause, may well be another mechanism for coping with an unstable social condition and a "great tradition" ideology which assumes that the deity knows what is best for humankind. Since God is considered perfect, the blatantly evil events and manifestly unjust and undeserved misfortune befalling the people of Israel in Shiraz must be caused by lesser, imperfect creatures, consciously or unconsciously frustrating divine will. The "great tradition" satisfactorally designates the proper relationship to the Divinity, but fails to provide adequate guidance with respect to the trials and tribulations provided by the forces of the mundane spirits. While the learned pious consciously snub the world of magic with its ideological contradictions of less than Divine omnipotence, they were observed to nevertheless participate in some of the "little tradition" practices of spirit avoidance.

---

[1] Sometimes a spirit "monster" referred to as "Lulu" is half-jestingly invoked by adults to intimidate naughty youngsters with supernatural punishment.

FOLK MEDICINE AND THE RELIGIO – MAGICAL TRADITION

Shirazi Jews subscribe to a disease theory deriving from the ancient Greek notion of "humors". Diseases are classified as "hot" or "cold" and appropriate treatment includes the prescription of a distilled *araq* or *sharbat* which "cools" the "hot" illness and "warms" the "cold" one. But the cause of the disease is often of magical or supernatural origin and this source of infection also requires attention. Likewise, the normal processes of maturation and birth require ritual attention to assure their healthy completion.

The *mama* ("midwife") while skillfully aiding the delivery often prays: "*khoda, khoda, komak bede*", i.e. "God! God! give help". Sometimes a more elaborate Hebrew/Persian prayer is offered:

> *El eḥad, rabi Me'ir ba'al hanes, rabi Shim'on bar Yoḥay, Avraham, Yiẓḥaq, David, Shlomo, vRaḥel mimenu ('imenu): yah hashem beman komak. Eliyahu hannavi zakhur lattov!*

> One God, Rabbi Me'ir – master of the miracle, Rabbi Shim'on bar Yoḥay, Abraham, Isaac, David, Solomon and Rachel our mother: Lord, God help me. Elijah the prophet be remembered for good! [1]

Whereas prayers are often recited at home and in *knisa* for the sick and the reading of psalms in the presence of a quorum is a frequent practice, healing ritual does not neglect the possibility of the evil eye or *gazand*. A Yeshiva graduate described the following rite conducted for the chronically ill:

A special room, not usually utilized, is selected in the patient's house. Special blinds or curtains are put up in the room. *Esfand*, "wild rue" is brought in and crushed to release incense. Every Saturday evening, after Shabbat is over, a feast in the presence of the patient, accompanied by dancing and singing, is held in this room. It is hoped that the *gazand* see the celebration and think it is on behalf of their victim. But it is done in secret behind the curtains so the spirits will not know exactly what is transpiring. During this feast some food and sugar are set aside and it is said that a transformation occurs whereby the sugar becomes food and the food sugar. In some mysterious way this change insures the recovery of the patient. [2]

---

[1] The names cited suggest some kabbalistic influence in this prayer.

[2] The informant indicated that many years ago an emissary from Israel came and collected all of the curtains used for these rites and burned them in a bonfire in the courtyard of *Knisa* Kohanim.

A procedure called *qal* (lit. "smelting") is used to ward off the *'ayin hara'*, especially in association with illness:

Some coal is heated red-hot. A pan is filled with water and a piece of bread is placed over the pan with a hole punched through the bread. The bread-covered pan is placed over the patient's head and the hot coal is dropped into the water through the hole. As the water sizzles a verse from the Tora is recited. As the coal sits in the water it assumes a shape and those present contemplate the shape in order to divine the cause of the illness. When there is a consensus about whom the coal resembles, the patient's kinsmen go to the suspect's doorstep and take some dust from the ground. They bring this home and place a dash of it in the sick man's mouth. This is said to make him healthy.

In these ways the Shirazi Jew traditionally united herbal/physical medicine with psychic/spiritual medicine in a procedure often effective in alleviating the patient's discomfort. It also allowed the patient's kinsmen to feel that they had actively done all that was within their power to speed recovery.

RITUAL CLEANLINESS AND FAMILY PURITY

Ritual ablutions used to be strictly observed by both men and women in Shiraz. Men used to dip in the *maqve* (ritual bath) after a nocturnal emission, on their wedding day and before Yom Kippur. Before and after each meal, there used to be a ritual washing of the hands and before entering *knisa* men would carefully wash their hands. Today, most men no longer observe these customs.

When a woman menstruates she is called *tame* (unclean) and is completely segregated from all male adults. For seven days the menstruating woman does not cook, handle food, touch her husband or even his clothing. A sister, mother or daughter takes over the household chores, but should no help be available, the menstruating woman may handle food while wearing plastic gloves. She is not permitted to light Sabbath or memorial candles, or to touch the Tora, and is excluded from all religious functions. An unmarried girl is subject to similar restrictions during the seven days. She does not cook nor come in contact with brothers, father or other male kinsmen. Men unashamedly ask women about their menses and carefully avoid a woman during this period. Women openly discuss their menses with other women, speaking of their pain and other side effects. After seven days, when menses cease, a woman goes to the *hamum*, washes her clothes and resumes her normal activities. But she has no intercourse with her husband until the fifteenth day after having first gone to the *maqve* for ritual immersion.

After the birth of a child, a woman is also considered unclean for different periods, depending on the sex of the child (Leviticus XII:1-5). Shirazis are very strict regarding the rules of family purity and scorn the Muslims for ignoring such regulations.

Birth control is avoided by pious men. The most common form of birth control is *jelo giri* (coitus interruptus) which the pious feel is of dubious validity under Jewish law. Because intercourse occurs on the fifteenth day of the cycle each month, during ovulation, conception is frequent.

KASHRUT

All of the Jews of Shiraz observe *kashrut* (ritual fitness of food), at home.[1] Kashrut is considered an important identification symbol for the Jew. Shirazis mock the Jews of the north who have, in large number, abandoned this practice.

The meat eaten by a Jew must be killed by a *shoḥet* and only those animals permitted by Jewish law (Leviticus XI) are considered fit. Except for liver and heart which can be made ritually fit only by broiling, the meat is cleaned and salted for a period of a few minutes to several hours, prior to cooking. The same utensils are used before and after salting and few women are aware that prior to salting, the meat is, strictly speaking, not yet fit (*cf.* Shulkhan Arukh, Yore De'a: 69—78). Meat is not soaked. Hind portions are skillfully dissected and the veins removed in accordance with Jewish law (*cf.* Shulkhan Arukh, Yore De'a: 55—56).

Meat products and utensils are called *gushti* or *gishti* (meaty). Dairy products are called *maasti* from the Persian word for yoghurt, the most commonly eaten dairy product. Jews buy milk, *maast*, *dukh* (a yoghurt drink) and ice cream from nearby stores. Only on Pesaḥ are Jews careful to buy their milk and milk products from a place where they can milk the cow or sheep themselves. Some Jews make their own *maast*. Cheese is bought only from a Jewish dairy product seller in the Mahalleh, as is *farini*, a popular dairy breakfast food.

For the most part, meat and dairy utensils are kept apart and there is no mixing of meat and dairy products in the same dish. Almost all of the cooking utensils are *gushti*, because few dairy products are cooked at home. Special metal bowls are set aside for eating *maast*. It was observ-

---

[1] A considerable number of the Shiraz elite eat non-kosher food outside of the house, but this is a new phenomenon, largely restricted to the young. Most Shirazis keep strict dietary laws even while traveling.

PLATE 79 An unusual *maqve* in Bushehr which fills with seawater at hightide and empties at low tide.

ed from time to time, that the same eating utensils were used alternatively for meat and dairy. Milk and meat may be served on the same cloth to different members of the family eating together, although no individual would eat from both at the same meal. There is, however, some uncertainty about what is considered meat and what is dairy:

Once, a thirteen year old girl brought us *kabab* (broiled meat) to eat when we were eating spaghetti and cheese. We told her that we could not eat it and that she should not put it on our plates because they were *maasti*. Seeing the cheese, she responded: "That is not *maast*, it is cheese – you can eat the *kabab* with that!"

There is no set waiting time after eating meat before one is permitted to eat dairy and vice versa. Usually an interval of several hours passes, but children were observed to run off to have ice cream a few minutes after eating meat. Despite such lapses, the intention is to maintain the separation of meat and dairy and, in all of Iran, only Yazdi and Mashhadi Jews seem to be more careful about it than the Shirazis.

ZIYYARAT (PILGRIMAGE)

The custom of making pilgrimages is popular among Shirazi Jews, as it is with other Middle Eastern Jews (Zenner, 1965; Deshen and Shokeid, 1974), and with the other religious groups of Iran. The usual purpose of a pilgrimage is to fulfill a vow made upon recovery from an illness or at the birth of a son. In the past, each pilgrimage brought the pilgrim a measure of honor varying directly with the distance of the site and the difficulty in reaching it. Today, due to good transportation and relative safety in travel, the pilgrim is no longer entitled to much prestige as a result of his journey.

Jerusalem used to be the most important pilgrimage site. The cost and difficulty involved in getting there were so immense that the successful returnee was granted the honorary title "*hajji*", the term for the Muslin pilgrim to Mecca. It remains the most esteemed pilgrimage, but being only a few hours away by air, numerous Shirazis have traveled there in the past thirty years and no special honor is paid to such pilgrims today.

The pilgrimage to Babylonia, to the tombs of Ezra the Scribe at Kurna and Ezekiel the Prophet at El-Kafal used to be undertaken by groups of young unmarried males. Being a hazardous journey of several months duration, its successful completion brought much joy and honor. These sites, located in present-day Iraq, are now inaccessible.

Hamadan is known to Jews as *shushan habbira* (Susa the capital) and its main attraction is the tomb of Esther and Mordecai. The most auspicious time for such a journey is in winter, in order that the pilgrim be there at Purim. Most Shirazis actually make the pilgramage during the hot summer months, as Hamadan is then pleasantly cool. The pilgrim to Hamadan also visits the tomb of the prophet Zekharia, near the bazaar. Frequently, the pilgrim concludes with a visit to the tomb of Habakkuk in nearby Tuserkan.

The Jews of Yazd in response to dreams or vows frequent the shrine of Eliyahu Hanavi at nearby Nasrabad (Fischer, 1973:326). The other local shrines: the tombs of Abraham ibn Ezra near Mashhad (Benjamin, 1859:241), Daniel at Shushtar, Isaiah at Isfahan and Zippora near Qom, once visited secretly because Muslims forbade unbelievers' attendance at these sites, are no longer viable sites for Jewish pilgrimage.

The most important Jewish pilgrimage site in Iran today is the shrine of Seraḥ bat Asher, located at Lenjan, thirty kilometers west of Isfahan. This is the nearest shrine to Shiraz, and has become the most popular one. Some 300 to 400 Shirazis visit there each year at Rosh Hashana.

According to tradition, it was at this place that Seraḥ, the daughter of

PLATE 80   Tomb of Esther and Mordecai in Hamadan.

PLATE 81   A carpet depicting Moses and the Ten Commandments adorns the wall of this tomb.

Asher the patriarch, made her mysterious appearance in Iran (see Appendix I). The site includes a grotto from which Seraḥ was said to have emerged in her journey from the land of Israel. Nearby is a "miraculous" oasis where water oozes from the mountainside and collects in a stone basin. About two kilometers away, at the edge of a stream, is the ancient Jewish cemetery at Lenjan, where Isfahani Jews are buried to the present day. At its edge is the sanctuary called *chele khune*, i.e. "the house of forty", the shrine proper, where Jews traditionally came at the beginning of the Hebrew month of Ellul and remained for forty days until after Yom Kippur. Between the *chele khune* and the stream is a small garden containing facilities which often house a thousand pilgrims or more at a time. In this horseshoe shaped compound, looking like an old caravansary, pilgrims share their quarters with kinsmen or neighbors from their native towns. Often the facilities are overcrowded and some pilgrims sleep outside on the ground. There is a small ritual bath and a well for drinking water, though most pilgrims drink from the stream. At one end of the compound is the *knisa* of *Ya'aqov Avinu* ("Our Father Jacob") where the more pious worship thrice daily.

The *ziyyarat* consists of visiting the grotto, where, to fulfill vows previously made, people crawl into the cave to a pit about 25 meters inside from where one can allegedly see the tunnel to the land of Israel. It is said that the heftiest of the righteous have no trouble negotiating the winding narrow tunnel, but the thinnest of sinners cannot comfortably squeeze through. Many pregnant women were observed to pull themselves into the grotto.

The other "cult" practice (aside from the normal High Holiday worship in *knisa* Ya'aqov 'Avinu) is a visitation, at least once, to the *chele khune*. It was there that Seraḥ bat Asher miraculously reappeared to deliver the Jews from their persecution at the hands of the Safavid Shah Abbas II (c. 1666):

One day, Abbas was watching a polo match in Isfahan's main square. Suddenly he spotted a beautiful white fawn and proclaimed a prize for its capture. The deer leaped over his head and ran away. Abbas chased it to Lenjan, to the site of *chele khune*. After crawling inside in pursuit, the stone door shut behind him, trapping him inside.

---

[1] Lenjan, in Jewish tradition, was a Jewish village once populated by gold and silversmiths. Although its population was forcibly converted to Islam in the seventeenth century, it nevertheless served as a refuge for Isfahani Jews fleeing the persecutions of Shah Abbas II (Fischel, 1937:284).

PLATE 82   Chel-e Khune — the shrine of Seraḥ bat Asher in Lenjan.

The fawn was transformed into an apparition of Seraḥ bat Asher, who told Abbas that he would die there unless he promised to protect the Jews of Persia and give them all of the land within 1000 parsecs[1] of Lenjan. This Abbas promised and the door opened allowing him to escape.

Pilgrims light candles and offer prayers of thanksgiving and petition. They marvel at the stone door emblazened with kabbalistic carving and the barrel-stone which is said to have once spun continuously until a ritually unclean woman touched it.

The ritual merit of *ziyyarat* while doubtlessly of crucial importance, should by no means obscure the social significance of the event. After the religious obligations of visitation to the *Kukulu* oasis, and the

---

[1] The exact nature of this measure could not be determined but the implication was a very large area was to be included. While the persecution of Jews did in fact cease, the distribution of land of course never came to pass.

PLATE 83   The stone entrance door that allegedly trapped Abbas II.

PLATE 84   The person whose coin sticks to this plaque will have his prayer answered.

PLATE 85 The stream flowing nearby the Chel-e Khune provides for bathing and clothes-washing while it supplies the pilgrims with fish and drinking water.

PLATE 86 Seraḥ bat Asher: fulfilling a hair-cutting *neder* (vow) immediately after Rosh Hashana.

lighting of a memorial candle, donation of charity and recitation of a personal prayer inside the *chele khune* pilgrims are generally free to enjoy themselves. Men sit and play cards, women cook and gossip, unmarried males and females flirt and even musical entertainment and dancing take place. *Ziyyarat* is an opportunity to renew kin ties between dispersed members of the *famil* now residing outside Shiraz and to evaluate members of the opposite sex as prospective mates.[1]

VARIOUS RITUALS AND RITUAL APPARATUSES

TFILLA

Tfilla, or "prayer", is held in the home or in *knisa* in the presence of a *minyan* (quorum of ten). There are three daily services: *shaharit* (morning), *minha* (afternoon) and *'arvit* (evening).

NEDER

Sacred vows are undertaken by Iranian Jews in response to the many crises they undergo. At the death of a first-degree kinsmen, a *neder* is made to hold the night-long Hoshana Rabba and Shavu'ot study in the house of the deceased. At the birth of a son, men and women often vow to visit a pilgrimage site and to perform the child's first haircut there as a testimony to the graciousness of God

TALLIT

This term is reserved for the small fringed garment worn under the outer shirt, known to Western Jews as the *'arba kanfot* or *tallit qatan*. Only the very pious wear the *tallit*; it is worn all the time, except during sleep.

ZIZIT

This is the large fringed shawl worn in *knisa* at morning worship. Except

---

[1] One result of this process has been the expansion of the potential marriage pool. While this had not effected substantial changes in marriage patterns as of 1968, as the ease of travel continues to increase, it is to be expected that an ever greater proportion of marriages will be intercity and *ziyyarat* will be an even more attractive event for young unmarrieds.

for two beggars, every male in Shiraz possesses his own *ẓiẓit*, made of wool, silk, or rayon.

TFILLIN

The phylacteries are worn during weekday morning worship. The illiterate and many of the young men do not possess *tfillin*. When *tfillin* are first put on, a small celebration may be held called *"ben miẓva"*. Like the *tallit* and *ẓiẓit*, the *tfillin* are imported from Israel. The winding of the leather straps, follows the tradition of the Oriental Sfardim.

MZUZA

The *mzuza* is a rolled-up parchment containing the biblical verses: Deuteronomy VI : 4–9, XI : 13–17. At least one doorpost in every building is supposed to have a *mzuza*, but many of the illiterates do not observe this practice. One is supposed to kiss the *mzuza* upon leaving the building, but only in *knisa* is this practice carefully observed. Those having a *mzuza* at home, usually put up the parchment without a case to protect it.

PE'OT

The *pe'ot* (side curls) have not been worn in Shiraz for at least several generations, although there are indications that is was a common practice in the nineteenth century (Alliance, 1902 : 60, 1903 : 110).

HEAD-COVERING

It is customary to pray with one's head covered in Shiraz. Brawer (1936:84) reports having observed the violation of this old practice and the author, too, observed that not everyone adhered to this practice strictly. There is no prescribed head-covering; *kippot* from Israel, knitted Kurdish caps and felt Western-style hats are the most popular.

TORA

The *Tora* is the holiest of ritual objects for the Shirazi. During its reading the congregation is especially quiet and attentive. At least 90% of those assembled do not understand the Tora, as it is read in Hebrew and is rarely translated into the vernacular. Indeed, hearing the words of the Tora is not nearly so important as *seeing* the object itself. When the

Tora is removed from the ark by someone who has pledged a donation
to the *knisa,* it is passed from person to person until it reaches the
reader's lectern. Everyone makes an effort to touch it. It is then lifted
and opened for the congregation to see the words. Someone points to the
opening verse for the current reading and the men, in turn, point to it
with their fringes, touching them to each eye several times alternately,
then kissing the fringes. Women cover and uncover their eyes several
times, then kiss their finger tips. Should a man or woman come into
knisa when the reading is over, but the Tora is still on the desk, they demand that the Tora be opened to the place, in order that they may see it
and go through the above described procedure.

It is a great honor to be called to the reading of *Tora* for an *'aliya.* In
Shiraz, they call *kohen, levi* and *yisra'el* in accordance with the order
followed the world over by Jews. However, on Sabbaths and holidays
when fifteen or more individuals may be called for this honor, the
traditional order breaks down. Shirazis see nothing wrong with calling
several *kohanim* in a row. First degree consanguines are rarely called
consecutively.

Tora reading is a big inducement to men and women to attend *knisa*,
though none could verbalize why it was good to hear and see Tora.

BRAKHA

A *brakha*, or "blessing", is recited at every opportunity by Shirazi
Jewish men. Anything that is drunk, eaten, smelled, heard or otherwise
experienced is an occasion to praise God. These blessings, the same ones
recited by pious Jews everywhere, are said by the literate and illiterate
alike. As is the case with prayer generally, it is the *quantity* of blessings
that is important, not the intensity of feeling accompanying them.
Women are excused from the recitation of blessings except over the Sabbath and holiday candles, at the Pesaḥ *seder,* and over the *lulav* and
'etrog on Sukkot.

In the *knisa*, the recitation of the *brakha* is frequently more important
than the event taking place. Thus the blessing over the Tora is con-
sidreed more important than listening to the reading. On Purim, women
come to hear the blessing over the *mgilla* but leave before the actual
reading. The blessing over the shofar on Rosh Hashana is as important
as its blowing. Women pack the *knisa* to hear the *sfira* blessing, and
only incidentally, the counting of the *'omer*.

Participation in the listening to these many blessings is necessary in
order that the individual may curry favor with the Almighty. At public
gatherings, the recitation of blessings by everyone present has the in-

tegrative effect of involving everyone present in the same activity while not overstepping rank differences. At gatherings of men of varied occupation, education and rank, uncomfortable moments of silence are quickly displaced for those otherwise uninvolved, by an activity all may share in: the recitation of blessings. The presence of various foods, flowers and drink encourages the individuals left out of conversation, to initiate such activity. They, in turn, are able to participate in the inevitable *ta'arof* by insisting that those higher in rank precede them in partaking of such objects and reciting the appropriate blessing over them.

PRIESTHOOD

In Iran, as elsewhere, Jews are divided into three segments: *kohanim, leviyim* and *yisra'el*. In Shiraz, the *yisra'el* are numerically predominant as is normally the case. The number of *leviyim* is very small, consisting of only about one-half dozen extended families. But the *kohanim* comprise more than one-third of the total Jewish population. Although the large proportion of *kohanim* is rather unusual, even in Iran, Shirazis were unable to explain why there should be so many.[1]

RITUAL FUNCTION

The *yisra'el* have no specific ritual role; religiously speaking: they can be considered the common masses.

The *leviyim* have one ritual function: aiding the *kohanim* in the latter's ritual ablutions. It is the role of the *levi* to pour water over the hands of the priests prior to the recitation of the priestly benediction in synagogue. Although this duty qualifies as a ritually meritorious act, *leviyim* of high rank abstain from its performance. Even the poor make an effort to avoid it. Equally incumbent upon all *leviyim,* the task of aiding in the priests' ablutions usually falls to a son or younger brother. It is not clear whether the reluctance to participate in these ablutions results from a disdain for this labor, which at home is the task wives perform for their husbands, or from the general fear of all non-*kohanim* of having too much contact with *kohanim*.

The ritual role of *kohanim,* in accordance with the Jewish "great tradition", is more complex than that of other Jews. Firstly, the *kohen* serves as representative of the priestly family in accepting the token

---

[1] Nearly 300 years ago, Tavernier reported: "The Jews of *Schiras* . . . boast themselves of the Tribe of Levi" (1684:248), i.e. the tribe from which the priests descend.

offering of the father of a first born *yisra'el* son at the *pidyon habben* ceremony, thirty days after birth. Secondly, each weekday morning, twice on Sabbaths, holidays and new moons, all of the *kohanim* in each *knisa* are called upon to bless the assembled congregation with the biblical verses, in Numbers VI : 24–26. The procedure is as follows:

After the recitation of the *qdusha* "sanctification" prayer, the *kohanim* walk to the rear of the *knisa,* where, with the help of *leviyim* they ritually wash their hands and dry them with a towel. There is no set pattern to these ablutions such as is found among other Jewish communities. Since their shoes are already off, they go to the front of the synagogue and face the western wall. In older, traditionally designed synagogues, they mount the carpet-covered stone benches. Non-*kohanim* leave the front of the *knisa* and move toward the middle of the sanctuary in order that they may be in front of the *kohanim* during the blessing. At the recitation of *modim 'anahnu lakh* ("we gratefully acknowledge . . .") the *kohanim* pull the *ẓiẓit* over their heads. After *hoda'a* (prayer of thanksgiving) the *shaliah ẓibbur* calls out *"kohanim!"* If the *shaliah ẓibbur* is himself a *kohen,* a *samikh* (assistant) takes over for him until the conclusion of the blessing. The *kohanim* recite their preliminary blessing, not attempting to synchronize with each other. Turning around, they face the congregation with arms extended, but their hands remain covered by the *ẓiẓit,* as does the head. The hands may be together or spread apart, extended upward or held dog-paddle style. Fingers may be together or spread. Palms may be flat out, slightly curved or loosely closed. In short, there is no established pattern for these positions as is found among other Jews (Idelsohn, 1932:193). The *kohanim* recite the benediction responsorially, word by word, with the *shaliah ẓibbur*; each *kohen* at his own pace and with his own melody.

During the recitation of the blessing, no one in the congregation looks at the *kohanim.* The learned say that it is no good to look upon the *shkhina* (the "presence" of the Almighty); the ignorant only know that there is danger in doing so. The congregants stand during the blessing and many recite appropriate verses posted on the walls of the *knisa.* Others cover their eyes with the right front fringe of their *ẓiẓit.* Women cover their eyes with their *chador* or with their hands. At the final word of the blessing, *"shalom"*, men lift the right front fringe from their eyes and in a sweeping motion arching from the right across their faces, bring it to their lips and kiss it. At the same time, the *kohanim* again face the western wall and uncover their heads.

The priests remain standing in place until the recitation of *qaddish,* at which time they walk around the synagogue in line. The *kohen* takes one fringe of his *ẓiẓit* in each hand; each non-*kohen* takes a fringe in his right

PLATE 87 The Priestly Blessing.

PLATE 88 Worshippers hide their faces from the *shkhina*, God's Presence.

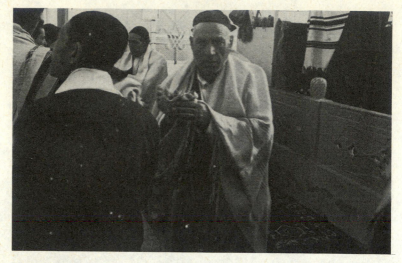

PLATE 89   The blessing completed, each *kohen* physically imparts the divine blessing as he greets other worshippers by clasping their hands in his and having their *ẓiẓit* fringes touch.

hand and places it between the two hands of the *kohen* and they allow the fingers to touch briefly. The *kohen* says "*titbarkhenu min hashamayim*" – (may you be blessed from heaven) or "*nitbarkhenu min hashamayim*" (may we be blessed from heaven). Then both *kohen* and non-*kohen* kiss the fringes.

Everyone must hear the blessing of the *kohanim*. The *kohanim* have the special power of blessing and those who hear it can hope to benefit from its efficacy. The *kohen's* direct link with God probably contributes to his relatively high prestige.

The Shirazi tradition that a *kohen* is worthy of great prestige is reminiscent of the ancient Israelite social order. In those days too, inter-marriage between priest and non-priest was discouraged (Epstein, 1927:73–74), producing an almost caste-like condition. On the island of Jerba, such a distinction remains to the present day. The *kohanim* have their own town, some seven kilometers from the larger community of non-priests (Slouschz, 1927:256). On Jerba it is believed that the *kohanim* have remained segregated since "the days when the *Cohanim* were still the religious heads of the communities" (Slouschz, 1927:267). Just as Shirazi Jews fear the power of the *kohen's* curse, the Jews of Tunis believe that the Jews of Jerba possess special magical faculties . . . and the Cohanim of the Isle of Jerba are both feared and respected. (Slouschz, 1927:283)

In Iran, the *Sayyids*, the descendants of the Prophet, are singled out by the Shi'a for special honor. They are believed to have the power of blessing as well as special healing ability (Donaldson, 1938:56-57, 68). The special powers of the *kohanim* in Shiraz, their high representation among Jewish sorcerers and importance in the community hierarchy suggest the possible borrowing of a tradition from the Muslim *Sayyids* of Iran. Slouschz points out, that

In the end, the tribes of Cohanim [in North Africa] came to model themselves very closely on the Mussulman tribes of the Shurefas, the descendants of Muhammad. (1927:290)

RELIGIOUS FUNCTIONARIES

EXTRA-SYNAGOGUE

The *dayan*, or "judge", lays claim to being the leading religious authority in the community (see Chapter IV). His function is the administration of justice in religious disputes or in cases involving Jewish litigants. The government recognizes the *dayan's* authority over Jewish marriage and divorce. The present *dayan* and current contenders for the position are not highly respected for their learning. As a result, although the *dayan* is theoretically the most important religious functionary in Shiraz, today, personages with other titles and even some untitled individuals have come to share his prestige. The role of *dayan* will probably resume its uppermost position on the hierarchy when it is assumed by an individual with recognized rabbinic ordination. In 1968, there were no ordained Rabbis in Iran as there was no tradition of rabbinical ordination there; positions and roles were inherited without formal ceremony or qualification.

The *mohel*, or "circumcisor" is a role frequently assumed by the *dayan,* but there is no necessity for a *mohel* to be any other kind of religious functionary. There are several Shirazi men skilled in performing this operation.

The role of *shoḥet*, or "ritual slaughterer", is another function traditionally associated with the *dayan*, but the present *dayan* is incapable of performing ritual slaughter. There are two categories of slaughterer in Shiraz; the slaughterer of fowl and the slaughterer of large animals.

No great skill is required to slaughter fowl and more than a dozen Shirazi men actively engage in such ritual slaughter. The slaughtering procedure is as follows: the bird is held under the left arm of the *shoḥet*, its head pulled back and grasped by the left thumb and forefinger.

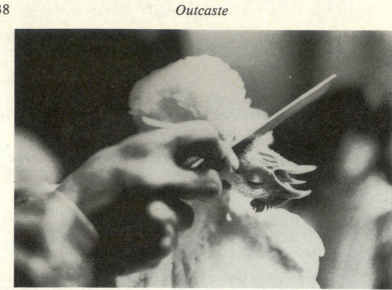

PLATE 90   A *shoḥet* slaughters a chicken.

PLATE 91   After *kappara* in the synagogue courtyard, the *shoḥet* reaches in to examine the steer's internal organs.

Feathers are plucked from the bird's throat where the incision is to be made. One or two strokes are made with a sharp knife at this point and the bird is thrown aside while its muscles contract reflexively. Most fowl slaughterers are not very careful about testing the blade for cleanliness and sharpness. Some of them, being unlearned in Judaica, are not trusted by the more pious. A fowl slaughterer receives but one or two *rial* for each bird slaughtered.

There are three men in Shiraz who are capable of slaughtering large animals. Large scale commercial slaughtering of kosher meat is conducted in a special section of the government built slaughterhouse, some five to six kilometers southeast of the Mahalleh.

Shirazi Jews differ from other Iranian Jews in their preference for beef over lamb; except for Rosh Hashana and Pesaḥ, sheep are almost never slaughtered. During the summer, cattle are slaughtered daily except on Shabbat, whereas during the winter, when meat keeps better, cattle are slaughtered three days per week.

The slaughterer of large animals uses a number of special long knives which are cleaned, honed and inspected before each use. The animal is thrown to the ground and held down by several butchers, one of whom holds the head back. One swift stroke of the knife severs the jugular vein. Care is taken to avoid touching any bone with the knife. The lungs of each animal are inspected. Postules on the lungs are cut open; if their liquid contents are clear the animal is declared "fit", but if blood or pus emerges the animal is declared "unfit".

Any time a negative ruling is made about an animal, the butchers who bought it curse, protest and even threaten the *shohet*, as they must now sell the animal to the *goyim* for a loss. Unfit animals have been rare in recent times, because butchers, seeking to avoid financial loss, choose their animals very carefully. At the same time, the *shohet*, fearing the wrath of the butchers, directs the benefit of his doubt in their favor. As a result, some of the pious would not eat commercially-slaughtered meat. They ate beef rarely, and only when they could arrange for private slaughtering by someone they could trust. Recently the pious prevailed upon the *dayan* to allow a Yeshiva graduate to slaughter on alternate weeks so that they, too, could buy meat from the butchers.

Commercial ritual slaughtering of large animals is under the control of the *dayan*. A tax of five *rial* per kilo of animal is to be paid to the *dayan*. Approximately 1500 Jewish families of Shiraz consume between 2 and 2½ kilos of meat per week; the hotels buy at least 500 kilos more, to which must be added the meat used in the school feeding program. It is suggested, therefore, that at least 4000 kilograms of kosher beef are consumed each week. The *dayan's* expected income from ritual slaughter is thus at least 20,000 *rial* per week; 1000 *rial* go to the *shoḥet* and a share goes to the *Anjoman*.

The profession of *sofer* (scribe) has all but vanished from Shiraz. In the past, while any learned Jew could write Hebrew and Judaeo-Persian texts, the scribe specialized in preparing *ktubot* (wedding contracts), *gittin* (bills of divorce), amulets, *mzuzot* and perhaps *tfillin* (phylacteries). Today, many of these items are obtained inexpensively from Israel. The only remaining *sofer* carves tombstones and writes amulets. For the latter practice, he is condemned by the pious who consider him a witch.

The role of *gabay* has been extensively discussed in Chapters IV and IX. There are several men considered official *gabayim* and many more unofficial ones. Unlike in Kurdistan (Feitelson, 1959:206), the Shirazi chief *gabay* is not chosen from among the wealthy and influential, but stands out as an honest man, famous for his integrity, in a society where such qualities are rare. The *gabay* in distributing funds acts as a purely secular agent of the *Anjoman* but by collecting funds for the poor, for *kappara* and for Israel his position as a religious functionary is assured.

The *morde shur,* or "body-washer", is a very necessary role usually performed by a Jew who is somewhat slow mentally or an out-of-towner. Because of his contact with the dead, he is not permitted to enter anyone's home and finds it nearly impossible to marry. The body-washer is a complete outcast and literally "untouchable". Should no *morde shur* be available, someone in the deceased's family must undertake this loathsome task, which is finally accepted with great bitterness. The pious and non-pious alike share a distaste and revulsion for this activity. Since the preparation of the dead for interment is an important religious duty for Jews, its avoidance may be attributed to the influence of Shi'a Muslims who likewise consider the *morde shur* untouchable (Waring, 1807:21). Shirazi Jews are somewhat more extreme in their attitude towards body washing than other Iranian Jews; in Kurdistan, Jews willingly participate in the washing of the dead (Brauer, 1947).

The *mulla,* literally "theological teacher", refers to a semi-literate Jew who earns small amounts of money for reading prayers in the house of mourning, chanting psalms for the sick or reading penitential prayers for Israel. *Mullas* form the core of those who spend the seven days of mourning, or *shiv'a*, with the mourners or who attend *mishmara*. This is their sole occupation. These *mullas* read Hebrew fluently, but understand very little. They are low ranked in the community, and it was often unclear whether they were called mulla out of politeness or in derision.

SYNAGOGUE FUNCTIONARIES – MAINTENANCE ORIENTED

The *ḥazzan*, or "overseer", is responsible for synagogue maintenance. He collects pledges made to the *knisa* and acts as synagogue *gabay*, collecting and distributing money to the poor.

Shirazi synagogues do not have large sums of money available, as seems to have been the case in Kurdistan (Feitelson, 1959:206). Most synagogues are dilapidated and in constant need of repair. It is the responsibility of the *ḥazzan* to bring to the attention of the congregation all needed improvements and to ask their approval for the expenditure of funds.

The *ḥazzan's* duties include the mediation of disputes between congregants and, sometimes, between religious functionaries. It is his prerogative to announce decisions to the *Anjoman* and to make other announcements of interest to the congregation. The *ḥazzan* is selected from among those who seem to be concerned about the *knisa*. The congregants agree to the selection by consensus. Each *knisa* has at least one *ḥazzan*, but may have more if there is more than one regular *minyan*. The *ḥazzan* is usually ranked among the *knisa's* elite, and is notable for his family and wealth rather than for piety and learning.

The *shamash*, or "beadle", is directly responsible to the *ḥazzan*. In return for acting as caretaker for the synagogue, he and his family are given an empty room on the synagogue grounds to live in. Appointment of a *shamash* by the *ḥazzan* is subject to approval by the congregation. One such appointment was the object of heated debate, because the candidate was a *morde shur* from Teheran who had left his family behind. Some congregants questioned the propriety of having a single man as a *shamash*. Single older women have an easier time being accepted. Today, some of the positions are filled by non-Jews, since there are no longer enough Jewish candidates for the position.

SYNAGOGUE FUNCTIONARIES – RITUAL ORIENTED

There are four or five men in Shiraz who regularly play the role of *darshan*, or "preacher". The *darshan* gives religious discourses in the *knisa* on Shabbat afternoons, on Saturday evenings, on Lag Ba'omer, Tish'a B'av and on other occasions. During *mishmara* he may be present to give a discourse in the house of mourning. When there is no *darshan* available, the *shaliaḥ zibbur* may fill in for him.

The *drasha* (sermon) is a highly developed art form, requiring oratory skill, originality, and superior knowledge of Judaica. These sermons frequently last more than an hour, while the audience sits in rapt atten-

tion listening to dramatic story-telling and clever exegesis. The main
material for these homiletics is the Bible, embellished by *gimatriyya*
(homiletic interpretation based on the numerical value of Hebrew letters)
and Midrash.

Shirazis greatly appreciate clever *gimatriyya,* especially when it is
used to prophesy the destruction of Jewry's enemies. Midrash (exegesis)
is so beloved by Shirazis, that even in the Otsar Hatorah schools, most
non-mechanical learning is spent in telling the children legends and anecdotes from the Midrash. Shirazis able to study Hebrew or Aramaic texts
ignore sections on law in order to study homiletical material. Shirazis
have developed their own Midrash and aside from religious poetry, this
is their other major contribution to Jewish literature. How Shirazi
Midrash compares with the indigenous Midrash of other Jewish groups
is unclear, but I have recently verified the claim of Professor Ezra
Melamed of the Hebrew University that a volume of his father's
homiletics is highly prized by Yemenite Jews.

The *darshan* is the master of sermons on ethics. Many men strive to
be accepted as *darshan*, but very few are sincerely urged to give discourses. Competition in giving sermons is one of the rare traditional intellectual outlets among Shirazi Jews – men actually close their stores
and visit each other to explain some new point they are developing to use
in the next sermon. In the past, the *dayan* was often a *darshan* of considerable renown.

The *shaliah zibbur,* or "precentor", leads the congregation in worship.
Every male able to read Hebrew is eligible to fill this position, and at
some time or other does so. The main task of the *shaliah zibbur* is to
chant the prayers, and, on occasion, to interpret them.

Each *knisa* has several "regulars" who perform as *shaliah zibbur*, one
of whom is looked upon as "chief" *shaliah zibbur*. His leadership in
prayer is desired on important occasions, otherwise the others substitute
for him. Leading worship is considered a great honor, and within the
knisa, the regular *shaliah zibbur* enjoys great influence. The chief
shaliah zibbur makes decisions regarding synagogue procedure and,
sometimes, regarding religious law. Such authority, occasionally brings
him into direct conflict with the *hazzan,* but the latter usually defers to
the superior learning of the *shaliah zibbur*. Sometimes, too, he may be
opposed by the majority of the congregation, but if he can swing one or
two substitute *shlihe zibbur* to his point of view, he can even prevail over
the wishes of the majority.

The most important criterion for acceptance of a *shaliah zibbur* is his
knowledge of Hebrew, i.e. his ability to read fluently and to communicate the meaning of the prayers. The better *shaliah zibbur*

translates and interprets prayers at sight from Hebrew to Judaeo-Persian, for the benefit of the illiterate worshipper. The position of *shaliaḥ ẓibbur* is usually inherited.

The *samikh*, or "adjacent one", is a very minor role in the synagogue. The *samikh* assists the *shaliaḥ ẓibbur* by leading certain prayers which, for some reason, the *shaliaḥ ẓibbur* is unable to lead. He also leads the congregational responses during worship.

HONORIFIC TITLES

The title *ḥakham* (sage), or *rabi* (rabbi), are honorific titles ususally reserved for the most learned of Shirazi Jews. As such, they are most often applied to the *dayan*. However, the title may be used in addressing or referring to anyone with considerable Jewish learning, but such usage is infrequent.

The *hajji*, or "pilgrim", is someone who made the pilgrimage to Jerusalem in the days before 1930 when such a journey could take up to two years to complete. *Hajji* is thus an honorific title given to one who has accomplished a specific difficult undertaking, and there are only a handful of Shirazis to whom the term is applied.

Mulla, or "theological teacher", is a respectful term of address or reference for any high religious functionary. It is the most widely used honorific title, applicable to any Jew learned in Judaica, whether he be a religious functionary or not. It is a title not usually applied to the *hazzan, shamash* or *morde shur*, who do not qualify, normally, as learned. Although we have seen that *mulla* also is the term applied to the low ranked prayer-reader, the usage of *mulla* like the usage of *ḥakham*, does not generally connote a specific role.

THE RELIGIOUS HIERARCHY

In Shiraz, where secular political activity was suppressed, activity in the religious domain was substituted for it. The struggle for position within the religious structure is intense, and it brings those who are successful, a measure of prestige and influence often out of proportion to their secular rank. The ranking of religious functionaries (Table 12) is separate from the other ranking scales, but may affect and be affected by them. Thus secular rank may be instrumental in helping one to obtain the position of *hazzan*, but not that of *darshan* or *shaliaḥ ẓibbur*. On the other hand, as we shall see, the position of *shaliaḥ ẓibbur* may be used to better one's secular ranking. Many religious functionaries fulfill several roles

TABLE 12
Ranking of Religious Functionaries

Synagogue– ritual oriented	Synagogue– maintenance oriented	Extra- Synagogue			Honorific
		Dayan		Ḥakham	
		X			
		X			
		X			
Darshan		X	Gabay		
		X	X		Hajji
Shaliaḥ Ẓibbur	Ḥazzan	X	X		
X	X	X	X		Mulla
X	X	Shohet	X	Mohel	
X	X		X		
X	X		X		
Samikh	X	Sofer	X		
	X		X		
	X		X		
Mulla	X		X		
	X		X		
	X		X		
	X		X		
	Shamash		X		
			X		
			X		
			X		
			X		
			X		
			X		
			Morde Shur		

Key
X
X represents measure of authority
X

simultaneously, but some roles appear to be mutually exclusive. A *morde shur* may also be a *shamash,* but nothing more; a *shamash* may be a *morde shur* or a *mulla;* a *hazzan* is often a *gabay* but rarely a *shaliaḥ ẓibbur* and a *dayan* may be *darshan, shaliaḥ ẓibbur, mohel, shoḥet* and *sofer.* Except for the *morde shur* and *shamash,* religious functionaries serve as members of the informally constituted "council of the pious".

THE KNISA

The only social institution in which the entire Jewish community participates is the *knisa*. There are eleven synagogues in the Mahalleh, three *tu khiyabun* and one at the Kosar school. Shiraz has a total of thirty-two sanctuaries, or rooms for worship. The old Yeshiva also had a sanctuary, but the new one did not since it was too far away from Jewish neighborhoods.

SYNAGOGUE CONSTRUCTION

The main sanctuary and the auxiliary ones, too, face on a large courtyard surrounded by a high wall, broken only by a heavy steel door opening into the *kuche*. Perhaps because Shirazi synagogues are relatively new structures, one does not enter them via long narrow tunnels culminating in a veritable fortress, as seen in Isfahan. The *knisa's* main windows open on the courtyard, and the few small ones look out over the *kuche* at a height of about five meters; some synagogues have skylights. In the courtyard are a pool and water tap.

Construction materials are similar to those used for residential dwellings, and synagogues are constantly being damaged by snow, heavy rain and earthquakes. Arch construction and vaulting, which have no doubt contributed to a synagogue durability of more than 250 years in Yazd and Isfahan, are absent in Shiraz. Roofs are supported by pillars, usually of wood and stucco, ranging in height from 6 to 15 meters. Roofs are the weakest element of *knisa* structure.

The buildings usually have one major sanctuary and at least one auxiliary. The main sanctuary is rectangular in shape and ranges in size from 6 × 6 to about 30 × 20 meters. Stone benches line the walls of the *knisa* and sometimes criss-cross the sanctuary. These benches may be supplemented by wooden ones. Benches and floors of wealthier synagogues are covered with carpets from Kerman, Mashhad or Shiraz. Other synagogues have *gelims*, (mats woven in tapestry), some with woven Hebrew letters, on the floor. Poorer synagogues have plain mats and partially exposed tiled or mud-plaster floors.

In the western wall, facing Jerusalem, is the *hekhal* (ark) containing the Tora scrolls. In many synagogues it is not located in the middle of the wall, but towards the southern extremity. An electric *ner tamid* (eternal light) is found above or inside the ark, but is lit only during worship.

The rectagonal or octagonal podium, measuring two to three meters in width, is usually made of stone, and located near the center of the

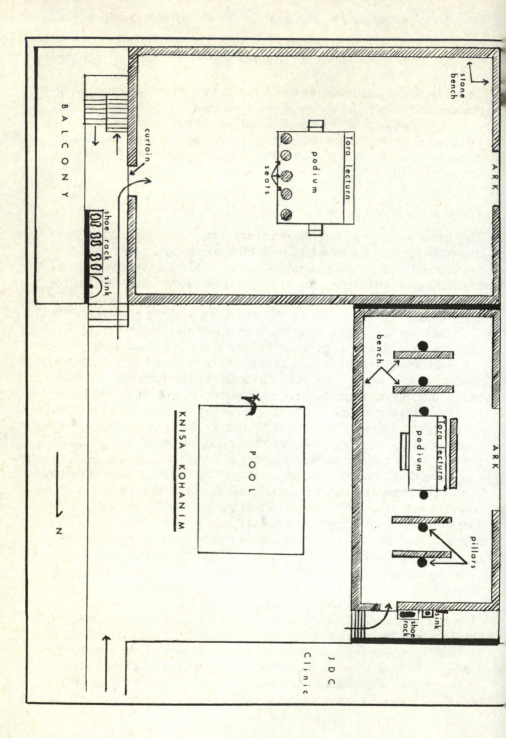

sanctuary. At its back or side are several steps leading up to it. The *shaliah zibbur* stands facing the western wall at a carpet-covered lectern extending the entire width of the podium. The Tora is read from this lectern and the congregation is addressed from it.

Near the entrance is a sink where the *kohanim* can wash their hands. The entrance, usually at the eastern wall, is covered by a tribal *gelim*. The worshipper enters the sanctuary, takes off his shoes and leaves them in a clutter near the entrance, or places them in racks specially made for the purpose. Nearby, there is at least one niche in the wall for lighting memorial candles.

Traditionally, the *knisa* did not have a clearly delineated section for women. Women occupied a section near the entrance and far from the ark, apart from the men, but without partition. Newer synagogues have balconies for the women, which are used primarily on Rosh Hashana and Yom Kippur when the *knisa* is overcrowded for long periods, otherwise women tend to sit downstairs in the rear of the main sanctuary. In warm weather, many women sit outside the sanctuary in the courtyard, near the open windows.

Significantly, there is no library or any sort of repository for books in the *knisa*; everyone brings his own prayer book. Old books, manuscripts and Tora scrolls are buried in archives under the floors or in walls of several synagogues.

KNISA DECORATION AND ARTIFACTS

The synagogues are plain, relatively undecorated and generally more poorly furnished than in communities to the north of Shiraz. One does not find beautifully tiled arks, such as the Isfahani one displayed at the Jewish Museum in New York City. Shirazis are, in general, not much concerned with synagogue aesthetics.

Knisa ceilings are sometimes painted with flowers and birds, or perhaps with the traditional twelve tribal symbols of Israel. Walls are frequently whitewashed and left nearly bare, aside from a few painted flowers, a Shield of David and, ever popular among oriental Jews, a grandfather clock. Older synagogues may have the original cornerstone inscriptions dating back as far as 500 years. There is little in the way of frieze work, such as is found in Rezayeh.

The western wall is covered by the kabbalistic rendering of the "Name of God" and the sixty-seventh Psalm written in the shape of a seven-branched candelabrum. A few of these decorations were hand painted in

FIGURE 3   Synagogue Floor Plan

PLATE 92   Knisa Mulla Rabi in Isfahan features a vaulted ceiling, horned lecturn and elaborate hand-printed ark curtain.

PLATE 93   A woman kisses the *tora* in Knisa Shokr as it is removed from the ark.

PLATE 94   *Nogle,* rice candy, is thrown into the air in honor of a bridegroom being called to the reading of the *tora.*

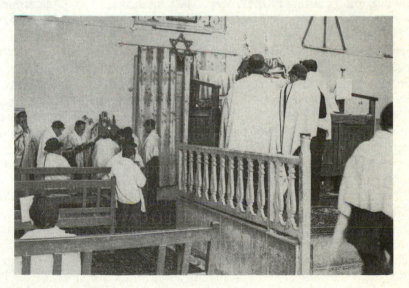

PLATE 95   Two *torot* being read simultaneously in Knisa Shokr so that a family may adequately memorialize a deceased loved one.

Shiraz, but most are printed copies from abroad. Green neon lighting shaped into the "Name of God" and seven-branched candelabrum, have become popular decorations. The ark looks like a simple closet, but may be covered by a velvet curtain, a *gelim* or a Kuwaiti carpet.

The most important ritual artifact, the Tora scroll, is protected by a hardwood box, as is the custom of Oriental Jews. The boxes are decorated with silver and are usually covered in green. The paired horn-like projections on the Tora box are decorated with silver crowns. The Tora pointer, is also of silver, but not so elaborately decorated as elsewhere in Iran. There is usually a silver vase containing greens and flowers, upon which the worshipper makes a blessing before leaving the sanctuary. The ark, containing the Tora and silver decorations, is kept locked, as is the *knisa* when not in use.

A recent innovation, of probable European-Israeli origin, is the painting of electric memorial lamps with the name of the deceased. Only a few synagogues have adopted this custom.

SYNAGOGUE MEMBERSHIP

On Yom Kippur, 100% of the adult population attend *knisa*. On Shabbat mornings 80% of the men attend, and during the week about 40% go at least once. Women usually go to *knisa* only for Tora reading, shofar blowing, and counting of the *'omer*. Male attendance too, is determined by such factors. Less then 50% of the women attend *knisa* regularly.

There is no synagogue "membership" as such, in Shiraz. One usually attends the *knisa* of one's father and is at least expected to go to that *knisa* on Yom Kippur, during mourning and for wedding and circumcision celebrations. Most people consistently attend the same *knisa* all year round. However, some of those living outside the Mahalleh find it easier to walk to a nearby synagogue than to undertake a fifteen-minute walk in order to reach their father's Mahalleh *knisa*; besides, it is more prestigious to attend *knisa* outside of the Mahalleh. Nevertheless, most of those living outside do attend *knisa* in the Mahalleh, while only a handful of Mahalleh dwellers attend outside synagogues.

Members change their *knisa* affiliation, not only for reasons of convenience, but because of disputes and for prestige purposes. Desertion of the traditional *knisa* is most common among the educated, younger generation and among social climbers who feel it degrading to go to a Mahalleh *knisa*. The switch is made simply by beginning regular attendance at the new *knisa* and purchasing *kvodot* (ritual honors) there. The members of the old synagogue object strenuously only when a wealthy member deserts them, as in the following case:

One young bridegroom, belonging to the wealthiest *khanevadeh* of Shiraz, refused to attend *knisa* at the Mahalleh *knisa* built by his *khanevadeh* and bearing its name, as is the custom on the Sabbath following one's wedding. The previous Yom Kippur no one from the entire *khanevadeh*, including the builder himself, attended *knisa* there. The membership was hurt and angry — both at the collective loss of prestige they all suffered by this rejection and the loss of financial support from the *knisa's* chief benefactor. The *ḥazzan* and a delegation of the *knisa's* notables, including affines of the builder, prevailed upon them to return. A part of the *khanevadeh* did so the following Yom Kippur when they purchased numerous ritual honors at high bids, thereby healing the rift which had been created.

On Shabbat, holiday, Monday and Thursday mornings, most of the synagogues are open. On other occasions, only a few are open, and many men must attend a *knisa* other than their own. It is customary for the visiting synagogue notables to vie with the *knisa's* indigenous leadership for ritual honors in an effort to clearly define the relative rank of notable worshippers.

Women do not necessarily attend the same *knisa* as their husbands. Often the choice is determined by the proximity of the *knisa* to their home as well as where their friends go.

WORSHIP

Pious Jews are present for worship three times per day, while others may be satisfied to attend on Shabbat only. During mourning and on special occasions, a *minyan* of ten men may pray in someone's home. Although there are prayers one should say at home by himself, the major daily services (*shaḥarit, minḥa* and *'arvit*) must be said at a *minyan* in a *knisa*. If one does not attend public worship, one does not pray.

One reason for the emphasis on public worship is quite pragmatic. One quarter of the men and most of the women are unable to read Hebrew. Of those who can read, 80% are functional illiterates who can read the texts fluently, but do not understand what is read. The illiterate worship fervently, reciting certain responses from memory. For their sake, the *shaliaḥ ẓibbur* translates prayers and other texts into Judaeo-Persian. For the sake of the illiterates, the custom has also evolved in Iran, for a *samikh* (literally "adjacent one") standing near the *shaliaḥ ẓibbur*, to recite normally silent prayers out loud. Thus, public worship prevents a religious schism between those able to read and those unable to do so.

CELEBRATIONS

In addition to holding worship, the *knisa* is the place where the community honors the bride and groom. Circumcision may be performed there and the occasional *ben miẓva* or important guest of the community, is honored in *knisa*.

MEETINGS

Community-wide as well as local private meetings are held in *knisa*. Business meetings of the *Anjoman* and its committees take place in the synagogue. The "council of the pious" meets there informally to proclaim fasts, special prayers and sacrifices. Youth Committee gatherings, political campaigning, elections, public meetings of all kinds take place in the synagogue. On Sabbaths and festivals the synagogue membership meets to decide on matters pertaining to the individual *knisa* or to one of the sanctuaries within it.

CHARITY

Most of the money given to the poor is collected in *knisa*. Pledge and bids for *kvodot* ("ritual honors") are collected for *knisa* maintenance. In Shiraz, money may be collected in *knisa* on Shabbat or the bid might be noted by the *ḥazzan* – in violation of Jewish law.

EDUCATION

In the past, religious school, the *koto*, was held in *knisa*, but now only occasional classes are held there for the young. Sermons are given in three of the synagogues every Sabbath afternoon, and in one synagogue on Friday evening. These are well attended and enjoyed, and serve as a substitute for story telling, so popular among all Iranians.

KAPPARA

Kappara (atonement sacrifice) of chickens is performed privately at home on the eve of Yom Kippur and at weddings. Shirazis also perform communal *kappara* on large animals, such as a calf or steer. The occasion of such slaughter is Tish'a B'av, the day preceding the new moon, or at sopecially proclaimed periods.

The announcement of an atonement sacrifice is passed by word-of-mouth throughout the community. The decision to hold such a sacrifice is made by the "council of the pious". The chief *gabay* then collects money from anyone willing to contribute and purchases one or more animals with the donations. The ritual slaughter performed by a *shohet* takes place after the afternoon worship in the courtyard of a *knisa*. After appropriate prayers, including one for the health of the Shah, for Israel, and for an honored individual, the animal is slaughtered and the meat distributed to the poor.[1]

The origin of this custom is difficult to determine. Many of the educated believe it is a Muslim custom adopted by the Jews.[2] On the other hand, animal sacrifice is a practice indigenous to ancient Judaism. Nevertheless, the Shiraz community is unique in the Jewish world in its regular performance of animal sacrifice.

The sin offering is an important aspect of Shirazi Jewish religion. Shirazis believe that their *galut*, or "exile", by which they mean their hard lot, is the result of sin. The "original" sin, so to speak, of Iranian Jewry, was their refusal to return to Israel in the fifth century B.C.E., when Ezra, the Scribe, asked them to do so. But other important social sins, including the sowing of seeds of communal disunity, prostitution and cheating fellow Jews, have all contributed to the *galut*. Personal disasters are blamed on one's personal sins or those of his kinsmen. Sins against Heaven are the most difficult to cope with, as one cannot be sure whether or not one has committed them. The fervent piety, and observance of ritual is in an effort to atone for sin.

Some effective ways of expiating sin are by giving *ẓdaqa* and by contributing to the *knisa*; relatively large sums of money are given away during the penitential period around Rosh Hashana. *Kappara* combines the giving of *ẓdaqa* — since the poor share the meat — with the biblical expiation of sin by animal sacrifice. Since the Bible is the law-code with which Shirazis are most familiar, there is a tendency to imitate its ancient procedures. Each individual contributing to the *kappara* is believed to be expiating his personal sins, while the community as a whole is atoning for sins, real or imaginary, committed by the community or even the whole Jewish people.

So many critical activities take place in the synagogue, that it is clear that it is the central institution in Shirazi Jewish life. Despite the large number of synagogues, there does not appear to be a tendency for the communal structure to fracture along the lines of *knisa* attendance, except that the rich attend synagogues outside the Mahalleh. The synagogues are not in competition with each other; their members work together and cooperate in community affairs. In smaller settlements such

---

[1] Kurdish Jews are reported to perform a similar rite on Tish'a B'av (Brauer, 1947:253).

[2] It has been the custom in this part of the world to sacrifice a sheep in honor of a distinguished guest or to welcome a ruler. Wills (1887:231) reports that Jews used to do so in order to obtain favor with the local governor.

as Burujerd, Nahawand and Kerman, one synagogue serves the entire community, but a single central building would be impractical for so large a settlement as Shiraz. Security, convenience and economics have brought about the evolution of the Shirazi synagogue and necessitated the development of several complementary institutions of differential wealth and prestige.

SYNAGOGUE BEHAVIOR

The core of synagogue behavior is *ta'arof* (see Chapter IX). Seating is arranged by rank; the highest ranked sitting closest to the ark. All synagogue activity is characterized by deference and attempts to bestow honor.

Ta'arof, as has been suggested, serves as an exchange mechanism. The *knisa* is the only place of public assembly not exposed to outsiders and here men lay claim to rank and demonstrate their prestige by means of honor exchange and purchase. Indeed, some of the most important social behavior affecting the dynamics of community structure, can be observed here.

One important process occurring in the *knisa* is the selection of a *shaliaḥ ẓibbur* to lead a particular service. Since this is a role much sought after for the honor it brings and the piety and knowledge it allows one to demonstrate, competition to obtain it is intense.

If the chief *shaliaḥ ẓibbur* is present, he usually begins with an offer to someone to accept the honor of leading the worship: "*aqaye* so-and-so, *bakhavod!*" – "Mr. so-and-so, with the honor!" Mr. so-and-so declines the offer by offering it back, or less often, by deferring to someone else. The chief *shaliaḥ ẓibbur* may now offer the honor elsewhere or he may persist with his original choice. This *kavod*, or "ritual honor", is first offered to the substitute *shliḥe ẓibbur*. It is then offered to others in order of general rank, but with somewhat more weight given to knowledge of Judaica and to piety than in secular *ta'arof* situations. One need not wait to respond to an offer, but may at any time take the initiative in offering it to others providing the target of the offer is literate. The non-literate are excluded from such exchanges, thereby reinforcing a rank differentiation between literate and non-literate.

The transaction usually lasts two or three minutes. Only eight to ten men, out of a much larger congregation participate in a given transaction of this kind. At any point, non-participants can, and do, inject themselves into the procedure. After the first exchanges, participants sense who is eventually going to accept the *kavod*. The eventual recipient's attempts at deferral are quieter and less convincing than are those of other participants. Instead of gesturing with an offer and look-ing towards a potential recipient whom he addresses, the eventual recipient studiously looks at the floor. If initial offers are not directed at him, he initiates his own offers to the others. In terms of the total number of offers made, the eventual recipient enjoys a plurality by offering more frequently than anyone else. In this way, he covertly proclaims that he wants the *kavod*, while his overt behavior demonstrates his modesty. He apparently only accepts the honor because everyone is deferring it to him.

Such *ta'arof* is a game, albeit a serious one. The object is for the in-dividual to accrue as much honor as possible. One "scores" by: (a) accepting an offer after much protestation, (b) deferring the honor up-ward, (c) magnanimously bestowing it on someone lower in rank, (d) pressing it on a near-equal. All participants in these exchanges gain honor, though in different measure depending on their rank, posture dur-ing the exchange and other variables. Non-participants suffer relative loss of honor.

All things being equal, the highest honor accrues to whomever accepts the offer after appropriate attempts at deferral. One cannot, however, accept an honor offered by someone very much higher in rank should he make the mistake of offering it, as he would appear to be mocking the recipient. This is frowned upon, and both parties share a consequent loss of honor. The proper strategy is to defer to someone else and thus es-cape the embarrassment. One may accept an honor offered from below, since such is one's due. Honor-gaining strategies also depend on mood. One may simply not want to act as *shaliah zibbur*, so one accepts a lesser honor by deferring. One of high rank may defer to one of lower rank who is more pious, learned, or has a better voice. The elite need not participate in such exchanges at all without penalty, for "just as capital assures credit, so the possession of honor guarantees against dishonor" (Pitt-Rivers, 1966:37). In a sense, it is the elite who are keeping score in these exchanges, since they possess prestige and wish to deny it to others.

One who is observing *yerze'it* or "memorial day", or is in mourning may claim the role of *shaliah zibbur* without regard to rank and without even perfunctory deferral, usually without loss of honor. Sometimes, though, one of low rank may simply walk up to the lectern and begin praying, thereby seizing the right to lead the worship. Such outright violation of the rules causes these mavericks to lose honor and they may be publicly asked to relinquish the role, by the *hazzan*. It is surmised that this behavior occurs mainly among those who have despaired of gaining honor and prestige in the eyes of the community, and merely want the spiritual merit brought by leading the worship.

Another example of a behavior pattern peculiar to the synagogue is the auctioning of *kvodot*. *Kvodot* (literally: "honors") are certain ritual acts and objects. Included are: the opening of the ark and removal of the tora, the various *'aliyot* (being called to the reading of the Tora), ownership — for specified periods — of various parts of the *knisa*, such as the eternal light, and the right to lead certain prayers.

The various *kvodot* are of unequal merit. Among *'aliyot*, for example, the last, "*haftara*", is the most important, followed by *mashlim* (next to last), *shlishi* (third), *samukh* (preceding *mashlim*), *rvi'i* (fourth) and so forth. The first *'aliya* belongs to the *kohanim* and a non-priest rarely buys it, since he cannot personally make use of it.

Anyone can purchase *kvodot*; the illiterate and poor are by no means excluded from the bidding. The auction is conducted by the *ḥazzan* who collects immediately from the winning bidder or records the name of the winning bidder and his obligation.

The buyer of *kvodot* demonstrates piety and wealth. By purchasing a *kavod*, one evinces reverence for *knisa* and Tora, because the money goes for synagogue maintenance and improvement. During mourning especially, when fear of the "souls" impels one to testify to his respect for the dead by purchasing ritual honors whose merit accrues also to the deceased, many *kvodot* are bought. Traditionally, to make a show of wealth by conspicuous consumption was possible only in the *knisa*. As was indicated earlier, property, household goods and carpets were kept to a minimum for fear of their seizure by Muslims. One could safely demonstrate wealth by means of auctions, within the confines of the *knisa*.

The elite, who need not support their claim to wealth in this manner, but who fear to express a lack of piety by total abstention from bidding, try to purchase *kvodot* at low prices. Everyone else tries to keep the bidding up to justify the expectations of greater prestige that is derived from greater wealth.

The importance of the synagogue in the dynamics of intra-community social ordering is shown by the behavior of the social climber. As *knisa* is Shiraz's only public forum, social climbers make most of their rank-seeking moves here. The social climber becomes a vigorous defender of synagogue improvement. His attendance, if previously erratic, becomes more regular. He tries to make friends among the elite, with the hope that he will eventually be invited to sit among them "up front". He may even leave the Mahalleh *knisa* of his family and join a more prestigious one outside.

The social climber endeavors to call attention to himself for the "right" reasons. He enters *knisa* a few minutes late, puts on his *ẓiẓit* and *tfillin* while loudly reciting the appropriate blessings. Worship is momentarily suspended and attention is drawn to him, as everyone is expected to reply *"amen"*. After receiving an *'aliya* to the Tora, he like everyone else, waves the fringe of his *ẓiẓit* over the congregation and wishes them: *"kulkhem tihyu brukhim!"* "may you all be blessed!" But afterwards, he goes to the elders of the congregation, touches the fringe to their heads and kisses it personally bestowing on them this blessing.

A social climber wishes to verify his claim to higher rank by making a display of his wealth. He may make outright public donations to the *knisa* in honor of some event and he actively participates in the auctioning of *kvodot*. His bids are conspicuously directed to the more meritorious honors. He has the audacity to challenge the very wealthy in the bidding, sometimes bidding far beyond his means in order to best them or at least force them to pay dearly for the honor. He demonstrates generosity, by outbidding someone and then bestowing the *kavod* on his opponent; alternatively, he may purchase the honor for one who cannot afford to bid for it. Such generosity obligates its target to reciprocate in some way.

A social climber clinches his claim to higher rank by showing that he is considered a near-equal by the elite, through public *ta'arof* exchanges with them. He makes strenuous efforts to be included in the process of selecting the *shaliaḥ ẓibbur* as previously described. When he accepts this honor, he demonstrates his piety and learning while showing his acceptance by the elite.

THE ROLE OF SACRED MUSIC IN STABILIZING THE RITUAL TRADITION

Despite the deviations inherent in the Shirazi version of Judaism, it conforms remarkably well to the "great tradition", falling well within the acceptable range of variation from the ideal. In lieu of the sporadic contact maintained with communities elsewhere over the past millennium, it is rather remarkable that so many traditions were preserved intact. At least one key to understanding the survival of Shirazi Judaism as a strong viable tradition comes from an evaluation of prayer and the liturgical musical practice.

LITURGY

Jewish liturgy throughout the world is similar in structure and text. Basic prayer structure is derived from Talmudic sources and texts are based on various model prayer books such as the *Siddur* of Rav Amram Ga'on (died in 874 C.E.). Nevertheless, whenever a prayer book is compiled and published it includes the "little tradition" of the locality of the compiler. Such variation as the insertion of additional prayers and even the alteration of text which scholars consider the unchangeable "coin of prayer" may be included. The major distinctions in these "little traditions" occurred before the invention of printing. Since the sixteenth century and especially in the past fifty years, the proliferation of local liturgical rites has greatly diminished. While some local traditions have been maintained orally, most textual differences have been eliminated by the adoption of printed text of a more widely accepted rite such as the Lvorno or Amsterdam rite.

A unique Persion liturgical rite once extended as far as China in the East and Babylonia in the West (Adler, E., 1898:601). This Persian rite differed from other rites by its adherence to the *Siddur* of Sa'adya Ga'on (died in 942 C.E.). A sixteenth century liturgical manuscript (Adler, E., 1898:603) shows that this rite was followed in Shiraz until at least the seventeenth century and might have existed until the nineteenth century. Within the broad expanse of this Persian liturgical tradition there were undoubtedly local variations.

Since about the seventeenth century, printed prayer books of Sfardic origin have trickled into Shiraz and manuscripts of the older rite have disappeared. Such total submission to a foreign liturgical rite might be explained as recognition by Persian Jews of the relative inferiority of their scholarship in Judaica. Yemen, a more scholarly Jewish community, resisted alteration of its unique rite more successfully.

Shirazis have gradually adopted the rite of Lvorno (Italy) as their own, as it was one of the earliest printed texts to reach Shiraz. Today an effort is being made to conform more closely to the Baghdad rite. Prayers from the pre-Sfardic period are still preserved, but they are recited mainly during the penitential season. Until recently, the Judaeo-Persian religious poetry of Shahin (fourteenth century) and Amrani (sixteenth century) was read regularly.

A PHILOSOPHY OF PRAYER

The author was unable to determine with any precision what the Shirazi attitude towards prayer had been in the past. In all likelihood, much more time was devoted to worship then and, no doubt, there was much elaborate interpretation of prayer text with musical embellishment. One indication of a changing attitude toward prayer in present day Shiraz is the length of time worship lasts in the most and least traditional synagogues. On Rosh Hashana, the traditional synagogue service lasted five and one-half hours while a less traditional service was an hour shorter. On the Sabbath, morning worship lasted two hours in the traditional synagogue as compared to an hour and one-half in the more modern synagogue. Young educated Shirazis have little patience for extended public worship and become argumentative when the *shaliaḥ ẓibbur* seems to take too long.

To the Shirazi, text is everything in prayer while the music is incidental. The author was impressed by the sheer volume of text recited. Every word of each text is recited *out loud*. A *shaliaḥ ẓibbur* is preferred for his mastery of the text, his ability to read it quickly and accurately, and to interpret it should the congregation so desire. Knowledge of prayer modes and vocal prowess is of less importance, nowadays, at least.

Only at special occasions, such as during the penitential season, is prayer a deeply emotional communal and personal experience for most Shirazis. The good *shaliaḥ ẓibbur* most at these times completely identify with the text and dramatically interpret it for the congregation. The performance requires weeping, haranguing and, rarely, expression of joy. Congregants respond appropriately to the performance by mimicking the mood of the *shaliaḥ ẓibbur*, who often takes liberties with the text in order to effect an empathic response from the congregation. One *shaliaḥ ẓibbur,* boasting of his performance prowess, told the author:

I am the last *shaliaḥ ẓibbur* in Shiraz who weeps while praying. On Rosh Hashana many women come to *knisa* only in order to hear me.

While the boast is not completely accurate, there is no doubt that highly emotional rendition of prayer is a disappearing custom, not observed elsewhere in Iran.

The practice of translating important texts into Judaeo-Persian is common all over Iran, in recognition of the high rate of Hebrew illiteracy. The translations are strictly word by word and follow the Hebrew sentence structure. They are recited within the melodic context appropriate for the Hebrew texts. There is no formal pattern of translation such as alternatively reciting a verse in Hebrew and then its translation. The *shaliaḥ ẓibbur* shifts from language to language at will. More literary poetic interpretations of text exist in manuscripts and in the books of Ḥayyim More (1921, 1924, 1927), and are used by some better educated *shliḥe ẓibbur.*

SYNAGOGUE MUSIC

Sacred music is essentially a creation of the synagogue. It is wholly
unacompanied by instruments, which are not allowed there. In style it
differs substantially from Fars's folk music and Persian classical music.
It is the author's impression that there is very little in the corpus of
Shirazi Jewish liturgical music that is related to Muslim sacred music —
possibly less than 5% of the total.

Elsewhere (Loeb, 1970) I have demonstrated that Shirazi sacred
music belongs to a greater Babylonian–Persian regional style of Jewish
music. Some of the framework of the style must have been diffused
throughout the region despite the poor communications of the past centuries. Other evidence suggests careful attention to the preservation of
the local tradition, through screening out secular and non-Jewish in-
fluences and venerating old melodies and fidelity to traditional *nusaḥ*, i.e.
liturgical music modes.

The process by which change is accepted in Shirazi sacred music is
most instructive. Two criteria dominate the selection. Firstly, only
liturgical melodies from bonafide Jewish religious leaders can be
countenanced. During the fieldwork period, melodies from Israel and
from Otsar Hatorah, emissaries were considered appropriate *no matter
the ultimate origin of the tune*. Secondly, secular tunes of Persian origin,
when suitably presented by certain respected religious functionaries were
considered acceptable by elite Jews *tu khiyabun*, though Mahalleh
dwellers were less receptive to such innovation.

Suffice it to say that none of the melodies of foreign import were ab-
sorbed intact. The following melody for the *yigdal*[1] prayer may have
been introduced into Iran about 1955; it seems to have reached Shiraz in
the early 1960s:

Example "A"

---

[1] A fourteenth century hymn attributed to Daniel ben Judah of Rome — sung on Friday
nights in Shiraz.

The version found in, example "A" is known in Teheran, Burujerd, Kermanshah, Sanandaj and Shiraz. In Kermanshah the informant claimed it as his own creation. (In fact it was! – he had forgotten all but the first few notes of the original melody.) A Kashani informant from Teheran insisted that it was an old version from Kashan, but another informant contradicted this, saying that he had personally brought the melody back from Israel. The melody is actually of European Sfardic origin (see example "B") and can be traced at least to Bayonne France (Benharoche-Baralia, 1961:71). Since all of the cities where it is sung have or have had Alliance schools, it may well have been spread by an Alliance emissary, but more probably was an Otsar Hatorah import.

Example "B"

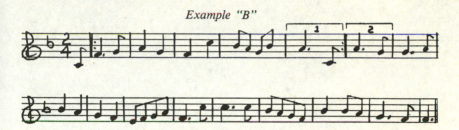

In Shiraz, everyone admits that this *yigdal* melody is a relatively new innovation. In the Mahalleh, people were still learning it in 1968, but sang it with great relish. Informants there could rarely repeat it the same way twice. Outside the Mahalleh, where they had been singing it for several years, the first verse was always sung in accordance with example "A", but the rest of the text was often sung to a melodic transformation invented by a young Yeshiva graduate. It is, stylistically typically Shirazi:

Example "C"

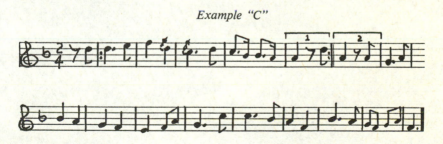

The sources of innovation in Shirazi liturgical music seemed to have been consciously limited in an effort to maintain the sacred music tradition. What is more, the process of absorption of melodies diffused from the outside caused them to be altered to conform to the local musical tradition. This process of stabilization carries over into the overall ritual tradition. The stability of the ritual tradition over the centuries has been the bedrock upon which a rich culture could continue to flourish in spite of the unfavorable social clime surrounding it.

CHAPTER XI

Redemption

Sound the great shofar of our freedom.
Raise on high the banner for the gathering of our exiles.
Assemble us together from the four corners of the earth.
Praised be You Lord, who gathers the dispersed of Your people
Israel.

(... from the daily petitionary prayer)

Redemption has always been understood by Jews to mean something concrete, not an intangible state of spirit. Jewish folk-literature abounds with stories about the messiah, his coming and life after that unprecedented event. But the central theme of Jewish redemption is the restoration of the people of Israel to their homeland, the land of Israel. While "little traditions" have embroidered on the fabric of redemption, its major theses vary little from community to community throughout the world.

The Jews of Shiraz, were the first Persian Jews to initiate the redemptive process, immigrating to the land of Israel in the decades preceding the rise of political Zionism in nineteenth century Europe. The initial group of emigrants from Shiraz left in 1815 and took a ship from Bushehr to Basra. From there they went overland by way of Baghdad and Damascus arriving half-dead from thirst and starvation. Some remained there, the rest went on to Safed and Jerusalem (Hakohen, 1970:48).

The first large scale *'aliya* (immigration to Israel) from Iran was undertaken in 1886. In 1892, the number of Shirazis in Jerusalem had reached 1000 (Mizrahi, 1959:202). The bulk of the early Iranian emigration was from Shiraz, whose citizens sought to escape the continual pogroms of the late nineteenth and early twentieth centuries. Exiles from the nearby towns of Lar and Jahrom arrived in Israel about 1910.

The usual group of emigrants numbered 50–100 and their journey was often the same undertaken by the handful of Shirazi Jews who made the *hajj* to Jerusalem. The group left Shiraz for a two-week or longer mule trip to Bushehr. At this hot, humid port on the Persian Gulf, they would wait weeks or even months for a ship to Egypt or perhaps Bombay. Eventually they would catch an Egypt-bound boat. After disembarking at Port Said they would make the caravan trip across the northern Sinai to Jerusalem. Time elapsed: six to twelve months!

From 1919 to 1948 some 3536 Jews from all of Iran settled in Israel (Gili, 1950:28) whereas, since then, more than 50,000 have gone there. Shirazis claim that since 1948 some 12,000 Jews left the city for Israel. The estimated Jewish population of Shiraz in 1949 was 15,000–20,000; by 1956 it had fallen to 8304 (Clarke, 1963:50). In that period, at least seven to twelve thousand Jews had left the city. In the following twelve years the population remained constant. Since the census population of Iran increased by about 41% from 1956 to 1966, some 3400 Jews, i.e. the potential increase from 1956 to 1968 must have left.[1] If a quarter of this total expected increase settled in Teheran[2] then about 2500 must have gone to Israel. Thus from 1948 to 1968 at least 9000–14,000 Shirazi Jews settled in Israel. Not surprisingly, all Shirazi Jews have large segments of their families in Israel with whom some degree of communication is maintained.

In the middle 1960s, *'aliya* was very low according to all sources: 1965 – 176, 1966 – 114, 1967 – 40 to 50, and 1968 – about 300. The 1968 rise in *'aliya* was due, in part, to the soccer riot in Teheran and the improved post-war conditions in Israel.

The large *'aliya* of the 1950s consisted primarily of the very pious and the destitute. Apparently the riff-raff went too, because until then, informants report that there were numbers of beggars and prostitutes, who have all but disappeared.

CONSEQUENCES OF 'ALIYA

It was previously suggested that since 1949 overcrowded living conditions in the Mahalleh had declined dramatically. One factor in this improvement most probably was the departure of at least half of the city's Jewish population. At the same time, the general standard of living of the

---

[1] No evidence was found suggesting that the birth rate among Shirazi Jews is lower than among the general Iranian population; infant mortality is most certainly lower among Jews, thanks to community medical facilities. The figures presented are, if anything, somewhat conservative.

[2] Shirazi Jews do not like to emigrate to the other cities of Iran; the bulk of emigrants prefer Israel.

Jewish community as a whole improved because a substantial proportion of emigrants were indigent.

Nevertheless, *'aliya* has wreaked havoc with many of the traditional
community institutions. In the forefront of the *'aliya* movement have
been the community's learned and pious religious leadership. Their
departure was noted as early as 1900 (Melamed, 1951:368) and has
been responsible in large measure for the general decline in the level of
religious knowledge and observance in Shiraz. Furthermore, there is a
noticeable dearth of scholarship and an absence of committed leadership
among the generally lackluster pietists remaining.

LOVE FOR ISRAEL

In a visit to Shiraz in 1945, an emissary from Palestine had a conversation with Mulla Aqajan, one of the community elders, The emissary urged him to go to the land of Israel, to the holy city of Jerusalem. Mulla
Aqajan replied: "Any place that is good to me — there is Jerusalem".
When asked, why in his prayers he said: "Next year in Jerusalem", he
answered: "Yes, in the prayers, yes. But it is also written: 'God will command me'; I am waiting for a sign from heaven". Not long after, when
somewhat inebriated, Mulla Aqajan began dancing and shouting: "Next
year in Jerusalem, yes, next year on Mount Zion". (Yishay, 1950:310).
All Shirazis pay lip service to *'aliya* and proclaim their intention to go to
Israel, someday. But whether they go or stay, all are sincere in their love
for Israel.

Eight p.m. each evening is consecrated to the Voice of Israel broad-
cast (in Persian) on the radio. Meetings and evening prayers are delayed
until its conclusion; Shabbat and holiday meals are interrupted to catch
it; in fact, all evening events are scheduled around the half-hour
program. All segments of the population, young and old, literate and illiterate, rich and poor, listen avidly. Bad news about Israel can evoke the
calling of a prayer vigil for the reading of Psalms and penitential prayers.
When, for example, news reached Shiraz that Moshe Dayan, then Israeli
Defense Minister, was injured in an archeological excavation cave-in, a
kappara accompanied by special prayers was performed to insure his
speedy recovery.

During the Six Day War, when Jews were too afraid to congregate in
synagogues, they spent hours in nearby homes praying for Israel's existence and victory, while comparatively large sums were raised and
donated for reconstruction and relief there. Preachers tried to weave the
Arab states and their leaders into Kabbalistic schemes designed to

reassure the congregation of Israel's ultimate triumph. In 1968, prayers were recited daily for the survival of the State of Israel. When the Asian Cup soccer matches took place that same year, Jews rooted for Israel against Iran, although many were afraid of the personal consequences should Israel have won.[1]

In a sense, Israel is an extension of each Shirazi Jew. Each Israeli success is considered a personal success and each failure a personal loss. Anything or anyone associated with Israel is considered of special merit. Israeli visitors to Shiraz are treated with the greatest reverence and respect. The study of spoken Hebrew has become most prestigious, motivating many middle and upper ranked Jews to pay for private lessons.

CULTURE HEROES

Whereas in traditional culture there was very little in the way of culture heroes, modern Shirazis found one in Moshe Dayan. After the Six Day War many of the sons born in Shiraz were named Moshe or Moshe Dayan. Shirazis view Moshe Dayan as everything they would like but are unable to be: brave enough to talk tough to Muslim Arabs, able to publicly ridicule them and strong enough to back up his words with force. The Yom Kippur War was no doubt most disappointing with respect to his image.

Shirazis were by no means nonplussed at the appointment of Golda Meir, a woman, as Israeli Prime Minister. As one informant put it, "Debora the prophetess was a woman who provided outstanding leadership for the Jewish people, and so, God willing, will Golda".

THE EMIGRATION PROCESS

The question of *'aliya* in a Muslim country is a very delicate one. The government places no major obstacles in the way of the emigrant to Israel, but it does keep careful watch on the operations of the Jewish organizations fostering *'aliya*. Public rallies to encourage *'aliya* are infrequent and must have police approval.

---

[1] Spicehandler (1970:16) reports riots in Teheran resulting from tension over an Israel-Iran soccer clash in the Autumn of 1967. To the best of my knowledge the only incident of that kind during the fieldwork period occurred May 21, 1968 when Iran bested Israel in an Asian Cup match on a disputed goal after which victory-intoxicated mobs rushed through the Teheran Mahalleh, damaging some property.

'*Aliya* affairs in Iran are handled by the "Sokhnut", or Jewish Agency which has a permanent representative in Shiraz. The latter does not actively search for immigrants, but waits for the potential immigrant to come to him. Depending on the economic circumstances of the immigrant, the "Sokhnut" may pay for the passport, plane fare, transport of possessions as well as all in-transit expenses. Transfer of capital is arranged and, in the past, males occasionally had to first be freed of their military obligation.

Once in Israel the Jewish Agency and various government offices provide the immigrant with housing, minimal furniture, employment and schooling for the children. Acculturation there is supposed to be constantly reinforced by social workers, but usually the new immigrants are abandoned to their own devices. Unable to speak the language, unused to strange customs and hard labor, immigrants write home of the hardships of adjusting. There is a small but steady stream of returnees to Shiraz.

The immigrants, many of whom had been denying themselves modern conveniences for years, take with them carpets and silver, with the hope of reselling these items in Israel. Some of the poor even purchase refrigerators and at least one family bought a large gas range, although for months they did not know how to make use of it. Modern western toilet facilities present a problem to the new immigrant. An Israeli architect reported that in immigrant housing he designed, the Iranian Jews were keeping the toilets constantly flushing, while watermelons were cooled in the flowing water. [1] The new settlers frequently hide their carpets and use only the few cots and stools provided by the Jewish Agency, in an effort to demonstrate their poverty to the social workers. Lower class parents strongly object to having their older sons and daughters in school and insist that they find work. Adjustment to Israeli life takes a number of years.

MOTIVATION AND OBSTRUCTION TO 'ALIYA: "IF NOT NOW, WHEN?" (Avot 1:14)

Most Shirazis, especially the lower class, realize that they could improve their financial position and provide their children with a more secure future in Israel. The worst living quarters in Israel are better than the lower and low-middle class Mahalleh homes. The daily (albeit minor)

---

[1] This is a common anecdote told about all of the oriental immigrants in Israel.

PLATE 96   Israeli emissaries discuss *'aliya* activity with the local Sokhnut representative.

PLATE 97   Knisa Kohanim packed with Mahalleh dwellers to hear a visiting Israeli emissary.

harassment at the hands of the Muslims in Iran is known to be absent in Israel. Why then has *'aliya* fallen to such low levels in the recent past?

The difficulty of adjustment to Israel, briefly outlined above, is further complicated by a considerable degree of prejudice among the Israelis toward the Iranian immigrants. The Iranians are said to be liars, cheaters and thieves. *"Farsi miduni?"* (do you speak Persian) is a favorite mocking question asked by the Israeli of the merchant who tries to cheat him. This hostility to the Iranian is not unfounded for their values with regard to honesty are not similar to Western values. Their illiteracy and ignorance of modern ideas are proverbial. The educational system in Iran is such that it contrasts starkly with the Israeli, i.e. rote learning versus comprehension and understanding; hence the Iranian trained teacher or engineer is at a distinct disadvantage in competing with the Israeli. Young people object that the Israelis do not accept Iranian professional diplomas. Children must often make up several years of school. Parents do occasionally send their teen-age children ahead to Israel on Youth 'Aliya to be educated and trained in Israel, in preparation for settlement.

The Shiraz elite have no intention of going to a place where their money would not buy them freedom from prejudice. Many have invested in Israel, but would emigrate only if necessary, and preferably to the United States. The elite are afraid, too, that their money would not allow them to live as well in Israel as they live in Shiraz; nor would they be accepted among the elite there.

The middle class people have no skills and often lack the capital to invest in a store in Israel. Many Shirazis say that the poor do not choose to emigrate because JDC makes things too easy for them in Iran. Why should they go to Israel and work hard, when they can stay home and make ends meet through relief? Shirazis, in fact, do complain that in Israel it is necessary to work hard. In Shiraz most Jews avoid manual labor and prefer to work no harder than is necessary to subsist.

Shirazi Jews are also afraid of the war. They will go to Israel just as soon as the war is over, they claim. The expansive press coverage given the Arabs by Iran radio, frightens the Jew and serves to more securely anchor him in Shiraz.

The Jewish Agency's passive approach to *'aliya* has borne little fruit. Occasionally an Israeli emissary is sent to Shiraz to stir up *'aliya* but the interval between these trips is too long to sustain interest. A team of Israeli engineers stationed in Shiraz was a potential motivating force, but the team's disdain for the Shirazi Jews whom they would not hire because they were "too lazy" and whom they generally avoided, effectively eliminated these Israelis from stimulating *'aliya*.

Family ties also hobble attempts at *'aliya.* A single girl cannot go to Israel, because it would be said that she was "bad" thus impugning family honor.[1] Children who go, often cannot resist their mothers' pleas to come back: "If you don't come back, my death will be your fault". The actual death of someone in the family often brings the mourner back from Israel; in all probability, he will be unable to sever the tie again. The objection of someone important in the family means that the entire family must stay put. In one case, a man, his wife and five children, plus his brother's family, could not go, because his wife's mother did not want them to do so.

One family of teen-agers and young adults did not go because their old father (who they all agree is a good-for-nothing) did not want to go. The mother wanted to go, so he said: "Go, I'll give you a *get*, 'divorce' ". They stayed, because the mother would have had to give up her *ktuba* money and the children would not go without her.

Many Jews have money lent out to Muslims or own property jointly with them. Muslim debtors are slow to return the money or refuse to do so; they also refuse to buy the Jew's property at a fair price. Shirazi Jews will forego pleasures and endure hardship, if to do otherwise would necessitate their giving up their claim to wealth.

Each negative remark about Israel received in the mail from relatives or friends, quickly becomes common knowledge. A *yored*, "returnee", does more to disrupt *'aliya* than all the Arab war threats, because it confirms the fears of the potential immigrant that he too will not succeed there. The *yored* bitterly complains of the hard work, and sometimes of the type of employment. Due to lack of vocational skills, most Shirazis on *'aliya* have to go into physical labor such as construction, house painting and street sweeping. The middle class immigrant always tries to set up a shop; Israel has too many shopkeepers and the competition is frequently too great for the new immigrant.

Hushang says: "We shall go in the autumn, so the children will not miss any school". The fall comes and passes and he says: "It is too cold in winter, we shall wait until summer". His wife becomes pregnant and he says: *"daste khoda",* ("it is the hand of God!"). We shall wait until the child is born and weaned." When this too passes, she may again become pregnant or he may say: "It is too late! Now our son must go into military service!" "Are you really going, Hushang?" ... *"Omide khoda!"* ("I hope to God"). "Why haven't you gone yet?" *"Qesmat!"* ("It is fate"). "When are you going?" *"Ensha'allah!"* ("God willing").

---

[1] In the past, girls suspected of prostitution were sent to Israel; so any single girl who is sent today is suspected of the same.

REVITALIZATION OR ASSIMILATION

And He said to me:
Son of man! Can these bones live?
And I replied:
Lord, God! You surely know!
(Ez. 37:3)

Though large numbers of Shirazis have emigrated since 1948, a considerable remnant appears to be unwilling to leave. In viewing their present circumstances, many Jews point to the considerable progress made by the Iranian government in removing the official stigma from the Jew. No longer are they a "pariah group" buffeted at the whim of those in a position to exploit them. The urban masses, occasionally spurred to open hostility by the harrangues of the *shi'a* clergy are constrained by the authorities from acting against the Jewish population. The growing political acceptance of real citizenship for the Jew has thus eased the pressure for emigration. But while some of the tension arising from traditional antagonism has abated, Shirazi Jews by no means feel totally secure or capable of relaxing their wary vigilance.

Informants report that there have been few radical changes since 1968, but that trends then evolving have rapidly developed. As of 1975, less than 20% of the Jews live in the Mahalleh and the atmosphere of the area is considerably less Jewish. While many of the community institutions, the synagogues, the butchers, the *maqve, hamum* and Joint clinic are still located within the Mahalleh, it is likely that future construction will take place *tu khiyabun*. The flow of emigration is not much changed, so that the overall population has remained stable or has even increased slightly. Jews moving out of the Mahalleh continue to settle to the west and northwest of the old quarter.

The importance and influence of Joint and Otsar Hatorah appear to be waning. The resident foreign director of Joint left in 1969 and the program has since been administered by locally trained Jews. The erratic feeding program no longer has the appeal it once had, since free schooling and feeding is one of the recent benefits offered the Iranian people as a result of the country's multifold-increased oil wealth. The schools and clinic continue, but there may be some question as to whether these institutions will be maintained as in the recent past. With the final closing of the Yeshiva in 1969, the major source of trained Hebrew teachers and religious reform has been eliminated. The return of Yizḥaq Ba'al Hanes as the community's first properly ordained Rabbi, has not had the impact it might have as the Anjoman has carefully circumscribed his role, severely restricting his function in the decisionmaking sphere by prohibiting him from serving as *dayan*. The Anjoman itself, has not become democratic in the manner prescribed in its charter, which has been a source of irritation for many of the young elite.

The occupational structure of Shirazi Jewry continues its shift towards professionalism as more young people finish high school, vocational school and college. Fewer Jews are becoming unskilled laborers, though large numbers are still opening up shops of every description, especially cloth, haberdashery, appliances, cameras, etc. Recent inflation has increased the poverty of some and there has been increasing unemployment for laborers and independent artisans. As young men increasingly seek employment outside of Shiraz, the available pool of unmarried females continues to expand while dowries skyrocket.[1]

Informants have not indicated whether Jews are entering industry or in what capacity they are involved in the cosmopolitization of metropolitan Shiraz, whose current population numbers about one-half million. But they do agree that modernization of Shiraz and the exposure to western ideas, is having a marked effect on religious observance.

Despite the long fossilization of Shirazi Judaism, Jews successfully resisted the easy escape from persecution and outcaste-status by conversion to Islam. In retrospect, Persian Jewish culture may long been seriously deficient in substance, innovation and scholarship, especially when compared with the rich spiritual cultures of Yemen, Morocco and Europe. Yet, somehow, ritual, symbolism and the religious structure itself always provided sufficient impetus for Jewish self-preservation.

Today, however, elite Shirazi youth, as their Teherani counterparts did ten years earlier, frequent the local nightclubs, where they are conspicuous in their consumption of non-kosher food. Observance of *kashrut* is in general decline as is the observance of the Sabbath and festivals. The disintegration of the bedrock of socio-cultural stability, i.e. the ritual tradition, especially where much of the potential leadership of the community has had little Jewish education, bodes poorly for the future of the community's ethnic and religious integrity. But social sentiment on behalf of the Jewish people and commitment to Israel remain consummate; there is as yet no evidence of Jewish participation in leftist or other anti-Israel groups. Support of the Shah also remains strong, though there may be some concern over the latter's recent rapprochement with Iraq, negative comments regarding Israeli attitudes and

---

[1] One informant on a visit to Teheran in the summer of 1976 reported that the situation there was far worse. Dowries had soared to 30 million *rials* in some cases and Jewish girls were said to be marrying gentile men.

behavior, and official support of the anti-Zionism resolution of the U.N. General Assembly in November of 1975.

The new social equilibrium which has continued to evolve in recent years has therefore evoked renewed concern about the internal well-being of the Shirazi Jewish community. The pious anxiously seek to revitalize religious life while assimilation insidiously tugs at the increasingly secular-minded youth. Israel continues to send emissaries as teachers and to stimulate *'aliya*, but efforts, both internal and external, to revitalize Iranian Judaism generally and Shirazi Judaism specifically, lie dormant. The indigenous leadership of Shiraz lacks the charisma and drive once provided by Natan Eli. Foreign Jewish religious and social institutions, emotionally and financially overcommitted to Israel are incapable or unwilling to undertake a new involvement in Iran. No doubt people will someday look back and view this as a costly wasted opportunity. But for the moment, it appears as if the future of Shirazi Jewry is to be left again to "the hand of God".

APPENDIX I

Outline of Iranian Jewish History

According to a well-known Persian-Jewish legend, the first Jew to have set foot in Iran was the biblical Seraḥ bat Asher, grand-daughter of Jacob, the patriarch. Her accidental arrival occured one day as she was tending sheep for her father in the Judaean hills. A lamb strayed into a cave and she pursued it in an effort to return it to the flock. The chase through the cavern seemed unusually long, but she persevered and caught up with the stray as it emerged from another cave opening – not far from present-day Isfahan!

The earliest written reference to Jewish settlement in Iran is biblical. In Kings II (17:6) we learn that Shalmaneser, king of Assyria,

took Samaria, and carried Israel away unto Assyria, and placed them in Halah, and Habor, on the river Gozan and in the cities of the Medes.

This exile took place in 722 B.C.E. There were several smaller banishments, beginning some thirty-five years earlier and extending for some years after the fall of Samaria. Most of the Jews were settled in the northern Zagros mountains, primarily in the region we know as Kurdistan.

In 597 B.C.E., Nebukhadnezzar, King of Babylon, conquered Judaea and

carried away all Jerusalem, and all the princes and all the mighty men of valour, even 10,000 captives, and all the craftsmen and the smiths; none remained, save the poorest sort of the people of the land. (Kings II, 24:15)

In 586 B.C.E., he destroyed the Temple of Solomon and exiled the remnant population (Kings II, 25:11). Various early Islamic scholars, such as Yaqut, Muqaddasi and al-Qazvini claim that Nebukhadnezzar settled many of these Jews in Isfahan, and that the city was called *al-Yahudiyya* (the Jewish city). It was further claimed that the Jews liked this area because the climate resembled Jerusalem's (Fischel, 1935:523–5). The Talmud gives a similar explanation for Jewish settlement at Tustari (Shushtar) in Khuzistan (Fischel, 1935:526).

274

Cyrus, the first of the Achaemenian kings of Persia, made Susa his capital. Iranian Jews maintain to the present day, that *shushan habbira* or "Susa, the Capital", was the city of Hamadan.[1] In 538 B.C.E., Cyrus agreed to the restoration of the Temple at Jerusalem and many thousands of Jews returned to Judaea. He thereby set an example of religious tolerance towards the Jewish minority, which was, for the most part, followed by succeeding Achaemenians. While Persian imperial policy encouraged preservation of national mores among its subject peoples, Persia's amicable relations with the Jews were further enhanced by the superficial similarity in their respective religious approaches (Baron, 1952:129)

From the book of Daniel we learn that Jews quickly ingratiated themselves with the various dynasties of Babylonian and Persian kings. The achievement of high rank and political influence by Daniel, who was appointed governor of Babylon (Daniel 2:48), and by Ezra the Scribe, and Nehemiah, who was made governor of Judaea (Nehemia 5:14), was regarded by these men as serving a divine purpose in the deliverance of their people. Their efforts were probably emulated by others too. Jewish influence in the Persian Empire was so great, that in 419 B.C.E., Darius II commanded all of the Jews in the kingdom to strictly observe the feast of Unleavened Bread (Baron, 1952:131).

However farsighted this policy of tolerance for ethnic minorities was, it nevertheless fostered the assimilation of minority groups within the Empire. Thus Jewish separatism was often viewed suspiciously by the Achaemenians and sometimes efforts were made to suppress it (Daniel 3:8–30, 6, Esther 3:8–15).

The first recorded attempt to destroy Persia's Jewish minority occurred in the reign of Aḥashverosh (Artaxerxes II? – 404–361 B.C.E.). Fortunately, Esther, a Jewish queen, managed to modify the attitude of the government, which then permitted the Jews to prepare a defense against their adversaries. The apparently well-organized Jewish communities defended themselves successfully (Esther 9:5–12), and Jewish political power reached new heights with the downfall of Haman, the chief vizier.

Many from among the peoples of the land became Jews; for the fear of the Jews was fallen upon them. (Esther 8:18)

---

[1] The evidence tends to refute this myth. Excavations at a large site in Khuzistan have convinced archeologists that it must have been Susa. It has been suggested, however, that Hamadan (Ecbatana) may well have been one of Cyrus's summer residences (Margolis and Marx, 1927:117).

Not long after, Persian–Jewish relations again deteriorated. *Circa* 340 B.C.E., Artaxerxes III Ochus forcibly deported many Jews to Hyrcania (Gilan-Mazanderan) on the Caspian, where they remained until at least the fifth century C.E. (Neusner, 1965:11). This action may have been a response to rebellion movements among the Jews of Persia (Baron, 1952:131). Little is known about the Hellenistic period following Alexander's conquest of Persia in 331 B.C.E.

The Parthian Arsacid dynasty ruled Persia and Mesopotamia from about 175 B.C.E. to 226 C.E. The Parthians were more flexible and tolerant in religious matters than the last Achaemenians. The good relations that Jews shared with the Parthians is attested to by the lack of complaint about them in Jewish sources; Jews in fact looked to the Parthians for aid in achieving national redemption (Neusner, 1965:68). For political reasons, the Parthians aided the Hasmonean kings of Judaea against the Seleucids and later against the Romans. Jews fought alongside the Parthians and some were reputed to be accomplished warriors (Neusner, 1965:39). The Parthians granted Jews a considerable measure of local autonomy.

During the first century C.E., a sovereign Jewish state existed for fifteen years near Nehardea, north of present-day Baghdad (Josephus, Antiquities: XVIII, 9:1–9). About the same time there was another Jewish satrapy at Adiabene, (in the northwestern Zagros), under Izates and Queen Helena.

Not very much is known about Jewish community organization during this period. As far back as Achaemenian times, genealogical scrolls were carefully kept and maintained. In all likelihood, they were reposited in archives and preserved for many centuries, as such collections "enhanced the orderliness and continuity of communal management" (Baron, 1948:72) by certifying succession and inheritance. Some Jewish communal authorities were officials of the Parthian government. They maintained large retinues and held the power of life and death over their co-religionists. By the end of the second century C.E., the Parthians recognized the office of Exilarch and granted its holder supreme authority in Jewish civil matters for the whole empire.

The Sassanians (226 to 646 C.E.), successors to the Parthians established their administrative capital at Veh-Ardashir, across the river from Ctesiphon in Babylonia. The religious center was located in the Sassanian home province of Fars, at Istakhr. Under the Sassanians, Jewish settlements were to be found at Susa and Shushtar in Elam (Khuzistan), on the shores of lake Urmia, on the Caspian Sea, at Hamadan, Nahawand, Isfahan and probably in Kurdistan and Fars.

The Sassanians took steps to annul Jewish legal autonomy and made it clear that their government would supervise the activities of Jewish courts as the Parthians never had. For a time, even the Exilarchy was weakened, but later on, this office regained its authority. At the height of his power, the Exilarch "ranked as the fourth highest officer of the empire, immediately following its two military chiefs"; he

was a member of the chief council of state, advising the Persian "king of kings" not only in matters directly relevant to the Jewish community, but also in state-wide affairs. (Baron, 1948:146–7)

The position was not always a secure one and the actual circumstances of the Exilarch varied greatly under each ruler. The influence of the Exilarch over Persian Jewry lasted until the thirteenth century when communications between Babylonian and Persian Jews seem to have been finally severed as a result of the Mongol invasions and their aftermath.

While Jewish scholarship was highly developed in Babylonia during the Sassanian period, it was not as well developed in Persia. Elam was said to produce students, but not teachers, of the law (Neusner, 1966:258). Already by the end of the third century C.E., a language schism was occurring, effecting a separation of Babylonian Jews from those in nearby Elam.[1]

The most serious problem facing Persian Jews during the Sassanian period was religious hostility. Mazdaism was made the state cult under Ardashir I (226–241) and it was he who established a church hierarchy. Neusner (1966:15) claims that these church officials "vigorously persecuted other religions." Under Shahpur I (241–272), his successor, more tolerance was shown towards minorities. However, his chief priest, Kartir, was extremely hostile towards Jews and other religious groups and is said to have instigated further repressive measures against them after the death of Shahpur I (Neusner, 1966:18–19).

The extent and nature of the Zoroastrian clergy's hostility to Judaism is not clear. Certain Jewish religious practices appear to have been objectionable. Thus the custom of lighting the Ḥanukka lamp so that it could be seen from the street was altered because of opposition from the Magi (Neusner, 1966:36)[2] Zoroastrians considered the burying of corpses a defilement of the earth. Jews had considerable difficulty in persuading the Sassanians that burial was a religious requirement; Shahpur II even demanded scriptural proof for this practice (San. 46b).

---

[1] A Talmudic text indicates the necessity of translating the scroll of Esther to Elamite, for the Jews living there (Meg. 18a).

[2] To this day Persian Jews light candles in windows facing the enclosed courtyard so that candlelight can not be seen from the street.

During the reign of Shahpur II (310–379), thousands of Jews were deported from Armenia and settled at Isfahan. Some sources suggest that Shushan-Dokht, daughter of the Exilarch Huna bar Nathan and wife of Shahpur's son, Yazdegerd I (399–421), founded the Jewish quarter of Isfahan (Fischel, 1953:112).[1] In any case, the forced removal of Jews to Isfahan suggests their importance as an economic asset to the Sassanians.

Meanwhile, religious intolerance of minorities by the Magi worsened, until, under Yazdegerd II (438–457) the clergy were given free reign. Jews were prohibited from reciting the *shma'*[2] in public (Mizrahi, 1966:23). Sabbath candles could not be lit because of the Zoroastrian reverence for fire; eventually Jews were forbidden to observe the Sabbath altogether, but they continued doing so secretly (Mizrahi, 1966:23).

These measures of suppression within a pervasive anti-Jewish atmosphere culminated in widespread and open hostility against Persian Jewry. Sparked by rumors of the murder of two Zoroastrian priests by Jews, riots broke out in Isfahan. Firuz (459–484), in an effort to placate the clergy and the mobs, ordered the execution of half of Isfahan's Jewish population and the forcible conversion of all Jewish children there. Elsewhere in the Empire, Jewish schools were closed, assemblies for teaching prohibited and Jewish legal autonomy suspended (Baron, 1957:55; Graetz, 1956: 629). In 471, the Exilarch, Huna Mari was executed along with some Jewish scholars. His son, Mar Zutra II, who succeeded him as Exilarch, set up an independent Jewish principality at Mahoza in Mesopotamia. It lasted for seven years, until 492, when the area was captured by the Persians and Mar Zutra and Mar Hanina (the head of an academy) were executed. It is quite possible that the flight of Jews from Persia and Babylonia to India's Malabar Coast, under Joseph Rabban, resulted from these persecutions.

Not long after these events, Persian Jews were faced with the Mazdakite upheaval with its emphasis on communal property and access to women, prompting the emigration of some Jews to Palestine. But in general, the situation was improved during the sixth century. Under Khosroe I (537–579), the Jewish tax burden was lightened by the

---

[1] A Pahlavi source cited in Baron (1952a:404) states; "The cities of Shus and Shuster were built by Shoshan-Dukht, wife of Yazdkart I, son of Shahpur. She was the daughter of the Resh Galuta, King of the Jews; she was the mother of Bahram Gur."

[2] The *shma'* is a biblical verse (Deut. 6:4) proclaiming the existence and unity of God Jews recite it every evening and morning and it is the last expression of faith recited by a Jew on his death bed. Whereas the complete *shma'* consists of several biblical paragraphs (Deut. 6:4-9, 11:13-21, Nu. 15:37-41), many Persian Jews know only the first sentence.

application of a universal poll tax (Baron, 1957:56). Towards the end of the century, most of Persia's attention was directed towards the military threat from Byzantium. Jews in the western provinces suffered greatly at the hands of the Christians who imposed baptism on the community of Melitene in Armenia, and who staged a pogrom at Maḥoza, near Ctesiphon.

ISLAM

By 642, the conquest of Persia by the Arab armies was almost complete. The conquerors were greeted with open arms by the Jews who had had no reason to esteem the deposed Sassanians. The Arabs showed their gratitude to the Jews by presenting the Exilarch, Bustani, with a captured Sassanian princess whom he subsequently married. Jews were granted the status of *dhimmi* (protected minority) as were the Christians and Zoroastrians. For the "protection" provided by Islam, and the privilege of remaining Jewish and maintaining semi-autonomy, Jews were obligated to assume a heavy tax burden. But for at least the first hundred years of Islam in Persia, the Jews suffered no persecution (Mizrahi, 1966:27).

During the Arab (Eastern Caliphate) and the later Turko-Mongol (eleventh to thirteenth century) periods, Jewish settlement was widespread throughout Persia. Large numbers were to be found in rural and urban locations in the southwestern quadrant of country which contemporary Arab geographers designated "Yahudistan", due to the numbers and influence of the Jews residing there.

Towards the end of the twelfth century, Benjamin ibn Tudela reported large Jewish populations in Hamadan, Shiraz, Isfahan, Tustar (Shushtar) and Rudbar (Qazvin), and smaller numbers in Nahawand and Neyshahpur (Adler, M., 1907). Rural Jews were living in the land of the Assassins, Tabiristan (Mazanderan) and Khorassan. In the latter province, Benjamin speaks of a mountain kingdom of Jews, ruled by a Jewish prince (Adler, M., 1907:59). Jews living in the north-western provinces ruled by the Assassins were brigands and allies of the latter. (Adler, M., 1907:54).[1] Yet they, like the Jews of Isfahan and the rest of Persia, were still considered under the ultimate authority of the Exilarch, in Baghdad (Adler, M., 1907:54, 58). Actually, the chief Rabbi of Isfahan, known as the Sar Shalom (Prince of Peace) was appointed by

---

[1] Inhabitants of the Kerend region, an area the Assassins once ruled, claim Jewish origin (Bishop, 1891:86).

the Exilarch to have jurisdiction over all of the Rabbis in the kingdom of Persia (Adler, M., 1907:58).

Isfahan appears to have been the main center of learning in Persia, but there may well have been a Talmudic academy in twelfth century Hamadan. In the tenth century, Isfahani scholars were known for their mastery of grammar and exegesis (Fischel, 1953:116). On the other hand, it was reported that

the Jews of Isfahan mispronounce the Hebrew language to such an extent as to make it unrecognizable. (Fischel, 1953:116)

Benjamin reports the presence of scholars throughout Persia (Adler, M., 1907). Eldad, the Danite, tells us that even the tribal Jews he found spoke Hebrew, and possessed the Mishna, Talmud and Haggada. Every Sabbath they read the Tora with accents *(ta'ame hammiqra)* in Hebrew and then translated the text into Persian (Adler, E., 1966:8). Jewish literacy was seemingly quite high during this period. Petaḥya of Ratisbon (1174–1185) observes:

There is no one so ignorant in the whole of Babylonia, Assyria, Media and Persia, but knows the twenty-four books (of the Bible), punctuation grammar, the superfluous and omitted letters, for the preceptor does not recite the scripture lesson, but he that is called up to the scroll of the law recites it himself. (Adler, E., 1966:70)

Jewish commercial interests were varied under Arab rule. Most Jews were engaged as artisans, dyers, weavers (Fischel, 1953:116) and in "humble trades such as those of cupping, tanning, fulling" and butchering (Mez, 1937:39). In Isfahan, Persia's most important city, the Jewish quarter was the business quarter. The Persian carpet industry, its headquarters located at Tustar, was largely in Jewish hands (Mez, 1937:478–9). The entire Persian Gulf pearl industry was controlled by a Jew. International trade was for the most part conducted by the Jewish "Radanites" who had access to otherwise restricted areas such as Kashmir. Jewish bankers in Baghdad served as court bankers and exerted much influence on commerce throughout Persia (Mez, 1937:479). Persian Jewish interests extended to Jerusalem, where they lived in large numbers (Goitein, 1955:113), and even to the Maghreb (Goitein, 1975:9).

Late in the seventh century, after fifty years of Arab rule, the first of a series of sporadic messianic and sectarian movements arose in the Persian capital of Isfahan. The first of these "Messiah's precursors", named Abu-Isa (Isaac Obadiah), an illiterate tailor, miraculously began to write learned religious tracts. He proclaimed the coming liberation of Persian Jewry, leading 10,000 adherents against the Caliph's army. Drawing a rope about his encircled followers, he declared that all within were safe from the enemy. While he defeated his foe on that occasion, he was eventually vanquished and himself felled in battle. His followers believed that he survived and was hidden in the mountains. Abu-Isa referred to himself as the "forerunner and awakener (Dai) who was to prepare for the coming of the Messiah" (Graetz, 1956a:124). There were to be five of these precursors of the Messiah, each more perfect than the previous one. He was the fifth and last of these to precede the Messiah. Abu-Isa promulgated a number of extensive reforms in Jewish ritual and theology. Worship was to be performed *seven* times daily instead of thrice, sacrificial worship was abolished, divorce was forbidden, the consumption of meat and wine proscribed, and Jesus and Mohammad proclaimed true prophets whose teachings were to be studied. Followers of Abu-Isa, called Issavites, still existed in tenth century Damascus (Dubnov, 1968:334–5; Graetz, 1956a:124–5).

A disciple of Abu-Isa, Yudgan of Hamadan, known as the "shepherd" (*al-rai*), founded a similar sect somewhat later. He rejected the observance of the Sabbath and Festivals, opposed biblical expressions of anthropomorphism and advanced the principle of free will in opposition to Muslim fatalism. Yudgan's disciple, Mushkhan led a holy war against his opponents and was slain in a battle near Qom.

The more important Karaite schism of the ninth and tenth centuries, found many protaganists in Persia. This sect's most important leaders were Persian, including Benjamin ben Moses of Nahawand who was strongly influenced in his opposition to Rabbinite Judaism by the philosophy of Yudgan, from nearby Hamadan. (Graetz, 1956a:150). Karaites were found in Khorassan, Jibal (north-western Iran), Fars, Tustar and Isfahan (Fischel, 1960:1150; 1953:116). In Fars, they survived until at least the fifteenth century (Fischel, 1953:115).

Another period of messianism occurred in the middle of the twelfth century. Benjamin of Tudela tells of a false Messiah, David Alroy (*al-rai*), who began his activities *c.* 1160 in Amadia, Kurdistan. By performing miracles, he gathered a large following, whom he led in rebellion against Persia. Opposed by the Exilarch and the Ga'on[1] of Babylonia, he was eventually slain by his own father-in-law and the rebellion was crushed (Adler, M., 1907:54–56). Not long after, in Isfahan, there arose a new messianic movement under the leadership of Abu Sa'id b. Daud. It was said that even Maimonides inquired about this would-be Messiah (Fischel, 1953:116).

---

[1] The Ga'on was the principal of the leading Talmudic academy in Babylonia and was the chief authority on ritual matters for Babylonian and Persian Jews.

While it is probable that there were far more sects than these, it is not clear what motivated all of this activity. Elements of Shi'ism and Zoroastrianism abound in these movements, but meaningful correlations with the circumstances of Jewish life in Persia in that epoch are as yet nil. In any case, they did serve to weaken the bonds between Mesopotamian and Persian Jewry, a trend which culminated in a complete language schism. By the twelfth century, it had become necessary for Jewish leaders in Baghdad to correspond with Persian communities in the Persian language (Fischel, 1960:1156).

MONGOLS

The Mongol invasions of Ghengiz Khan swept through Persia, beginning in 1220. The inhabitants of Neyshahpur, Merv, Zanjan, Qazvin, Hamadan, Rey, Sava, Qom, and Kashan were massacred (Sykes, 1930:80, 83–4). From 1258, after the sack of Baghdad, the Mongols held sway over the entire Persian empire.

> The Jews of this our time a rank attain
> To which the heavens might aspire in vain,
> Theirs is dominion, wealth to them doth cling,
> To them belong both councillor and king.
> O people, hear my words of counsel true;
> Turn Jews, for heaven itself hath turned a Jew! [1]
> Yet wait, and ye shall hear their torment's cry,
> And see them fall and perish presently.
> (Tarikh-i-Wassaf, cited in Browne, 1920:32)

Penned in response to the favorable treatment the Jews received at the hands of the pagan Il-Khans, this poem aptly describes the typical rise and fall of Jewish fortunes at court.

In 1289, Sa'ad ad-Daula, a Jew, was made the grand Vizier of Arghun, the il-Khan. He appointed his brother to be governor of Baghdad. Jews were also appointed as governors of Azerbayjan, Mosul and Shiraz. Contemporaries tell of the efforts of Sa'ad ad-Daula on behalf of his fellow Jews. One apostate Jew, Bar Hebraeus writes:

Jews who were on the fringes of the world gathered together with him and they all with one mouth said, "Verily by means of this man the Lord hath raised on high the horn of redemption and the hope of glory of the sons of the Hebrews in their last days." (Fischel, 1937:106)

---

[1] Cf. Esther 8:18.

He further reports that

the man who could confer a favour or benefit or could do harm was never seen at the gate of the kingdom unless he was a Jew. (Fischel, 1937:110)

Sa'ad ad-Daula's enemies leveled many libels against him. He supposedly sent blacklists to Shiraz and Khorassan for the execution of prominent opponents and was supposed to have planned an attack on Mecca to convert the Ka'ba into a heathen temple. Sa'ad ad-Daula finally suffered the fate of many court Jews and was executed in 1291. According to Bar Hebraeus

the trials and wrath which were stirred up against the Jews at this time neither tongue can utter nor the pen write down. (Fischel, 1937:117)

In 1293, Rashid ad-Daula, a Jewish physician, served as advisor to the II-Khan. He supported the kingdom's failing treasury out of his own pocket for some time, but fell quickly from power when his money ran out. In 1318, the apostate Jew, Rashid ad-Din, scholar, financier and physican, who had also served as grand Vizier, was murdered.

The widespread persecution of Jews following the fall of these men, also severed the final direct links between Babylonian and Persian Jewry. Excepting occasional merchants and emissaries, Persian Jewry was largely on its own until the late 19th century.[1]

The fourteenth century was a period of intense creativity in Persian-Jewish literature. Amina (Binyamin ben Misha'el), noted for his 'Aqedat Yiẓḥaq (The Binding of Isaac) wrote religious poetry still popular among Persian speaking Jews. The great Maulana Shahin of Shiraz, wrote poetical commentaries on the Bible, imitating the epic style of the Persian master-poets. However, aside from these works of literature, almost nothing is known about Persian Jewry from the fourteenth through the sixteenth centuries.

THE SAFAVIDS

The Safavids ousted the latest of foreign conquerors, the Turkomans. For the first time in over 800 years, Persia was free of foreign domination. In a nativistic spirit, Shah Isma'il proclaimed the Twelver or Imami sect of Shi'a Islam as the state religion. In 1502 the capital was shifted

[1] One interesting exception to this generalization occured in the early eighteenth century, when two Jewish soldiers in the Turkish army attempted to arrange an accommodation with the Jews of the then besieged city of Hamadan. (See Bacher, 1907:101.)

from Tabriz to Qazvin, where its extensive commercial opportunities attracted many Jews. Shah Abbas I (1587–1629) later transferred the capital to Isfahan, which then became the main center of Persian Jewish life. For economic reasons, Abbas settled Armenians in new Julfa outside of Isfahan, while Georgian Jews were established in Farahabad in Mazanderan. In the early years of his reign, other foreign Jews were attracted to Persia for trade and settlement.

The Jewish population of Persia was estimated at eight to ten thousand families during the reign of Abbas I (Teixeira, 1902:252). During the reign of Abbas II, Chardin likewise estimated the Jewish population at nine to ten thousand families or thirty to thirty-five thousand people (Fischel, 1937a:276). This Jewish population was widely dispersed throughout the country and included settlements at: Abarquh, Ardebil, Ashraf, Asterabad, Bandar (*sic*), Demavend, Farahabad, Gilar (Gilan?), Golpaygan, Hamadan, Hormuz, Isfahan, Jahrom, Kashan, Kerman, Kermanshah, Khonsar, Khorassan, Lar, Nahawand, Natanf (Natanz?), Qazvin, Qom, Shiraz, Shushtar, Tabriz, Teheran and Yazd (Fischel, 1937a:276–7). The above sites are documented. but no doubt there were many other locations in which Jews resided.

The adoption of a strict, sectarian form of Islam as Persia's state religion had important economic and social consequences for the *dhimmi* population in general and for Jews in particular. On the one hand more stringent interpretation of the laws of ritual purity prevented Jews from engaging in food production or sale, while on the other hand, more scrupulous adherence to religious law meant that Muslims could no longer manufacture liquor or wine, nor engage in music-making or moneylending. Competition between Jews and other minorities to fill such vacant occupational niches was intense.[1] Thus, at first, the Jews were the most important usurers (Chardin, 1735:427), but Banians from India soon surpassed them (Tavernier, 1684:202). A contemporary traveler also observed that

the country trade is in the hands of the Persians and the Jews, [while] the foreign traffic is in the hands of the Armenians only. (Tavernier, 1684:229)

Occupations associated with Jewish men of this period included: wine maker, silk farmer, druggist, doctor, magician, fortune teller, tailor, miller, goldsmith, jeweler, musician, clown, funeral wailer, and dancer. Jews were also shopkeepers, moneylenders, itinerant peddlers, peddlers of secondhand goods and of "produire des femmes" (Chardin,

---

[1] Refer to Chapter V and Loeb (1976).

1735:427). Jewish women also engaged in commerce in order to service the confined Muslim women. Despite the variety of economic activity, Chardin considered their situation desperate:

> They are everywhere destitute. I have not seen a single family in the entire kingdom that one could call rich, and which, to the contrary, was not subsisting on the lowest of levels. (1735:427, trans. mine)

The Safavid period was a time of great anxiety for the entire Persian Jewish community. It is not clear whether a decline in Jewish scholarship resulted from the stresses of the period or whether Persian Jews were, as Chardin claims, "the most ignorant in the whole world" (1735:428). The Bible, *Siddur*, Mishna, Talmud, Shulkhan Arukh (code of Jewish law) and *Sefer Razim* (a kabbalistic work) were known and used (Bacher, 1906:272), but scholarship was limited to biblical translation and chronicle poems such as the *Kitab-i Anusi* of Babay ibn Lutf. Centers of Jewish learning, such as there were, existed in Lar, Isfahan and Kashan.

Ritual observance was not as it should have been either. Babay ibn Lutf chastises the Jews for numerous transgressions, such as, eating bread without reciting a blessing, not fasting on appropriate occasions, not helping the poor, not assembling a *minyan* (quorum) for prayer and mourners *qaddish* and not properly observing the holidays (Fischel, 1937a:288). But these oversights may have resulted from the zealous persecution of Jews under Abbas I and II.

In 1617, during the reign of Shah Abbas I, an intracommunal dispute occurred in the city of Isfahan. The community elders accused the *Nasi* (community leader), Siman Tov ben David, of cheating his customers by short-weighing their meat. When the elders appealed to the Shah to redress their wrong, Siman Tov converted to Islam and intimated to the Shah that the Jews were using a book of magic to work evil against the Shah.[1] Elders of the community were brought before the *Diwan* (a government office for Jewish affairs) and asked to convert to Islam. Upon their refusal they were thrown to the dogs and killed. Thereupon all holy books in the community were thrown in a pile in the main square and the whole community was forced to convert. In 1622, several men who had been secretly practising Judaism were executed. The community was finally permitted to return to Judaism by Shah Safi (1629–1642).

---

[1] Abbas I may well have been a military genius, but descriptions of his religious fanaticism and brutality *vis-à-vis* his own sons, to me suggest a rather unstable personality. The events described occur late in his life while he suffered some painful disability which may well have clouded his judgement.

This happy occasion was named *Hag Ḥabbsora*, "the holiday of good tidings", (Mizrahi, 1966:37).

In 1622, a Jew from Lar, Abul Hassan Lari, was accused of selling improperly slaughtered meat. On Yom Kippur he converted to Islam and, to exact vengeance, enlisted the support of the Shi'a clergy to enforce restrictive measures against the Jews. In Lar, Isfahan, Kashan and elsewhere, these restrictions were put into effect. Eventually, the stricture of Abul Hassan were incorporated into the *Jam Abbasi*, a more extensive code instituted by Abbas I (see Appendix II). From 1622 to 1925, Persian Jews were required to wear a special hat or piece of colored cloth as an identifying "badge of shame". A "Law of Apostasy" was promulgated permitting any Jewish convert to Islam to inherit all of the property of his relatives, even from those of distant degree.

In the reign of Shah Abbas II, from 1653 to 1666, almost all of the Jews of Persia were forced to become Muslims. According to Jewish sources, the cause of these persecutions was the theft of a silver dagger belonging to the Shah, by his gardener. One of the jewels from its handle was found in the possession of two Jewish merchants. On this evidence, the vizier attributed the crime to the Jews and received permission from the Shah to convert all of the Jews of Isfahan as punishment. One Sabbath eve, the Jews fled from Isfahan and took refuge at the shrine of Seraḥ bat Asher (see Chapter X). Eventually, Jews in Lar, Shiraz, Kashan, Qom, Khonsar, Golpaygan, Hamadan and elsewhere were compelled to convert. In the ensuing disorder, many Jews committed suicide or were killed or expelled. Jews fled from Hamadan to Kurdistan, Baghdad and even Palestine (Bacher, 1906:88). Only the Jews of Yazd escaped conversion because the Muslims of that city, for economic reasons, intervened on the Jews' behalf when the latter threatened to emigrate to Kabul (Bacher, 1906:247).

Jewish resistence to the decrees of Abbas II was mostly passive. The conversions were without conviction. Chardin tells us that a Jew questioned about his conversion replied:

I? A Muslim? Not at all. I am Jewish. It is true that they gave me two *Tomans* to swear a false oath. (1735:427, translation mine)

Jewish sources say that soon after conversion to Islam, most Jews went back to observing the Sabbath; even the execution of those caught doing so did not deter the others. Finally, Abbas II relented and permitted Jews to return to their religion upon repayment of the bribe given them, renewed payment of the poll tax retroactive to the time they converted to Islam and the donning anew the "badge of shame" (Fischel, 1937a:287).

Their redemption from this oppression must have seemed nothing short of miraculous, as, indeed, the folklore bears out.[1] The Jews of Mazanderan must, therefore, have been particularly elated, in 1666, when word reached them of the coming of a new Messiah, Shabbtay Zvi. The Jews of this region made swift preparations to go to Palestine, but were restrained by the pragmatic governor of the province who requested payment of their unpaid taxes. The Jews agreed to wait three months for the Messiah's arrival at which time they would be free to go without payment. It was further stipulated that should the Messiah fail to appear within that span, they would be obliged to pay a large penalty tax to the governor. Reportedly they were forced to raise the money demanded by the governor, and they never did go to Palestine (Chardin, 1735:428).

Despite the government's permission to return to Judaism, many Jews must have remained converts to Islam. Muslim villagers in the Isfahan area are reputed to still light candles on Friday evening as is the Jewish custom. Lenjan, the village near the shrine of Serah bat Asher and site of the Isfahani Jewish cemetery, has no Jewish inhabitants although it must be assumed to have had some earlier. Many of the Afghans claim that they were Jews until converted under Abbas II (Ben-Zvi, 1961:188). There is also linguistic evidence to support the contention that some Iranian Muslims were Jews before the Safavid period. [2]

The later Safavids were nearly as cruel as the earlier ones. As an example, during the reign of Shah Suleyman, in 1678, Jewish notables of Isfahan were falsely accused and murdered, and their corpses thrown into the main square (Carmelite Chronicles, I:408)

The Afghan sacking of Isfahan (1722) marked the end of Safavid rule. Although one observer indicated that the Jews welcomed the new conqueror (Alexander, 1936:648), a Jewish source claims:

We have only fallen into the hands of new enemies, because at those times when Muslims kill, the lives of Jews are even less secure. (Fischel, 1937a:293, trans. mine)

In fact, there were new persecutions in Kashan in 1729 while the Jews of Golpaygan were fortunately able to buy-off their enemies. Nevertheless, the Afghan period was, by comparison, something of a respite from the Safavid oppression.

Nadir Shah (1736–1747) was a Sunni and well disposed towards the

---

[1] See Chapter X and the discussion of the pilgrimage site of Serah bat Asher.

[2] "It is interesting to note that in two of the villages (in the vicinity) of Isfahan, at Sedey and at G'ez, the Iranians call their language *zeboni ibri,* the Israelite tongue" (Abrahamian 1936:2, trans. mine).

Jews. For economic reasons he settled some forty Jewish families from Qazvin in the holy city of Mashhad in 1734 (Fischel, 1936:52). A translation of the Tora and book of Psalms was undertaken at his direction by Babay ben Nuriel of Isfahan and completed in 1740 (Fischel, 1960:1173). There is also a tradition that one day, when Nadir Shah was listening to the reading of the Tora, he was so moved by the story of Ẓalafḥad's daughters (Nu. 36) that he wished to further improve the lot of the Jew, but was prevented from doing so by his ministers and officers (Levi, 1960:496).

Under the Zands (1750–1794) there was no reported violence against the Jews, despite considerable anti-Jewish propaganda in Shiraz, the capital. The only clear case of their exploitation was at the personal whim of Lotfali Khan, who abducted five Jewish girls from Isfahan and eight from Shiraz to be added to his harem (Levi, 1960:496).

THE QAJARS

Under the Qajars (1796–1925) many of the restrictions of the Safavids were reimposed upon Iranian Jewry. Since the central government was usually weak and the provinces locally autonomous, the Jews of the outlying regions were often left to the mercy of the local population.[1] As has been shown elsewhere (Loeb, 1970:424–430), this period could rightfully be characterized as "an uninterrupted sequence of persecution and oppression" (Fischel, 1950:21)

The most significant development for Persian Jewry during this 130 year span was the re-establishment of communications with world Jewry. In 1858, Jewish organizations began to pressure the French and British Ministers in Teheran to intervene on behalf of the Jews. In 1865, Sir Moses Montefiore considered making a personal visit to Persia, but was dissuaded from doing so by the British Foreign Office. After the famine of 1871, large sums of relief money were distributed among the Jews of Iran by representatives of the British government (Fischel, 1950:129). In 1873, when Nasser ad-Din Shah visited Europe, he was confronted everywhere by concerned Jewry. Adolphe Cremieux appealed to the Shah on behalf of the Alliance Israélite Universelle to allow them to open schools in Iran and was given permission to do so (Fischel, 1950:132).

Until the first Alliance school opened in Teheran in 1898, Jews either

---

[1] After a pogrom in 1839, the entire surviving community or Mashhad was forcibly converted to Islam. They remained crypto-Jews until after W.W. II.

had no secular education or went to missionary schools. Missionary activity succeeded in converting small numbers of Jews to Christianity in Hamadan, Isfahan and Teheran, while larger numbers became Bahais. Jewish religious knowledge and literacy was very low despite occasional emissaries from Baghdad and Jerusalem, who had been coming to Persia since the early eighteenth century. The cities of Kashan, Shiraz and Yazd [1] were the leading religious centers.

The 1906 constitutional movement did not bring any immediate benefits to Iranian Jewry, although eventually Jews were enabled to choose their own representative to *Majles* (parliament). Some of the official discriminatory regulations were removed, but such legislated improvement in conditions was too slow to practically affect the daily life of the Persian Jew.

THE PAHLAVIS

The Pahlavi period, instituted by Reza Shah's seizure of power in 1925, has been the most favorable era for Persian Jews since Parthian rule. Jews have their own deputy in Majles who effectively serves the Jewish community *not* by active participation in public debate, but by means of personal influence with the Shah. In this way the "Law of Apostasy" was abrogated about 1930. While Reza Shah did prohibit political Zionism and condoned the execution of the popular liberal Jewish reformer Hayyim Effendi, his rule was on the whole, an era of new opportunity for the Persian Jew.

Hostile outbreaks against the Jews have been prevented by the government. Jews are no longer legally barred from any profession. They are required to serve in the army and pay the same taxes as Muslims. The elimination of the face-veil removed a source of insult to Jewish women, who had been previously required to have their faces uncovered; now all women are supposed to appear unveiled in public.

Although the Pahlavi government officially discouraged the spread of Alliance schools, ostensibly because of their emphasis on the French language, there were 23 of them serving 8000 pupils in 1951 and 34 such schools by 1958 (Schechtman, 1961:244). Secular educations were made available to Jewish girls as well as to boys, and, for the first time,

---

[1] The latter was known as "*Yrushalayim Haqqatan*", "little Jerusalem". Similar claims implying piety and scholarship were made by informants in Burujerd, Hamadan and elsewhere and, indeed, the claim of one's community being "*Yrushalayim Haqqatan*" was one of the most widespread initial statements made by informants upon making my acquaintance.

Jews could become government-licensed teachers. Otsar Hatorah eventually assumed responsibility for Jewish religious education in Iran, with apparent Pahlavi acquiescence.

Since the ascendance of Mohammad Reza Shah Aryamehr in 1941, the situation has further improved. In 1947, the American Joint Distribution Committee commenced operations in Iran through providing aid to education, medical services, feeding programs for the children and sanitation programs to clean up the Mahalleh. Indeed, their efforts, together with the emigration impetus provided by the Jewish Agency, has raised the standard of living among the remaining Jews to a point where it is now substantially higher than that of the non-Jewish population. Not only has the number of poor been reduced, but a new bourgeoisie is emerging. There are even Jewish millionaires. For the first time Jews are spending their money on cars, carpets, houses, travel and clothing. Teheran has attracted provincial Jews in large numbers and has become the center of Iranian Jewish life.

The Pahlavi era has seen vastly improved communications between Iranian Jewry and the rest of the world. Hundreds of boys and girls attend college and boarding school in the United States and Europe. Israeli emissaries come for periods of two years to teach in the Jewish schools. Improved roads, postal and telephone service have greatly increased contact between Jews in the provinces and those in Teheran. Rural Jews and small-town dwellers who, only forty years ago, may have constituted 25% or more of the total Jewish population are now less than 2%. Radio, TV, the phonograph, movies and magazines are markedly affecting Iranian Jewish life.

A small Jewish publication industry has arisen since 1925. Religious texts in Judaeo-Persian were edited and distributed in the 1920s by Hayyim More, originally of Kashan. Books on Jewish history, Zionism, the Hebrew language and classroom texts have since been published. The Jewish newspapers *Ha-G'ula* and *Haḥayyim* were sporadically issued for some years, and the Jewish Agency regularly distributes a newsletter.

On March 15, 1950, Iran extended *de facto* recognition to Israel. Relations with Israel are good and trade is growing. Israel provides Iran with technical aid and produce, such as eggs and food stuffs: in return, Israel receives petroleum, landing rights for El Al, and until recently, discrete unofficial sympathy from the Iranian government in its struggle against the Arabs.

Despite the favorable attitude of the government and the relative prosperity of the Jewish community, all Iranian Jews acknowledge the precarious nature of the present situation. There are still sporadic outbreaks against them, because the Muslim clergy constantly berates Jews, inciting the masses who make no effort to hide their animosity towards the Jew. Most Jews express the belief that it is only the personal strength and goodwill of the Shah that protects them: that plus God's intervention! If either should fail. . . .

APPENDIX II

Restrictive Codes

RESTRICTIONS OF THE SAFAVID PERIOD

BEHAVIOR CODE OF ABUL HASSAN LARI (1622)

1. Houses that are too high (higher than a Muslim's) must be lowered.
2. Jews may not circulate freely among the Believers.
3. In their stores, Jews must sit on low stools, in order that they not see the purchaser's face.
4. Jews must wear a specially constructed hat of eleven colors.
5. Around this hat they must sew a yellow ribbon, three meters long.
6. Women must tie many little bells on their sandals.
7. Jewish women must also wear a black *chador*.
8. When a Jew speaks to a Muslim, he must humbly lower his head.

(Bacher, 1906, 52:237)

THE *JAM ABBASI*, INSTITUTED BY ABBAS I (C. 1618) AND ADMINISTERED IN SOME MEASURE UNTIL 1925

1. Jews are not permitted to dress like Muslims.
2. A Jew must exhibit a yellow or red "badge of dishonor" on his chest.
3. A Jew is not permitted to ride on a horse.
4. When riding on an ass, he must hang both legs on one side.
5. He is not entitled to bear arms.
6. On the street and in the market, he must pass stealthily from a corner or from the side.
7. Jewish women are not permitted to cover their faces.
8. The Jew is restricted from establishing boundaries of private property.
9. A Jew who becomes a Muslim, is forbidden to return to Judaism.
10. Upon disclosure of a disagreement between Jew and Muslim, the Jew's argument has no merit.
11. In Muslim cities, the Jew is forbidden to build a synagogue.
12. A Jew is not entitled to have his house built higher than a Muslim's.

(Mizrahi, 1966:36)

RESTRICTIONS OF THE NINETEENTH CENTURY QAJAR PERIOD

"OPPRESSIONS" NOTED BY A JEWISH TRAVELER

1. Throughout Persia the Jews are obliged to live in a part of town separated from the other inhabitants; for they are regarded as unclean creatures, who bring contamination with their intercourse and presence.
2. They have no right to carry on trade in stuff goods.
3. Even in the streets of their own quarter on the town they are not allowed to keep any open shop – they may only sell spices and drugs, or carry on the trade of a jeweler.
4. Under the pretext of their being unclean, they are treated with the greatest severity, and should they enter the street, inhabited by Mussulmen, they are pelted by the boys and mob with stones and dirt.
5. For the same reason they are forbidden to go out when it rains; for it is said the rain would wash dirt off them, which would dirty the feet of the Mussulmen.
6. If a Jew is recognized as such in the streets, he is subjected to the greatest insults. The passers-by spit in his face, and sometimes beat him so cruelly, that he falls to the ground, and is obliged to be carried home.
7. If a Persian kills a Jew, and the family of the deceased can bring forward two Mussulmen as witnesses to the fact, the murderer is punished by a fine of 12 tumauns (600 piastres) but if two such witnesses cannot be produced, the crime remains unpunished, even though it has been publically committed, and is well known.
8. The flesh of animals killed according to Hebrew custom, but as *trefe* declared, must not be sold to any Mussulmen. The slaughterers are compelled to bury the meat, for even the Christians do not dare to buy it, fearing the mockery and insult of the Persians.
9. If a Jew enters a shop to buy anything, he is forbidden to inspect the goods, but must stand at a respectful distance and ask the price. Should his hand by accident touch the goods, he must take them at any price the seller chooses to ask for them.
10. Sometimes the Persians intrude into the dwellings of the Jews and take possession of whatever pleases them. Should the owner make the least opposition in defense of his property, he runs the danger of atoning for it with his life.
11. Upon the least dispute between a Jew and a Persian, the former is immediately dragged before the Achund, and, if the complainant can bring forward two witnesses, the Jew is condemned to pay a heavy fine. If he is too poor to pay this penalty in money, he must pay it in his person. He is stripped to the waist, bound to a stake and receives forty blows with a stick. Should the sufferer utter the least cry of pain during this proceeding, the blows already given are not reckoned, and the punishment is begun afresh.
12. In the same manner the Jewish children, when they get into a quarrel with those of the Mussulmen, are immediately led before the Achund, and punished with blows.
13. A Jew who travels in Persia is taxed at every inn and caravan-serai he enters.
14. If ... a Jew shows himself in the street during the three days of the Katel (feast of mourning for the death of the Persian founder of the religion of Ali [probably *ashura*]) he is sure to be killed.

(Benjamin, 1859:258–60)

EDICT OF PROHIBITION ISSUED TO THE JEWS OF HAMADAN IN 1892

1. It is forbidden to Jews to leave their houses when it rains or snows.
2. The Jewish woman must appear on the public streets with her face uncovered.
3. She is required to be wrapped in an *izar* (*chador*?) of two colors.
4. Men are not permitted to wear handsome clothing, the only material permitted is blue cotton.
5. It is forbidden to wear matching shoes.
6. Every Jew must wear a piece of red material on his chest.
7. A Jew must never pass a Muslim on a public street.
8. It is forbidden for him to speak loudly to a Muslim.
9. A Jewish creditor of a Muslim ought to claim his debt in a trembling and respectful tone.
10. If a Muslim insults a Jew, he (the Jew) is obliged to lower his head and remain silent.
11. A Jew who buys some meat must wrap it and conceal it carefully out of respect for Muslims.
12. It is forbidden to erect beautiful buildings.
13. One is forbidden to have a house higher than his Muslim neighbor.
14. Neither may one whitewash his rooms.
15. The entrance of his house must be low.
16. The Jew is not permitted to arrange the folds of his coat, but must be content to wear it twisted under the arm.
17. He is forbidden to have his beard cut, even to slightly trim it with scissors.
18. Jews are not permitted to leave the city, nor to take a walk in the country.
19. Jewish doctors are not permitted to ride a horse.
20. A Jew suspected of having drunk liquor is not permitted to appear in the street; if he appears, he is immediately put to death.
21. Jewish weddings must be celebrated in great secrecy, so that what transpires is not heard outside.
22. Jews are not permitted to consume good fruit.

(Alliance, 1892:49–59)

APPENDIX III

Judaism under Shi'a Islam

Jews survived under Islam with differential success, dependent on numerous socio-historical factors. But, as Goitein (1955) pointed out in his comparative research of Jews and Arabs, the long-term survival of Jews in areas under the control of sectarian Islam presented a formidable challenge. Goitein focusses primarily on the Jews of Yemen, who responded with considerable ingenuity to the fanaticism of Shi'a Islam. Facing somewhat comparable circumstances, Iranian Jewry developed differently, with cultural attainments and social structures of a very different order than those of Yemen. A proper evaluation of these two adaptive strategies must await the availability of more complete historical and ethnographic materials from both societies (*cf.* Loeb, 1970).

Yet, the different cultural adaptations of Iranian and Yemenite Jews may be partially attributed, to the distinctive cultures of their respective dominant populations. Thus Yemenite Jews are like the Zayidi Shi'a Arabs in their predilection for a strong patrilineal kinship system and legal scholarship, whereas Iranian Jews are more bilateral in their kinship and stress epic poetry and mysticism as do the Imami Shi'a. The relatively superior economic position of the Yemenite Jew and the wealth of his material culture may result from what Hitti (1960:449) considers the more tolerant Sunni-like orthodoxy of the Zayidis.

The comparatively difficult situation of Jews under Shi'a rule as compared with Sunni rule may be explained in part by the nature of Shi'a Islam itself. Bernard Lewis (1960:71) points out that Shi'a Islam was taken over soon after its inception by the discontents of the Mawali. Theoretically the equals of Arab Muslims, the Mawali Muslims, who were not full members by descent of an Arab tribe, were treated as social inferiors (Lewis, B., 1960:70). The Mawali flocked to Shi'a Islam as a religious expression of opposition to the orthodox Sunni Arab elite. Ivanow (1948:12–20) indicates that Shi'a Islam arose as a class struggle between the lower class village poor and upper class town elite. The battle over language further deepened the split in Persia, where Arabic became associated with the elite (Ivanow, 1948:16).

Shi'ism with its ideals of idyllic theocracy, justice and equity for everybody, personal safety, freedom from oppression and exploitation, unlimited and unending, was particularly attractive to the masses. (Ivanow, 1948:19)

Thus Shi'a Islam was soon taken over by the Persian masses and became their expression of defiance against upper class orthodoxy. Since the masses preserved many Zoroastrian beliefs and practices, Shi'a Islam

resuscitated the worst and most anti-social ideas of the Zoroastrian priests about the "purity" or "impurity" of everything in life. (Ivanow, 1948:29–30)

It would seem, therefore, that the application of the myriad of restrictions on Jews by the Shi'a of both Yemen and Iran may be ultimately traced to Persian Zoroastrianism.

APPENDIX IV

Comparative Kinship Terminology of Iranian Jews

Relationship	Shiraz	Yazd	Kerman	Isfahan	Golpaygan	Kashan	Hamadan	Burujerd	Nahawand
father	buwa; aqa	baba; /piyar-/	baba; /pedar-/	buwa; baba	aqa; baba	per	aqa; bowa	aqa; bova; /-nar/	bova; /-nar/
mother	mava; mama	mama; /mari-/	mama; /madar-/	mavi; madha	nane	mar	dada	nana	nana; /madhda/
brother	kaka; /berd-/	kaka; /baradar/	kaka; ka; /baradar-/	bedhar	aqachi; b (e) rar	berar	bra; /bre-/	dashi; /-bra/; /-berar/	brar; /-berar/
sister	dada; kha	khahar	khar	khokh	dada; kha	khar	kha	khuwar	khuwar
son	poth	por	por	pir	pir	pir; pur	pir	pir	pür
daughter	doft	dokht	dokht	dot	dot	dot	dot	dot	dot
husband	mera; /-shi/	mero	mero; /-shu/	mere	mire	shi	mire	mira; oy; /shi-/	mire; /shu-/
wife	dhen	zino	zino; /-zan/	jan	jan	jan	jen	jan	jan

(cont.)

APPENDIX IV
Comparative Kinship Terminology of Iranian Jews

Relationship	Shiraz	Yazd	Kerman	Isfahan	Golpaygan	Kashan	Hamadan	Burujerd	Nahawand
fabr	amu	omu	omu	amu	amu	amu	amu	amu	amu
fasi	ama	omo	omo	ame	ame	ame	ame	ama	ame
mobr	da'iy	da'iy	da'iy	da'iy	da'iy	dayiy	da'iy	dayiy	a'dayiy
mosi	khala	khalo	khalo	khale	khale	khale	hale	khala	khale
fafa; mofa	buwa-bodhorg; buwakhaje	aqababa	aqababa	babjun	babajun	bakhaje	baba-massar	aqajani-baba	bovamassar; aqamassar
momo; famo	bivi; nane; mamani	bibi	bibi; mama-gondegi	manjun	bibi; nanebibi	mamajun	nene	nanajan; nane-bozorg	nanabibi
grandchild	nava	navo	boche-zadi	neve	nevi	neve	neve	nava; bechaza; pirza; dotsa	pürza; dotsa
sowi	arith	bori	bori	arith	aris	arith	aris	arus	arus
dahu	dumad	dumad	dumad	dhumat	dumad	dhumad	dumad	domad	damad
co-wife	ahu	hove	zino-hamshu	havu	hovu	ha'u	howu	howu	ha'u

Relationship	Shiraz	Yazd	Kerman	Isfahan	Golpaygan	Kashan	Hamadan	Burujerd	Nahawand
brwi	dhene-kaka	zinokaka; bori	zinokaka	jane-bedhar	jenaqachi	jeneberar	jenebra	jan-brar	jan-brar
sihu	meredada	mero-khahar; dumad	merokhar	merekhokh	miredada	shi-khar	mirekha	mire-khuwar	mire-khuwar
hufa	buwayishi; buwa	piyarmero	pedarshu	buwamere; amu	baba-khesure	pershi	qaynbowa	khesure-nar; amu	khesure nar
humo	maveyishi	marimero	madarshu	khorsi; jan-amu	nane-khesure	marshi	qayndada	khesure-nana	khesure-madhda
wifa	buway dhenabuwa	piyarzino	pedarzan	buwajan	baba-khesure	perejan	qaynbowa	khesure-nar; janamu	khesure nar
wimo	mavey-dhena	marizino	madarzan	khorsi; madhajan	nane-khesure	marjan	dadajan	khesure-nana; jan-amu	khesure-madhda
hubrwi	amarith; dhene-berdishi	hambori	hambori	jane-bedhar	yadiye	janberar-shi	hambo	hambivi; jandashi	hambivi
wisihu	amrish; mere-khadhena	hamdumad	merezino?	mere-khokhejan	mire-khajan	shikhar-jan	mirekha-jene	bajenaq	mire-khuwarjan

APPENDIX V
Demographic Data

JEWISH POPULATION OF SHIRAZ

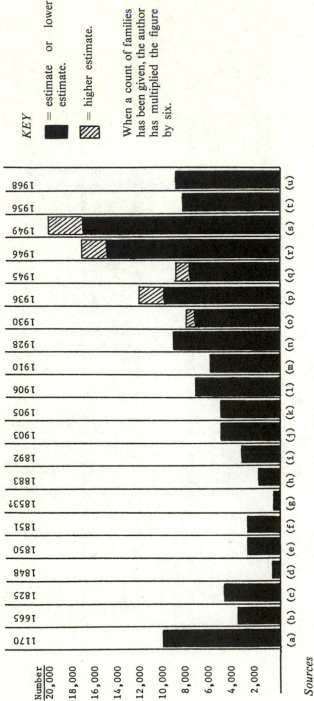

KEY

■ = estimate or lower estimate.

▨ = higher estimate.

When a count of families has been given, the author has multiplied the figure by six.

Sources

a) Adler, M. 1907:58
b) Clarke 1963:50 (citing Tavernier)
c) Fischel 1944:210
d) Benjamin 1859:229
e) Stern 1854:129
f) Binning 1857, I:270
g) Petermann 1861, II:176

h) Wilson 1916:16
i) Curzon 1892, I:510
j) Alliance 1903:104
k) Descos 1908:298
l) Wilson 1916:16
m) Alliance 1910:230
n) Kopellowitz 1930:42

o) Ben Zvi 1936:148
p) Ben Zvi 1936:147 (citing H. Levi)
q) Yishay 1951:308
r) Landshut n.d.:63
s) Levi 1960, III:1010; informants
t) Clarke 1963:50
u) Author's estimate

Glossary

KEY
heb. = Hebrew
j.p. = Judaeo-Persian
pers. = Persian

aberu	honor (pers.)
"abu'aben"	father of the (circumcised) son (j.p.)
'afiqoman	dessert, piece of maza eaten at the end of the seder (heb.)
aggada	legend, text read on Pesah (heb.)
akhond	Muslim clergyman, theologian (pers.)
'alaqiye	a mixture of fruits, nuts, spices and vinegar eaten in Shiraz on Pesah (j.p.)
'aliya	going up: immigration to Israel, being called to the reading of the Tora (heb.)
ama	father's sister (pers.)
'amida	standing prayer, central to all Jewish worship (heb.)
amu	father's brother (pers.)
anderun	harem (pers.)
anjoman	council, Shirazi Jews "central committee" (pers.)
aqa	sir (pers.)
araq	hard liquor (pers.)
'arelim	uncircumcised, i.e., the Christians and Zoroastrians according to Shirazi usage (heb.)
arith	bride, daughter-in-law (j.p.)
'arvit	evening worship (heb.)
bakhavod	with the honor (j.p./heb.)
bala	up front (pers.)
bat yisra'el	daughter of an Israelite (heb.)
befarmayid	please! (pers.)
ben mizva	Bar Mitsvah (heb.)
bet din	court (heb.)
brakha	blessing (heb.)
brit mila	circumcision (heb.)
buwa	father (j.p.)
chador	tent, all enveloping cloak worn by women (pers.)
chele khune	house of forty, the shrine of Serah bat Asher (j.p.)

301

da'iy	mother's brother (pers.)
daleleh	match maker (pers.)
darshan	preacher (heb.)
dayan	judge (heb.)
dhimmi	protected minority (arab.)
diwan	government ministry, for Jewish affairs (pers.)
divune	crazy (pers.)
dohedhar	two rial (j.p.)
dohol	two headed wooden drum (pers.)
dombak	single headed drum (pers.)
drasha	sermon (heb.)
dukh	yoghurt drink (pers.)
dumad	groom, son-in-law (j.p.)
'ene ha'eda	eyes of the community, i.e., a council of elders (heb.)
erusin	betrothal (heb.)
'etrog	citron (heb.)
famil	kindred (pers.; of French origin)
farini	a breakfast cereal (j.p.)
gabay	treasurer, collector of money (heb.)
galut	exile, namely the Shirazi Jews' "hard lot" (heb.)
gelim	mat woven in tapestry (pers.)
get, gittin	(pl.) bill of divorce (heb.)
gimatriyya	homiletic interpretation based on the numerical value of Hebrew letters (heb. – greek)
giveh	woven peasant's shoes (pers.)
goyim	nations, Shirazi usage denotes Muslim or Muslims (heb.)
g'ulat bkhor	redemption of the first born (heb.)
gushti, gishti	meaty (pers./j.p.)
haftara	selection from the Prophets (heb.)
hajj	"pilgrimage" to Mecca; Jewish usage – to Jerusalem (arab.)
hajji	"pilgrim" to Jerusalem (arab.)
ḥakham	sage (heb.)
ḥaliẓa	drawing off the shoe of the levirate (heb.)
ḥalla	dough set aside for the priests; a special Sabbath bread (heb.)
hamum	bath (pers.)
ḥaroset	a condiment eaten on Pesah night (heb.)
ḥatam	mosaic maker (pers.)
hattarat ndarim	dissolution of vows (heb.)
hattarat qlalot	dissolution of curses (heb.)
havdala	ceremony at the end of the Sabbath by means of which one distinguishes between the holy and profane (heb.)
ḥazzan	overseer of a synagogue (heb.)
hekhal	ark (literally: temple) (heb.)
hosha'na rabba	The Great Salvation, seventh day of Sukkot (heb.)

hosha'not	prayers of salvation (heb.)
ḥuppa	canopy – the bridal chamber (heb.)
jadid al-islam	new Muslim (pers.)
jam abbasi	code of restrictions enacted against the Jews by Abbas I (pers.)
jaziyeh	poll tax (pers.)
jud	Jew (pers., derogatory)
jud baazi	Jew game (pers.)
jud kosht	Jew murder (pers.)
judi	the Shirazi Jewish dialect (j.p.)
kabab	broiled meat (pers.)
kadkhoda	head man (pers.)
kalantar	chief civil magistrate (pers.)
kalimi	Jew (pers.)
kappara	atonement sacrifice (heb.)
karguzar	agent in charge of Jewish affairs (pers.)
kashrut	ritual fitness (heb.)
kavod, kvodot	(pl.) ritual honor (heb.)
kelele	cheers of approval, a vocalization common to the Middle East.
kemanje	spiked fiddle (pers.)
khala	mother's sister (j.p.)
khalebibi	special Sabbath porridge (j.p.)
khamis	soured, leaven (j.p.)
khanevadeh	household, extended family (pers.)
khazanadar	treasurer (pers.)
kippot	skull caps (heb.)
knisa	synagogue (pers.)
kohen, kohanim	priest(s) (heb.)
kolah	hat (pers.)
korsi	traditional Persian room heater (pers)
koto	school (j.p.)
kudakistan	kindergarten (pers.)
kuche	alley (pers.)
letra'i	not Tora, a Judaeo-Persian jargon (j.p.)
leviyim	Levites (heb.)
lulav	palm branch (heb.)
luti	rogue (pers.)
maast	yoghurt (pers.)
mahalleh	area (pers.)
mahalli	local (pers.)
majles	Parliament (pers.)
makkot	blows (heb.)
maktab	school (pers.)
mama	midwife (j.p.)
maqve	ritual bath (j.p./heb.)

mashlim	complete — the last called to the Tora reading before the *haftara* (heb./j.p.)
mava	mother (j.p.)
mazza	unleavened bread (heb.)
mgilla	scroll of Esther (heb.)
midrash	homiletical commentary on scripture (heb.)
mila	circumcision (heb.)
minḥa	afternoon worship (heb.)
minyan	quorum of ten men (heb.)
mishmara	vigil in house of mourning (heb./j.p.)
mishna	collection of oral law (heb.)
misped	funeral oration (heb.)
misqal	dry measure equal to about 4.7 grams (pers.)
mo'ed	season, appointed time, name give to Pesah by Shirazi Jews (heb.)
mohar habbtulot	bride price of virgins (heb.)
mohel	circumcisor (heb.)
morde shur	body washer (pers.)
motreb	musician (pers.)
mulla	master, theologian, teacher (pers.)
musaf	additional worship (heb.)
mzuza	doorpost, parchment containing biblical texts placed at entrance to a Jewish house (heb.)
najas	impure, unclean (pers.)
nakara khane	house of the kettle drum, music guild (pers.)
nane	mother (j.p.)
nasi	prince, chief, head of the community (heb.)
nay	flute, wind instrument (pers.)
nayab re'is	vice-president (pers.)
neder	vow (heb.)
ner tamid	eternal light (heb.)
nshamot	souls, spirits (heb.)
'omer	sheaf (heb.)
ostad	master, head of guild (pers.)
pe'ot	side curls (heb.)
pesaḥ	Passover (heb.)
piddyon habben	redemption of the son (heb.)
pul	money (pers.)
qaddish	sanctification of God's name, recited by mourners (aramaic)
qanun	trapezoidal zither (pers.)
qeri	nocturnal pollution (heb.)
qesmat	fate (pers.)
qinot	dirges (heb.)
qiddush	sanctification over wine (heb.)
qiddushin	wedding ceremony (heb.)
qom	tribe, relative (pers.)

rabi	Rabbi (heb.)
re'is	chief, president (pers.)
rḥiza gdola	great washing (heb.)
rial	Persian coin exchanged at 75 rial to the U.S. dollar (pers.)
rvi'i	fourth (heb.)
salam	salute (pers.)
samikh	adjacent one, assists the *shaliaḥ ẓibbur* (heb.)
samukh	adjacent, the Tora honor preceding the last before the haftara (heb.)
sandaq	godfather (heb.)
santur	dulcimer (pers.)
sayyid	descendant of Mohammad (pers.)
seder	order, the service and meal for the first two evenings of Pesah (heb.)
setar	long necked lute (pers.)
sfira	counting of the 'omer from Pesah to Shavu'ot (heb.)
shabbat	Sabbath (heb.)
shaharit	morning worship (heb.)
shakh	roof greens for the sukka (heb.)
shal	shawl worn by Shirazi Jewish mourners (pers.)
shaliaḥ ẓibbur, shliḥe ẓibbur	precentor(s) (heb.)
shamash	beadle, caretaker (heb.)
sharab khane	wine house (pers.)
sharbat	cooling drink, syrup (pers.)
shavu'ot	Feast of Weeks, Pentecost (heb.)
sheheḥeyanu	who has kept us in life – a blessing made by a Jew at any auspicious occasion (heb.)
sheva' brakhot	seven benedictions made for the bride and groom (heb.)
shhita	ritual slaughter (heb.)
shiv'a	seven day period of mourning (heb.)
shkhina	presence of the Almighty (heb.)
shlishi	third 'aliya to the Tora (heb.)
shloshim	thirty day period of mourning (heb.)
shma'	hear!, biblical verse proclaiming the unity of God (heb.)
shmini 'azeret	Eighth day of Assembly (heb.)
shofar	ram's horn (heb.)
shoḥet	ritual slaughterer (heb.)
shoma	you, polite second person plural (pers.)
shovavim	wild ones (heb.)
shubkolah	night cap (pers.)
shulkhan 'arukh	The Prepared Table, a code of Jewish law (heb.)
siddur	prayer book (heb.)
simḥat tora	Rejoicing of the Law (heb.)
sliḥot	penitential prayers (heb.)
sofer	scribe (heb.)
sukka	tabernacle, booth (heb.)
sukkot	holiday of booths (heb.)

ta'arof	offer, the code of Persian polite behavior (pers.)
ta'aziyeh	Muslim ritual performance during Muharram (pers.)
tallit	small prayer shawl (heb.)
tame	unclean (heb.)
tar	fretted long necked lute (pers.)
tashlikh	cast away, ceremony of casting away sins on Rosh Hashana (heb.)
tfilla	prayer (heb.)
tfillin	phylacteries (heb.)
to	you, familiar second person singular (pers.)
toman	ten rial (pers.)
toranit	scholar(ly) (heb.)
tu khiyabun	in the streets, outside of the Mahalleh (pers./j.p.)
yerže'it	memorial day of mourning (from German)
yeshiva	academy (heb.)
yeshuva	sitting, usually nightime vigil in house of mourning (heb./j.p.)
yibbum	leviratic marriage
yisra'el	Jew, self-identification by Iranian Jews (heb.)
yored	returnee from Israel (heb.)
yrusha	inheritance (heb.)
żaddiq	righteous man (heb.)
zaqarun	memorial day, Ninth of 'Av (j.p.)
zarb	single headed hand drum (pers.)
żdaqa	charity (heb.)
ziyyarat	pilgrimage (pers.)
żiżit	prayer shawl (heb.)
zurkhane	house of strength (pers.)

References

Abrahamian, Roubene (1936) *Dialectes des Israélites de Hamadan et d'Ispahan et dialecte de Baba Tahir*, Paris: Libraire d'Amerique et d'Orient, Adrien-Maisonneuve.

Adams, Reverend Isaac (1900) *Persia by a Persian*. Washington D.C.

Adler, Elkan Nathan (1898) The Persian Jews: their books and their ritual. *Jewish Quarterly Review*, **10**, 584–625.

Adler, Elkan Nathan (1905) *Jews in Many Lands*. Philadelphia: Jewish Publication Society of America.

Adler, Elkan Nathan (1966) *Jewish Travelers*. Second edition. New York: Herman Press.

Adler, Marcus Nathan (1907) *The Itinerary of Benjamin of Tudela*. London: Oxford University Press.

Alberts, Robert C. (1963) *Social Structure and Culture Change in an Iranian Village*. Madison: University of Wisconsin (unpublished Ph.D. dissertation).

Alexander, Friar (1936) The Story of the Sack of Ispahan by the Afgans in 1722. Translated by H. Dunlop, *Journal of the Royal Central Asiatic Society*, **23**, 643–653.

Alliance, *Bulletin Mensuel de l'Alliance Israélite Universelle*.
    (1889) 49–51.
    (1892) 48–54.
    (1896) 101–102, 171–175.
    (1897) 70–73, 86–87.
    (1898) 135–141, 194–196.
    (1899) 8–9, 85–87, 105–106, 181–182.
    (1900) 8–10, 160–162, 211–214.
    (1901) 42–45, 57–58, 69–70, 113–115, 163–167, 179–189.
    (1902) 23–24, 59–63, 90–92, 186–201, 209–210.
    (1903) 14–17, 31–33, 100–118, 230–239.
    (1904) 29–39, 124–136.
    (1905) 62–66, 94–100.
    (1906) 16–18, 159–168.
    (1907) 51–56, 77–92.
    (1908) 88–92.
    (1909) 71–77, 131–138.
    (1910) 18–21, 36–37, 57–69, 228–246.
    (1911) 62–64.

American Jewish Year Book. (1967) Volume 68. Morris Fine, Milton Himmelfarb and Martha Jelenko, editors. New York: American Jewish Committee, Philadelphia: Jewish Publication Society of America.

Arasteh, A. Reza and Josephine (1964) *Man and Society in Iran*. Leiden: E. J. Brill.

Arberry, Arthur J. (1960) *Shiraz: Persian City of Saints and Poets*. Norman: University of Oklahoma Press.

Arnold, Arthur J. (1877) *Through Persia by Caravan*. Volumes I and II. London: Tinsley Brothers.

Avery, Peter (1965) *Modern Iran*. London: Ernest Benn Ltd.

Bacher, Wilhelm (1904) Un episode de l'Histoire des Juifs de Perse apres les chroniques poetiques de Babai Loutf et de Babai b. Farhad. *Revue des etudes Juives*, **47**, 262–282.

Bacher, Wilhelm (1906) Les Juifs en Perse au XVIII et au XVIII siecle d'apres les chroniques poetiques de Babai Loutf et de Babai b. Farhad. *Revue des etudes Juives*, **51**, 121–136, 265–279; **52**, 77–97, 234–271; **53**, 85–110.

Bacher, Wilhelm (1908) *Zwei Judishe-Persische Dicter (Schahin und Imrani)*. Strassburg: Karl J. Trubner.

Baron, Salo W. (1948) *The Jewish Community*. Volume I. Philadelphia: Jewish Publication Society of America.

Baron, Salo W. (1952) *A Social and Religious History of the Jews*. Revised edition. Volume I. New York: Columbia University Press, Philadelphia: Jewish Publication Society of America.

Baron Salo W. (1952a) *A Social and Religious History of the Jews*. Revised edition. Volume II. New York: Columbia University Press, Philadelphia: Jewish Publication Society of America.

Baron Salo W. (1957) *A Social and Religious History of the Jews*. Revised edition. Volume III. New York: Columbia University Press, Philadelphia: Jewish Publication Society of America.

Barth, Fredrik (1961) *Nomads of South Persia*. Oslo: Oslo University Press.

Barth, Fredrik (1966) *Models of Social Organization,* Royal Anthropological Institute, Occasional Paper No. 23.

Bemont, Fredy (1969) *Les Villes de l'Iran*. Volume I. Paris.

Benharouche-Baralia (1961) *Chants Traditionnels Hebraiques*. Biarritz.

Benjamin, Israel Joseph (1859) *Eight Years in Asia and Africa – from 1846 to 1854*. Hanover.

Ben-Zvi, Yitẓḥaq (1936) *Zikhronot Vrishimot – Kitve Yiẓḥaq ben-Zvi*, Volume I. Tel Aviv: Mizpe (Hebrew)

Ben-Zvi, Yitẓḥaq (1937) *Okhluse Erez Yisra'el – Kitve Yiẓḥaq ben-Zvi*, Volume V. Tel Aviv: Mizpe (Hebrew).

Ben-Zvi, Yitzhaq (1958) Mqorot ltoldot yhudey paras. *Sefunot*, **2**, 190–213.

Ben-Zvi, Yitzhaq (1961) *The Exiled and the Redeemed*. Philadelphia: Jewish Publication Society of America.

Binning, Robert B. M. (1857) *A Journal of Two Years Travel in Persia, Ceylon etc*. Volumes I and II. London: William H. Allen and Co.

Bishop, Isabella L. Bird (1891) *Journeys in Persia and Kurdistan*. Volumes I and II. London: John Murray.

Black, Jacob (1972) Tyranny as a strategy for survival in an "egalitarian" society: Luri facts versus an anthropological mystique. *Man* n.s., **7**, 614–634.

Brauer, Erich (1934) *Ethnologie der jemenitischen Juden*. Heidelberg: Carl Winters Universitätsbuchhandlung.

Brauer, Erich (1947) *Yhude Kurdistan*. Completed, edited and translated by R. Patai. Jerusalem: The Palestine Institute of Folklore and Ethnology. Studies in Folklore and Ethnology. Volume II. (Hebrew).

Brawer, Avraham (1936) Mipparashat massa'i bfaras. *Sinai*, **3**, 72–87 (Hebrew).

Brawer, Avraham (1946) *'Avaq Drakhim*. Vol. II – "Paras". Tel Aviv: Shaharut, Am Orer, Davar (Hebrew).

Briggs, Lloyd Cabot and Norina Lami Guede (1964) *No More Forever – A Saharan Jewish Town*. Papers of the Peabody Museum of Archaeology and Ethnology. Cambridge, Massachusetts: Harvard University. Vol. LV, No. 1.

Browne, Edward G. (1920) *A History of Persian Literature*. Volume III: Under Tartar Dominion, A.D. 1265–1502. Cambridge: At the University Press.

Browne, Edward G. (1950) *A Year Amongst the Persians*. London: Adam and Charles Black.

Carmelite Chronicles (1939) *A chronicle of the Carmelites in Persia and the Papal Mission of the XVIIth and XVIIIth Centuries*. London. Eyre and Spottiswoode.

Chardin, Sir John (1735) *Voyages du Chevalier Chardin en Perse et autres lieux de l'orient*. Nouvelle edition. Four volumes. Amsterdam.

Chardin, Sir John (1923) *Sir John Chardin's Travels in Persia*. London: Argonaut Press (London: 1686 edition).

Clarke, John I. (1963) *The Iranian City of Shiraz*. Research Paper Series No. 7. Durham: Department of Geography, University of Durham.

Curzon, G. N. (1892) *Persia and the Persian Question*. Two volumes. London: Longmans Green and Co.

Deshen, Shlomo and Moshe Shokeid (1974) *The Predicament of Homecoming*. Ithaca: Cornell University Press.

Descos, Leon Eugene Aubin Coullar (1908) *La Perse d'Aujordhui – Iran*. Paris: A. Colin.

Donaldson, Bess Ann (1938) *The Wild Rue: A Study of Muhammadan Magic and Folklore in Iran*. London: Luzac and Co.

Dubnov, Simon (1968) *History of the Jews*. Volume II. Translated by Moshe Spiegel. S. Brunswick, New York, London: Thomas Yoseloff.

Epstein, Louis (1927) *The Jewish Marriage Contract*. New York: Jewish Theological Seminary of America.

Evans-Pritchard, E. E. (1937) *Witchcraft, Oracles and Magic Among the Azande*. London: Oxford University Press.

Feitelson, Dina (1959) Aspects of the Social Life of Kurdish Jews. *The Jewish Journal of Sociology*, **1**, 201–216.

Feldman, David M. (1974) *Marital Relations, Birth Control and Abortion in Jewish Law*. New York: Schocken Books.

Fischel, Walter J. (1935) Yahudiyya – Ireshit hayyshuv hayyhudi bfaras. *Tarbiz*, **6**, 523–536 (Hebrew).

Fischel, Walter J. (1936) Qhillat ha'anusim bfaras. *Zion*, n.s., **1**, 49–74 (Hebrew).

Fischel, Walter J. (1937) *Jews in the Economic and Political Life of Medieval Islam*. London: Royal Asiatic Society Monographs, Volume XXII.

Fischel, Walter J. (1937a) Toldot yhude faras bime shalshelet hassafavidim bme'a hashva' 'esre. *Zion*, n.s., **2**, 273–293. (Hebrew).

Fischel, Walter J. (1944) The Jews of Kurdistan a Hundred Years Ago. *Jewish Social Studies*, **6**, 195–226.

Fischel, Walter J. (1950) The Jews of Persia: 1795–1940. *Jewish Social Studies*, **12**, 119–160.

Fischel, Walter J. (1953) Isfahan: the story of a Jewish community in Persia. In *The Joshua Starr Memorial Volume*. Jewish Social Studies Publication. Volume V. Pp. 111–128.

Fischel, Walter J. (1960) Israel in Iran. In *The Jews*. Louis Finkelstein, editor. Third edition. Philadelphia: Jewish Publication Society of America. Volume II. Pp. 1149–1190.

Fischel, Walter J. (1960a) *The Jews in India*. Translated by Ya'aqov Hason. Jerusalem: The Ben-Zvi Institute (Hebrew).

Fischer, Michael M. J. (1973) *Zoroastrian Iran between Myth and Praxis*. Chicago: University of Chicago (unpublished Ph.D. dissertation).

Fischer, W. B. (editor) (1968) *The Land of Iran*. The Cambridge History of Iran, Volume I. Cambridge: Cambridge at the University Press.

Francklin, William (1790) *Observations made on a tour from Bengal to Persia in the year 1786–1787*. Second edition. London: T. Cadell in the Strand.

Fraser, James B. (1825) *Narrative of a Journey into Khorassan in the years 1821 and 1822*. London: Longman, Hurst, Rees, Orme, Browne and Green.

Fryer, Sir John (1912) *A New Account of East India and Persia being Nine Years' Travels, 1672–1681*. William Crooke, editor. London: Hakluyt Society, Volumes II and III (Series II, Vols. 20 and 39).

Gili, B. (1951) *Dappe 'Aliya*. Jerusalem: Jewish Agency for Israel (Hebrew).

Goitein, S. D. (1955) *Jews and Arabs*. New York: Schocken Books.

Goitein, S. D. (1975) The Origin and Historical Significance of North Africa Jewry. In *Proceedings of the Seminar on Muslim–Jewish Relations in North Africa*. New York: World Jewish Congress. Pp. 2–13.

Goodman, Philip (1962) *The Passover Anthology*. Philadelphia: Jewish Publication Society of America.

Graetz, Heinrich (1956) *History of the Jews*. Volume II. Philadelphia: Jewish Publication Society of America.

Graetz, Heinrich (1956a) *History of the Jews*. Volume III. Philadelphia: Jewish Publication Society of America.

Grey, Charles (n.d.) *A Narrative of Italian Travels in Persia in the 15th and 16th Century*. New York: Burt Franklin.

Haas, William S. (1946) *Iran*. New York: Columbia University Press.

Hakohen, Rfa'el Ḥayyim (1970) *Avanim Baḥoma*. Jerusalem: Rfa'el Ḥayyim Hakohen Press.

Heilman, Samuel c. (1975) The Gift of Alms: Face-to-Face Almsgiving Among Orthodox Jews. *Urban Life and Culture*, 3, 371–395.

Herbert, Sir Thomas (1677) *Some Years Travel into Diverse Parts of Africa and Asia the Great*. London.

Hertz, Joseph H. (1948) *The Authorized Daily Prayer Book*. New York: Bloch Publishing Co.

Heschel, Abraham J. (1952) *The Sabbath*. Cleveland and New York: The World Publishing Company; Philadelphia: Jewish Publication Society of America. (Meridian edition – 1963.)

Ibn Battuta (1962) *The Travels of ibn Battuta*. Translated by H. A. R. Gibb. Volume II. Cambridge: At the University Press.

Idelsohn, A. Z. (1932) *Jewish Liturgy and its Development*. New York: Henry Holt and Co. (Sacred Music Press.)

Iran Almanac (1968) Seventh edition. Teheran: Echo.

Josephus, Flavius (n.d.) *The Complete Works of Flavius Josephus*. Translated by William Whiston. Philadelphia: John E. Potter.

Kafih, Joseph (1963) *Jewish Life in Sana*. Jerusalem: Ban-Zvi Institute (Hebrew).

Kopellowitz, Jehudah (1930) The Jews of Persia. *Menorah Journal*. Pp. 42–51.

Lamm, Maurice (1972) *The Jewish Way in Death and Mourning.* Revised edition. New York: Jonathan David.

Landshut, S. (n.d.) *Jewish Communities in the Muslim Countries of the Middle East.* London: The Jewish Chronicle.

Levi, Habib (1960) *Tarikhe Yahud-e Iran.* Volume III. Teheran: Berukhim and Sons (Persian).

Lewis, Oscar (1966) *La Vida.* New York: Random House.

Loeb, Laurence D. (1970) *The Jews of Southwest Iran: a study of cultural persistence.* New York: Columbia University (unpublished Ph.D. dissertation)

Loeb, Laurence D. (1974) The Jewish Wedding in Modern Shiraz. In *Studies in Marriage Customs.* Jerusalem: Folklore Research Center Studies. Volume IV. Pp. 167–176

Loeb, Laurence D. (1976) Dhimmi Status and Jewish Roles in Iranian Society. *Ethnic Groups.* 1:89–105.

Malcolm, Napier (1905) *Five Years in a Persian Town.* New York: E. P. Dutton.

Malinowski, Bronislaw (1954) *Magic, Science and Religion and Other Essays.* Garden City: Anchor Books.

Manzur, Saleh Y. (1951) *Maḥzor Tfillat Ysharim Hashalem Lyom Kippur.* Jerusalem (Hebrew).

Margolis, Max and Alexander Marx (1927) *A History of the Jewish People.* New York: Meridian Books; Philadelphia: Jewish Publication Society of America.

Masse, Henri (1954) *Persian Beliefs and Customs.* New Haven: HRAF.

Melamed, Ezra (1951) Hayyhudim bfaras lifne shishim shana. *Sinai,* 29, 359–370 (Hebrew).

Mendelson, Rebekah Z. (1964) *The Bokharan Jewish Community of New York City.* New York: Columbia University (unpublished M.A. thesis).

Mez, Adam (1937) *The Renaissance of Islam.* Translated by Salahuddin Khudda Barksh and D. S. Margoliouth. First edition. Patna: Jubilee Printing and Publishing.

Millgram, Abraham E. (1959) *Sabbath: The Day of Delight.* Philadelphia: Jewish Publication Society of America.

Milligram, Abraham E. (1971) *Jewish Worship.* Philadelphia: Jewish Publication Society of America.

Mizrahi, Hanina (1957) Tish'a b'av bfaras. In *Sefer Hammo'adim.* Yom Tov Levinsky, editor. Tel Aviv: Oneg Shabbat Society and Dvir. Volume VII. Pp. 369–372. (Hebrew).

Mizrahi, Hanina (1959) *Yhude Faras.* Tel Aviv: Dvir (Hebrew).

Mizrahi, Hanina (1966) *Toldot Yhude Faras Umshorrehem.* Jerusalem: Rubin Mass (Hebrew).

More, Ḥayyim (1921) *Sefer Derekh Ḥayyim.* Teheran (Judeo-Persian).

More, Ḥayyim (1924) *Sefer Gdulat Mordkhay.* Teheran (Judeo-Persian).

More, Ḥayyim (1927) *Sefer Yede Eliyahu.* Teheran (Judeo-Persian).

Morier, James (1812) *A Journey through Persia, Armenia and Asia Minor to Constantinople in the Years 1808 and 1809.* London: Longman, Hurst, Rees, Orme and Brown.

Morier, James (1818) *A Second Journey through Persia, Armenia and Asia Minor to Constantinople between the Years 1810 and 1816.* London: Longman, Hurst, Rees, Orme and Brown.

Mounsey, Augustus H. (1872) *A Journey through the Caucasus and the Interior of Persia.* London: Smith, Elder and Co.

Murdock, George P. (1949) *Social Structure*. The Macmillan Company.

Musleah, Ezekiel N. (1975) *On the Banks of the Ganga*. North Quincy: The Christopher Publishing House.

Mustafi, Hamd-Allah (of Qazvin) (1919) *The Geographical Part of the Nuzhat-al-Qulub*. Translated by Guy Le Strange. E. J. W. Gibb Memorial Series XXIII: 2. Leyden: E. J. Brill; London: Luzac.

Nadel, S. F. (1952) Witchcraft in Four African Societies; an Essay in comparison. *American Anthropologist*, 54, 18–29.

Neusner, Jacob (1965) *A History of the Jews in Babylonia: The Parthian Period*. Leiden: E. J. Brill.

Neusner, Jacob (1966) *A History of the Jews in Babylonia: The Early Sassanian Period*. Leiden: E. J. Brill

Neusner, Jacob (1968) *A History of the Jews in Babylonia: From Shapur I to Shapur II*. Leiden: E. J. Brill

Neibuhr, Carsten (1778) *Reisbeischreibung nach Arabien und andern umliegenden Landern*. Three Volumes. Kopenhagen: Nicolaus Moeller.

Ouseley, Sir William (1819) *Travels in Various Countries of the East: More Particularly Persia*. London: Rodwell and Martin.

Paine, Robert (1974) *Second Thoughts about Barth's Models*. Royal Anthropological Institute Occasional Paper No. 32.

Patai, Raphael (1947) Marriage among the Marranoes of Meshhed. *Edoth*, 2, 165–192 (Hebrew).

Petermann, Julius H. (1861) *Reisen im Orient*. Volume II. Leipzig: Veit and Co.

Peters, Emrys (1960) The Proliferation of Segments in the Lineage of the Bedouin of Cyrenaica. *Journal of the Royal Anthropological Institute*, 90, 29–53.

Pitt-Rivers, Julian (1966) Honor and Social Status. In *Honour and Shame*. J. Peristiany, editor. Chicago: University of Chicago Press.

Polak, Jakob Eduard (1865) *Persien: Das Land und seine Bewohner*. Two volumes. Leipzig: F. A. Brockhaus.

Rakower, J. (1973) Tuberculosis among Jews. In *Ethnic Groups of America: Their Morbidity, Mortality and Behavior Disorders. Volume I – The Jews*. Ailon Shiloh and Ida Cohen Selavan editors. Springfield: Charles C. Thomas.

Sassoon, David S. (1949) *A History of the Jews of Baghdad*. Letchworth: S. Sassoon.

Sassoon, David S. (1955) *Mas'a Bavel*. Jerusalem: Azriel (Hebrew).

Schechtman, Joseph B. (1961) *On Wings of Eagles*. New York–London; Thomas Yoseloff.

Schwartz, Richard M. (1973) *The Structure of Christian-Muslim Relations in Contemporary Iran*. St. Louis: Washington U. (unpublished Ph.D. dissertation)

Schrire, T. (1966) *Hebrew Amulets*. London: Routledge and Kegan Paul.

Sjoberg, Gideon (1960) *The Preindustrial City*. New York: The Free Press.

Slouschz, Nahum (1927) *The Jews of North Africa*. Philadelphia: Jewish Publication Society of America.

Spicehandler, Ezra (1970) *Contemporary Iranian Jewry*. Jerusalem: The Institute of Contemporary Jewry, Sprinzak Division – Hebrew University. (Heb)

Spooner, Brian (1965) Kinship and Marriage in Eastern Persia. *Sociologus* n.s., 15, 22–31.

Stern, Henry A. (1854) *Dawnings of Light in the East*. London: Charles Purday.

Stirling, Paul (1965) *Turkish Village*. London: Weidenfeld and Nicolson.

Stuart, Charles (1854) *Journal of a Residence in Northern Persia*. London: R. Bently.

Sykes, Ella (1910) *Persia and its People*. London: Methuen and Co.

Sykes, Percy M. (1930) *A History of Persia*. Third edition. Two volumes. London: Macmillan and Co.

Tavernier, John Baptista (1684) *The Six Travels of John Baptista Tavernier, Baron of Aubonne, through Turkey and Persia to the Indies – in the Space of forty years*. English by J. P. London.

Teixeira, Pedro (1902) *The Travels of Pedro Teixeira*. Translated and edited by William F. Sinclair. Notes and introduction by Donald Ferguson. London: Hakluyt Society, Series II, Volume IX.

Thaiss, Gustav E. (1973) *Religious Symbolism and Social Change: The Drama of Husain*. St. Louis: Washington University (unpublished Ph.D. dissertation).

Thevenot, J. de (1687) *The Travels of Monsieur de Thevenot into the Levant*. London

Trachtenberg, Joshua (1939) *Jewish Magic and Superstition*. New York: Behrman's Jewish Book House.

Tylor, Edward (1958) *Religion in Primitive Culture*. New York, Evanston, London: Harper and Row.

Vambery, Hermann (Arminus) (1865) *Travels in Central Asia*. New York: Harper and Row.

Vambery, Hermann (Arminus) (1884) *His Life and Adventures – written by himself*. New York: Cassell and Co.

Wankert, Yosef (1975) *The Jews of Iran Today*. Jerusalem: American Jewish Committee. *Tefutsot Israel*, **13**, No. 1. (Heb.)

Waring, E. S. (1807) *A Tour to Sheeraz*. London: T. Cadell.

Weber, Max (1952) *Ancient Judaism*. Glencoe: Free Press.

Weber, Max (1964) *The Sociology of Religion*. Translated by Ephraim Fischoff. Boston: Beacon Press.

Wilson, A. T. (1916) *Report on Fars*. Simla/catalogue –P–53 Con. serial –105./India (British Army Publication).

Wills, C. J. (1883) *In the Land of the Lion and Sun, or Modern Persia*. London: Macmillan and Co.

Wills, C. J. (1887) *Persia as it is*. Second edition. London: Sampson, Low, Marston, Searle and Rivington.

Wolff, Reverend Joseph (1832) *Journal of the Reverend Joseph Wolff for the year 1831*. London: James Fraser.

Wolff, Reverend, Joseph (1846) *Narrative of a Mission to Bokhara in the Years 1843–1845, to ascertain the fate of Colonel Stoddart and Captain Conolly*. Third edition. London: John W. Parker.

Wulff, Hans E. (1966) *The Traditional Crafts of Persia*. Cambridge, Mass. and London: The M.I.T. Press.

Ya'ari, Avraham (editor) (1947) *Massa B'ereẓ Haqqedem: Me'et Efrayim Neumark*. Jerusalem: Levine-Epstein Brothers (Hebrew).

Yishay, M. (1950) *Zir Blo To'ar: Rishme Shliḥut Umassa Bfaras*. Tel Aviv: N. Tavarski (Hebrew).

Zenner, Walter (1965) Saints and Piecemeal Supernaturalism Among the Jerusalem Sephardim. *Anthropological Quarterly*, **38**, 201–217.

Zimmels, H. J. (1958) *Ashkenazim and Sephardim*. London: Oxford University Press.

Geographic Index

Name and Subject Index